SPIES, LIES, AND CYBERCRIME

ALSO BY ERIC O'NEILL

Gray Day: My Undercover Mission to Expose America's First Cyber Spy

SPIES, LIES, AND CYBERCRIME

CYBERSECURITY TACTICS TO OUTSMART HACKERS AND DISARM SCAMMERS

ERIC O'NEILL

FORMER FBI SPY HUNTER

WILLIAM MORROW
An Imprint of HarperCollins*Publishers*

Without limiting the exclusive rights of any author, contributor or the publisher of this publication, any unauthorized use of this publication to train generative artificial intelligence (AI) technologies is expressly prohibited. HarperCollins also exercise their rights under Article 4(3) of the Digital Single Market Directive 2019/790 and expressly reserve this publication from the text and data mining exception.

The material on linked sites referenced in this book is the author's own. HarperCollins disclaims all liability that may result from the use of the material contained at those sites. All such material is supplemental and not part of the book. The author reserves the right to close the website in their sole discretion following October 2025.

All statements of fact, opinion, or analysis expressed in this book are those of the author. Nothing in this book should be construed as asserting or implying US government or FBI endorsement of this book's factual statements and interpretations. The names and identifying details of some individuals have been changed to protect their privacy.

SPIES, LIES, AND CYBERCRIME. Copyright © 2025 by Eric M. O'Neill. All rights reserved. No part of this book may be used or reproduced in any manner whatsoever without written permission except in the case of brief quotations embodied in critical articles and reviews. For information, address HarperCollins Publishers, 195 Broadway, New York, NY 10007. In Europe, HarperCollins Publishers, Macken House, 39/40 Mayor Street Upper, Dublin 1, D01 C9W8, Ireland.

HarperCollins books may be purchased for educational, business, or sales promotional use. For information, please email the Special Markets Department at SPsales@harpercollins.com.

hc.com

FIRST EDITION

Designed by Michele Cameron

Spy hunter logo courtesy of the author

Library of Congress Cataloging-in-Publication Data has been applied for.

ISBN 978-0-06-339817-7

Printed in the United States of America

25 26 27 28 29 LBC 5 4 3 2 1

To my father,

John O'Neill.

My first hero.

CONTENTS

Prologue: The Deepest, Darkest Cave — 1

Introduction: It's Now or . . . *It's Now!* — 11

Part I: Think Like a Spy — 19

Chapter One: The House Is Burning Down — 21

Chapter Two: The Cloak-and-Dagger Game — 30

Chapter Three: Deception: How an Email Launched a War — 42

Chapter Four: Impersonation: How to Skip School — 53

Chapter Five: Impersonation: Deepfakes — 66

Chapter Six: Infiltration: The Trojan Horse — 78

Chapter Seven: Infiltration: Indomitable Weeds — 93

Chapter Eight: Confidence: "I Want to Believe" — 109

Chapter Nine: Confidence: Question Everything — 120

Chapter Ten: Exploitation: Spelunking into a Nightmare — 132

Chapter Eleven: Exploitation: No Blank Pages — 151

Chapter Twelve: Destruction: Inside the Fishbowl — 166

Chapter Thirteen: Destruction: Up at Night — 190

Part II: Act Like a Spy Hunter 205

Chapter Fourteen: Intro to PAID   207

Chapter Fifteen: Prepare   211

Chapter Sixteen: Assess   229

Chapter Seventeen: Investigate   242

Chapter Eighteen: Decide   254

Chapter Nineteen: Congratulations, Spy Hunter   261

The Spy Hunter Tool Kit 267

Acknowledgments   279

Notes   283

SPIES, LIES, AND CYBERCRIME

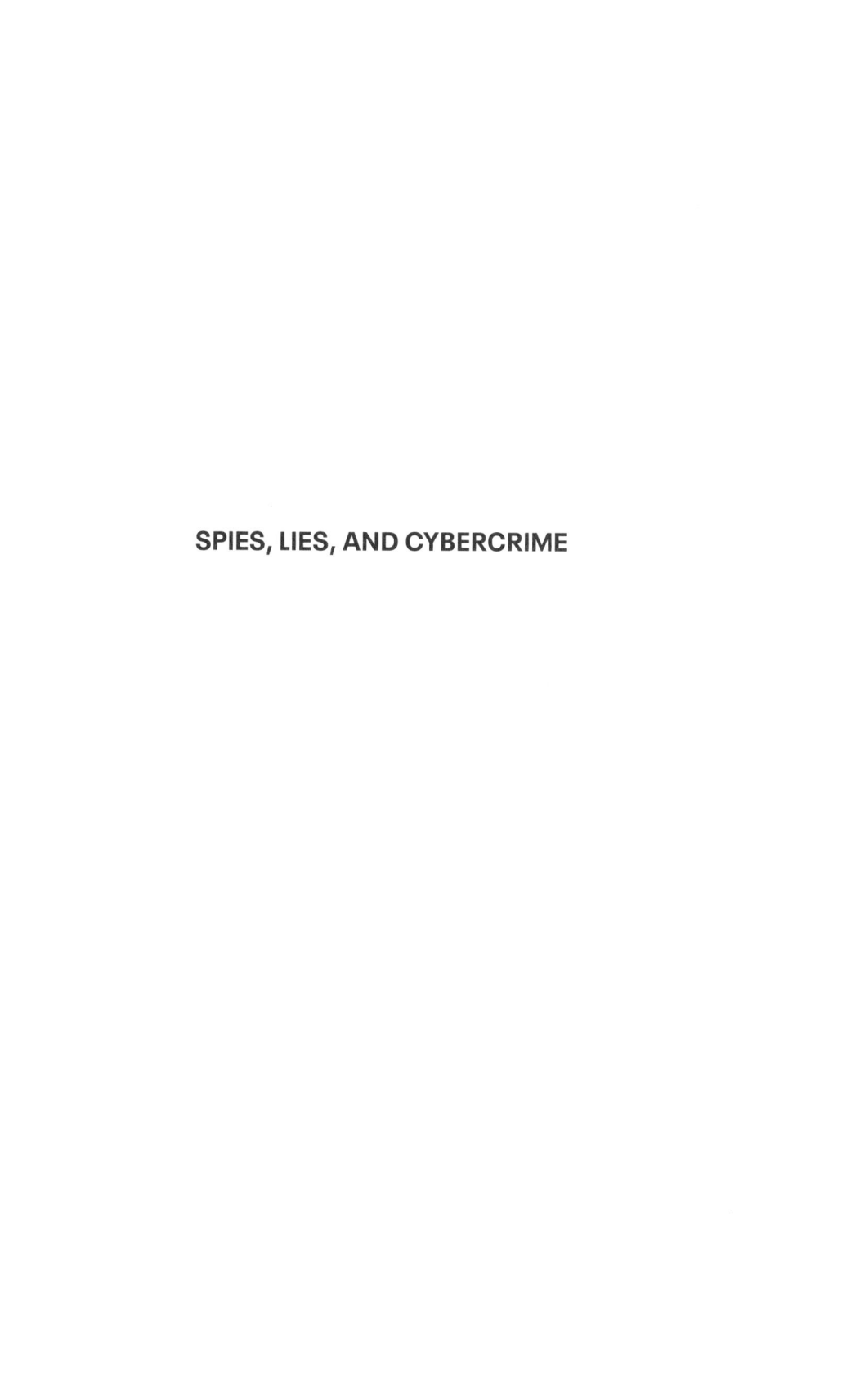

PROLOGUE

The Deepest, Darkest Cave

On a sunny day in October, when Washington, D.C. was painted in a riot of color, our friend Josh convinced my wife and me to follow him into a cave.

Josh had spent a year in his late teens learning to guide tourists through complex cave systems in South America and emerged with a preternatural sense of direction in darkness that could challenge a bat. I've long suffered from claustrophobia, and the thought of delving into a cave peppered my arms with goose bumps. Aside from a one-time guided tour with my Boy Scout troop as a kid, I'd never stepped foot into a cave and certainly not gone to the depths that Josh described.

We drove an hour southwest to where historic Harper's Ferry nestles strategically at a juncture of the Potomac and Shenandoah rivers in West Virginia. Prior to the Civil War, the United States Army used Harper's Ferry as a military arsenal. In October 1859, John Brown, an abolitionist from Kansas, captured the arsenal with twenty-one men, including freed slaves, to instigate an armed slave uprising in Virginia. The revolution lasted less than thirty-six hours, as long as it took then-Colonel Robert E. Lee and a company of U.S. marines to arrive and quell it.

Josh parked his van beside some railroad tracks just past Harper's Ferry, and we set out on foot along the steel rails. I couldn't help humming Ben E. King's "Stand by Me" and wondering whether this particular adventure would lead us to a dead body, like in Stephen King's titular story. We must've looked an odd sort to anyone watching from the middle of nowhere, with Josh wearing brilliant yellow caving overalls while I, my wife, Juliana, and our friend Rich opted for cheap army fatigues purchased from a nearby thrift store. Josh had made us duct tape the bottom of our pants to our boots. "It gets muddy," he'd said, smirking.

Finding the cave took some work. As the legend goes, John Brown and his cohorts had hidden in the cave before launching their attack on Harper's Ferry. Unfortunately, over the years, the popularity of the attraction made many wannabe cavers arrive without a Josh to guide them, and some got lost, hurt, or even died. Caving can be a dangerous sport, particularly when a cave descends miles into darkness.

Outside the cave, Josh settled his fancy red miner's helmet and fired up his carbide headlamp. A flame burst alight, dancing in front of a mirrored surface. The steady glow suffused the cave with light so brilliant, I felt its warmth deep within the place in my chest where fear had gained ground. Josh led the way downward on hands and knees, the brightness of his helmet drawing us forward.

* * *

IF THE INTERNET is a shining beacon for global communications, collaboration, information sharing, and the engine for all our modern contrivances (or Josh lighting our way), the dark web is a parasite that creates pustules and grows with its host.

The winding, branching, and ever-growing cave system of the internet is packed with information. In 2024, humans consumed an incomprehensible 149 zettabytes of data. By 2028, experts predict that we will post, tweet, binge, share, buy, and search our way to over 394 zettabytes of information—that's the number 394 followed by 21 zeros! To make sense of such a number, let's try an analog analogy. One zettabyte is equivalent to 1,000 exabytes or 1 billion terabytes. If you stacked sheets of printer paper filled with information 35 feet high (the size of a standard telephone pole), you might have approximately

1 gigabyte of data (1,000 megabytes). One terabyte is equivalent to 1,000 gigabytes, or 35,000 feet of stacked paper. That is nearly the distance one would need to dive to reach the bottom of the Mariana Trench, the deepest location on earth, 7 miles under the sea. One terabyte of stacked paper would leave the Milky Way and stretch about one light year to the Andromeda Galaxy. One hundred forty-nine zettabytes of stacked paper would leave the Andromeda Galaxy in the dust and arrive at K2–18b, a habitable-zone exoplanet found by the James Webb Space Telescope in the constellation Leo.

Every minute of every day, two thirds of humanity—more than 5 billion people—spend more than 25 million hours online. In that time, humanity streams nearly 1.2 million hours of videos (i.e., Netflix and YouTube). We also share more than 300,000 photos across Instagram and Facebook and countless other platforms. Every sixty seconds means 360,000 more tweets, 167 million more TikTok videos, and more than 2 million Snapchat snaps. In sixty heartbeats, 6 million people shop online, spend $455,000 on Amazon, and exchange $463,000 through Venmo. Every minute of every day, humanity sends 241 million emails.[1] All of this grows the internet.

Most who think of the internet are referring to just the relatively comfortable entrance—akin to where we first entered John Brown's Cave. We can stand there, meander, look at the graffiti that tourists have painted on the walls, and feel comforted by the sunlight still streaming through the entrance. Only about 10 percent of the internet is the so-called surface web, or the data indexed and searchable through search engines like Chrome, Safari, and Edge. This includes all the information that we *want* others to find, information that lives on websites, social media posts, and all the Wikipedia-like history, encyclopedic knowledge, and how-to guides of human experience.

The remaining 90 percent of the internet delves deep in the earth below, appropriately called the deep web. This underground portion includes sensitive and confidential information that is protected with passwords and security and hidden from web crawlers. It contains critical data like medical records, electronic bank statements, memberships, confidential corporate websites, private chats, emails, direct messages, social media accounts, and everything you wouldn't want someone accessing through a search engine. This level of the internet is indexed, controlled, and difficult to access for those without authorization. This is also the data that spies and criminals are desperate to steal. This last point is most crucial of all.

Finally, at the very bottom of the internet's cavernous system lies the dark web. And *here there be monsters*. The dark web has infected the bottom 5 percent of the internet, accessed through the most difficult crawls, and is host to some macabre and heartrending virtual storefronts. One example is the Body Parts Bazaar, a clearinghouse for organ sales that targets the world's most desperate patients who aren't on the coveted lists for transplants. There are roughly ten thousand illegal organ transplant surgeries every year. The more vital the organ, the more it will cost you. Need a new heart? You'll have to scrape up $200,000. A new set of eyes runs $1,200. I can't imagine why someone would want someone else's hands or feet, but they cost around $500 apiece.

Even *people* are for sale on the dark web. The United Nations Office on Drugs and Crime has estimated that 2.5 million victims are trafficked by criminals at any given time. According to UNICEF, children account for nearly one third of human-trafficking victims. The scum of the earth find one another on dark web marketplaces where they buy and sell children. Especially girls. Obtaining accurate statistics on dark web human trafficking is challenging due to the clandestine and often encrypted nature of the marketplaces, but since 2020, most of the U.S. Justice Department's sex-trafficking prosecutions involve dark web advertising.

There are some images in life that burn your eyes indelibly and terrifyingly. Though I'll carry pictures from investigations into some of the most horrendous terrorists on earth in the back of my mind, I'll never unsee a legal case that required me to review the laptop of a criminal suspected of child pornography. The dark web is full of pornography, illegal arms trading, gambling, online stores for every illegal drug, and so much more. The worst is the human marketplace. You can buy a teenage girl for a few thousand dollars, negotiate the hotel she will be delivered to, and purchase a PDF of instructions to build a soundproof basement dungeon.

***

WE DESCENDED FOR hours, the dark graduating from an abstract description to a presence that walked beside us. Stalked us. Perhaps more than a mile below the morning sun, Josh had us turn off all our lights. In that moment I learned that darkness is a rare occurrence in a world of streetlamps, smartphones, and starlight. This darkness breathed in my ears and tickled the hair at the back of my neck. It didn't take long for me to feel the urge to switch on my light and push away the discomfort.

I followed the spear of light from my headlamp and the distant scuffle of my wife's boots into the unknown, breathing shallowly. "It opens up here!" Josh's distant shout from far ahead gave me hope. But it also occurred to me that our intrepid friend did not know what he'd find after minutes of traversing a narrow gap. What if he reached a dead end? If we couldn't turn around, would we need to back out?

I choked back emotion and pushed forward over a rocky protuberance. My headlamp cracked against the rock above and sudden darkness severed the thin string of confidence that pulled me forward. I froze and did the worst thing imaginable. I tried to stand.

***

THE DARK WEB finds its origin story in espionage. In 1995, David Goldschlag, Mike Reed, and Paul Syverson at the U.S. Naval Research Lab (NRL) sought to design a way to use the internet under a cloak of anonymity. They created the first prototype of "onion routing" to protect the identities of American spies who used the internet to communicate. If internet traffic could be routed through multiple servers and encrypted each step of the way, a spy could communicate home through monitored internet hubs without fear of being detected. A few years later, in the early 2000s, Syverson and computer scientists

A cross-section of an onion.

Roger Dingledine and Nick Mathewson expanded the original NRL research and began the Onion Routing Project, aka Tor.

Onion routing makes internet traffic anonymous by layering encryption around a message. When we connect to a website, our path crosses through a guard, middle, and exit node. The guard node is the entry point that first encrypts your data; the middle node adds extra encryption while passing it along; and the exit node decrypts it just enough to reach the intended website—keeping the whole path anonymous using a Tor router. Only the guard to a website knows the unique Internet Protocol (IP) address assigned to every internet traveler. In general, government agencies, investigators, hackers, and internet service providers can easily track a user's journey online through an IP address. Tor encrypts this information throughout each node. Indeed, only the exit node knows the content of a user's online communication, and because the internet has no borders, that exit node can exist *anywhere in the world*. Even if an investigative government agency determined a user's IP address at the guard node, the middle and exit node might be routed to servers in other countries, where international search warrants are unavailable. In fact, some of the dark web server farms are hidden on actual pirate islands, operated by wealthy criminals, far from law enforcement's reach. This makes determining the origin of a message near impossible.

In October 2002, Syverson, Dingledine, and Mathewson released the source code for the Tor network as free and open software. Today, there are over six thousand worldwide network relays. Although the founders of the Tor network intended to provide a digital haven for speech and the exchange of information, even the best intentions are corruptible. Criminals soon learned that decentralized content could be hidden behind anonymous addresses made of numbers and letters followed by the Tor network's signature .onion extension. The dark web was officially born.

* * *

FEAR MAKES US irrational. In the contest between me and the rock scraping my back, the cave won and drove the air from my chest. I hyperventilated, lost in the dark, miles below the earth, hands clawing at the stone beneath me. I was a spelunker who had descended too deep.

I visualized an open sky above instead of the coffin I lay in and considered my dilemma. I've always practiced what I preach, and planning for pressure situations before the event is a core precept. With a contortion that might have wrung a nod from a Cirque du Soleil performer, I slid a hand along my body down to my kneepad, where I had stashed a glow stick. I snapped the plastic and chemical light illuminated the tunnel ahead in a ghoulish green glow. The light must have switched on the rational part of my brain. "I'm coming!" I shouted and crawled forward.

The unfortunate reality of security is that law enforcement tends to lag behind crime. Criminals will launch innovative attacks mercilessly until cybersecurity discovers how to stop them. While security works around the clock discovering the cause of the attack and how to prevent it in the future, criminals have already begun dreaming up the next unexpected way to breach security. When an attack is no longer effective, criminals move on to the next innovation they've learned or perfected, sending cybersecurity back into their repetitive cycle, always one step behind their dupers.

Cybercriminals are not just government spies looking to dig up data and intelligence on other countries, as in the spy wars of the Soviet era. They work either in tandem or independent of agencies, and they are everywhere. They are busy too. In 2024, the year kicked off with a bang as the mother of all data leaks appeared on a dark web database as a smorgasbord for future criminal cyberattacks. Twenty-six billion records from such critical companies as LinkedIn, Dropbox, X (née Twitter), Adobe, Canva, and Telegram are available for criminals to peruse and use for email phishing attacks, identity theft, and credential mining of usernames and passwords to access confidential accounts. Accounts like yours.

To make matters worse, a few months later, a second breach became the data breach to end all data breaches—literally. Up to 2.9 billion people had their personal lives dumped onto the dark web for criminals to browse, like Amazon Prime for fraudsters. Names, Social Security numbers, addresses, phone numbers—you name it, it's out there. The culprits? A hacker group charmingly calling themselves "USDoD," who cracked into National Public Data, a background check company, and posted the stolen data for all the shady characters of the dark web to enjoy. The breach was so massive that lawsuits piled

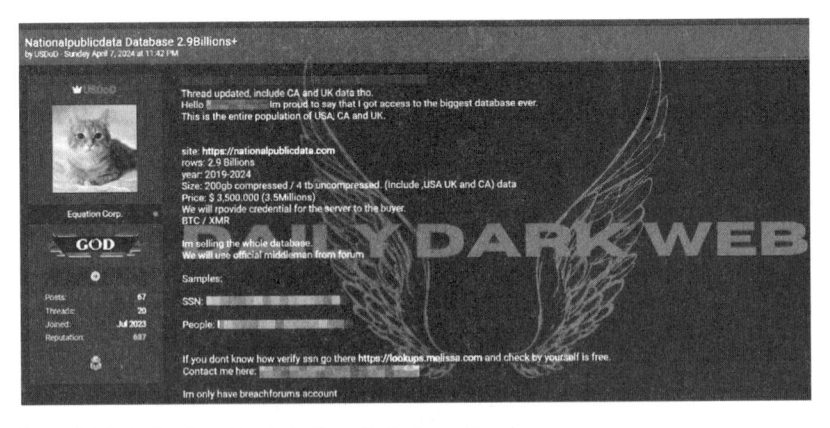

https://dailydarkweb.net/usdod-allegedly-leaks-national-public-data-database-exposing-2-9-billion-records/.

up faster than the company could file bankruptcy papers, which—surprise—they did. This is yet another grim reminder that once your data is out there, it's out there for good—and the dark web has no return policy.

We are currently trapped in the depths of John Brown's Cave, struggling to breathe. Unless we find a light, we'll stay trapped there and continue to lose trillions of dollars—not to mention personal value, time, and emotion—to cybercrime. Protecting the data that is the currency of our lives will require struggle. If we want to make the world safe from cyberattacks, we'd better start crawling.

INTRODUCTION

It's Now or . . . *It's Now!*

Sebastian worked for an innovation lab headquartered in Palo Alto, California. He wasn't a scientist or cutting-edge programmer who dreamt up new technologies that would change the world, but rather a finance controller who earned an honest living. He processed the invoices, paid the vendors, and made certain that all the financials were accurate, down to the penny. Meanwhile, the company's CEO, Chloe, was young, vibrant, and formidable. Her revolutionary ideas fed the twenty-four-hour news cycle that catapulted her into social influencer status. Sebastian followed her social media accounts, subscribed to her YouTube videos and podcast, and just might have had a small crush on her. Despite his infatuation, they'd never met. Sebastian worked remotely from his flat in Berlin, Germany, while Chloe jetted around the world.

Late one evening, Sebastian's dream of interacting with his influencer boss came true when he received a text from her asking to FaceTime. They'd never communicated, but he determined that it was reasonable that she'd have access to his cell number. She was the CEO, after all. He eagerly clicked to agree to the chat, and within seconds Chloe's smiling face appeared. The warm and congenial conversation was everything Sebastian had hoped for. She asked after him and shared some anecdotes about her experiences in Berlin, such as her favorite biergarten and what she saw during the long walks she took along the Spree River. Maybe one day they could walk together?

When she got to the point of the call—an immediate transfer of 5 million euros to a subcontractor he'd never heard of—Sebastian never questioned the request. Chloe was on his screen personally requesting the transfer. Her smile assured him of this.

Later investigation would reveal that Chloe had never contacted Sebastian. Not once. When asked, she did not know his name, the fact that he worked in Berlin, or that the company employed a German finance controller. It turned out that a sophisticated cybercrime syndicate hidden within the dark web's countless anonymous servers data mined all of Chloe's many media interviews, social media posts, and YouTube videos and cloned her voice using a subscription-based online AI model. After spending a few weeks surveilling the company through LinkedIn and Twitter, the criminals identified all the personnel in finance and discovered a Chloe superfan in Sebastian. They located his personal cell phone number and called using the AI avatar. Sebastian thought he'd spoken to the woman of his dreams. Instead, he'd spoken to Artyom, a twenty-two-year-old Belarusian computer engineer. Artyom typed what he wanted Chloe to say in his AI chat function and the avatar mimicked Chloe's voice and face with near precision. Within hours of the deposit, the 5 million euros disappeared from the "subcontractor's" bank account and melted away into untraceable cryptocurrency wallets owned by Artyom's dark web cybercriminal friends.

This *Black Mirror*–like scenario is a real-life example of our current cybersecurity crisis. It isn't an example of what *could* happen in some distant future if we're not careful; it's an example of what's occurring every day, all around the world. Soon, we will not be able to trust everyday mediums like texts, FaceTime, Google Meet, Teams, and other social and work platforms. These attacks have already begun to replace the most common spear phishing email threats. The best AI avatar attacks are already indistinguishable from real life—all because of the unchecked, innovative rise of cybercrime. By 2026, 90 percent of the internet will be synthetically generated.[1] Trust has become an uncommon commodity.

We have progressed into a global society that relies on technology to learn, experience, communicate, collaborate, work, and play—a tele-everything world—where all interactions of every sort occur online. This fact fed steam to the engine of the dark web's train. And this train has no brakes. Global cybercrime syndicates adopted the espionage tradecrafts of impersonation, bullying, greed, and the human propensity to trust others as a means to launch cyberattacks against us. They research our social media, befriend us when we are lonely, trick us with investment opportunities by exploiting our heartstrings, cloak themselves in our identities, ransom sensitive information, and exploit our most critical data. Cybercrime has become a business with growth verticals to rival the largest corporate juggernauts, its grandiosity protected by the anonymity of the dark web, the deepest and most secret layer of the internet. We are all future customers—ready or not.

To exploit our vulnerability, criminals have flocked into the dark web's hidden depths to launch ransomware attacks, line their pockets with billions of dollars in criminal fraud, upset and weaken critical infrastructure, and share tips and tools to train the next generation of bandits. The cost of cybercrime is skyrocketing exponentially and increases by an average of 15 percent year over year. In 2023, global cybercrime exceeded $12 trillion. At its current growth, the cybercrime industry will exceed $20 trillion annually by 2026 and potentially $30 trillion by 2028! Measured as gross domestic product, the dark web generates enough cybercrime to make it the third-largest economy on earth, exceeding both Germany and Japan combined. This represents the greatest transfer of wealth in world history, exceeds the global damage costs from natural disasters in a year, and is more profitable than global gains from the trade of all major illegal drugs combined. Let that sink in for a moment.

Threat actors of all stripes and colors—from nation-state spies to new criminal syndicates—have invested in new business ventures to steal the data that moves, shapes, and informs humanity. Like spies, they use our data to improve rival economies, steal technology, undermine democracy, and prepare for future warfare. Espionage has evolved from the cloak-and-dagger dead drops of the past to a relentless series of cyberattacks that confound security and defy counterintelligence. To prevent spies and criminals from igniting a data doomsday, cybersecurity demands spy hunters like me.

My career began in the FBI's counterintelligence trenches as an undercover operative. Protected by false identities, I shadowed spies and terrorists along the wide boulevards and cracked alleys of Washington, D.C., the unofficial spy capital of the world. I investigated trusted insiders who betrayed every oath, and I tracked and dismantled terrorist cells before they could plan attacks.

The capstone of my origin story as an FBI Ghost (what operatives are known as) was my undercover work to bring down Robert Hanssen, a decorated FBI Supervisory Special Agent who spent over two decades spying for Russia. Working against a ticking clock, I covertly assembled evidence against Hanssen while working overtly with him to build the FBI's first cybersecurity division. My efforts led to the smoking gun that closed the case on Robert Hanssen and sent him to prison for life.

Hanssen's legacy as the most notorious and damaging spy in U.S. history may never be exceeded. It took the FBI over two decades to identify the mole, but only after Hanssen had thoroughly undermined the United States' most carefully hidden secrets. It took me three months to catch him. The sensational story became the basis for Universal Studio's critically acclaimed thriller *Breach* and the basis for my first book, *Gray Day*.

I've since spent decades as a national security attorney, corporate investigator, national cybersecurity strategist, and part of internal threat response teams for several cybersecurity companies. I speak between twenty-five and thirty times a year to thousands across the globe, inspiring audiences to protect themselves and join the struggle to make the world safe from cyberattacks. As spies evolved, I also had to. In the last decade, no threat actor has caused more damage than cybercriminals that emulate, and often surpass, the spies that had once emboldened and inspired them.

The COVID-19 lockdowns emboldened them further. A forcibly distributed workforce dove into the deep end of technology adoption before cybersecurity could learn to swim. While lockdowns closed restaurants, shopping malls, churches, gyms, and entertainment venues, e-commerce transactions surged. Businesses of all stripes and sizes, including most restaurants, innovated with curbside pickup and invested in web portals and phone applications that accepted digital orders. Within an hour, and all from apps on my phone, I could pick up dinner at Five Guys, a new backup drive at BestBuy, a prescription refill at CVS, and a growler of beer from Seven Locks Brewery.

The largesse from cyberattacks seeded the dark web with a bounty of usernames, passwords, and personally identifying information. Criminals bought this data for pennies through online auctions and used it to launch further attacks. While most of society was unprepared to live online, the criminals had already perfected their craft.

In the years since COVID-19 scourged the world, a vicious circle of pandemic-made vulnerabilities—exploits crafted by espionage units; pressure situations that overburdened cybersecurity; and the growth of the dark web as a resource, payment clearinghouse, and collaborative think tank for criminals—has allowed crime to surge and security to fail.

According to a recent report from the World Economic Forum, a global catastrophic mutating event (GCME) will occur before the end of 2025. Among five potential GCMEs, a global critical infrastructure cyberattack is cited as most likely. A lack of adequate cybersecurity measures, resources to protect against cyberthreats, and international cooperation and regulation has made attacks easier for cybercriminals (threat actors). At the same time, nation-state sponsored cyberattacks (particularly from China, Russia, Iran, and North Korea) have increased as diplomacy fails, which will have catastrophic global implications as warfare moves to the cyber battleground.

Where spies employed by foreign nations have spent the last decade probing critical infrastructure to ready their trigger for a GCME, rogue criminals have exploited our reliance on power, water, gas, food, and communications (everything our society cannot live without) to make their fortunes. In the past five years, criminals have left gas stations without fuel, held power and water for ransom, prevented food from reaching our tables, shut down hospitals, and prevented our children from attending school—all to make some Bitcoin.

Some solutions to the problem are extreme. The most critical infrastructure, our nuclear energy reactors, have taken extraordinary steps to prevent catastrophic cyberattacks. Operational systems are so air-gapped (removed from any connection to the internet) that legacy systems are updated using floppy disks. The most secure information in government systems exists in locked vaults that do not allow anything more technologically advanced than a paperclip inside. Secret spy rooms buried in embassies around the world hold meetings in soundproofed plexiglass chambers, suspended off the floor to reduce sound vibrations. I have brilliant friends who have tossed out their smartphones and have chosen to write on aged, mechanical typewriters, all to protect their most critical information. Others have replaced their recorded voicemail messages with the generic robotic message because AI can now clone a voice with only a few seconds of sound. These steps are an extreme response to an often baffling problem. But for most, opening our eyes to the threat and understanding how to fight back will be enough to demystify the dark web.

To protect against this future, we must change the way we think about cyberattacks. We must divorce ourselves from a defensive mindset and become threat hunters instead. We must become as tireless as the cybercriminals—but for the purposes of a good, safer, more favorable world. We must take back the tactics that cybercriminals have exploited and learn to beat them at their own game. Only then can we avoid a data doomsday.

This book is your field manual for the current cyber war, helping you take up arms instead of fleeing as the village burns. But before we can begin our counteroffensive, we must learn about and understand the tool kit used by cybercriminals. **Part I: Think Like a Spy** will expose and demystify these tools, including **Deception, Impersonation, Infiltration, Confidence, Exploitation**, and **Destruction**

(DI²CED). I will pry into each of these tools so that you'll learn how spies, grifters, scammers, hackers, and cybercriminals exploit our innate trust in others. Every great lie surrounds a kernel of truth, and this truth is the hook that spies and criminals use to deceive human targets into handing over access to secrets.

It turns out no one is safe. Even my background and training have not immunized me from cyberattacks. I've survived numerous ransomware attack attempts, clever spear phishing schemes, and even phone calls from criminals posing as clients—all of which you'll read about. Still, I've learned from the near hits of previous attacks and have developed concrete defenses that have saved my data and secured my wallet. And once you're finished reading, these defenses will serve as your tools in a personal cybersecurity arsenal.

That's where **Part II: Act Like a Spy Hunter** applies. Once you understand the tactics that cybercriminals employ to disrupt your wallet and your emotions, you'll be primed to do something about it.

Most spies are highly trained, continually cover their tracks, and deploy countersurveillance in an attempt to spot the spy hunter. A single mistake can lead to devastating consequences. For that reason, careful tactics of **Prepare, Assess, Investigate, and Decide (PAID)** are the prescriptive keys to successfully catching a spy.

PAID provides context—critical insight into the attackers' tactics, motivations, and objectives—that allows threat hunters to defeat attackers. Context is both an enemy and savior. If you have it, you are golden. Without it, everything comes crashing down. Context grants intrinsic knowledge of where your most critical data resides and how it may be accessed. Imagine a dojo where the martial arts master knows every corner of every floorboard, knows his balance across the mats, and can fight blindfolded without touching a wall or hitting a beam. Any challenger that enters the dojo will have a hard time defeating the owner. PAID will help turn my readers into grand masters responsible for their own data.

In recent years, cybercrime has grown so bloated that law enforcement is impotent to stop it. This means that cybersecurity must continue to evolve to compete in an arms race with attackers. Individuals, businesses, and organizations can protect themselves from cyberattacks by opening their eyes, understanding the threat, and preparing for the worst *before* an attacker strikes.

If enough of us become covert agents and learn to safeguard our personal data, we can also make the world safe from cyberattacks. This is how we start. One data point at a time.

PART I

THINK LIKE A SPY

(DI²CED)

Deception: The espionage art of deception refers to the deliberate use of misleading tactics, misinformation, and subterfuge by intelligence agencies or operatives to manipulate adversaries, conceal true intentions, or gather information covertly.

Impersonation: The espionage art of impersonation involves assuming the identity of another individual or entity, typically for the purpose of gaining access to restricted areas, obtaining sensitive information, or carrying out covert operations.

Infiltration: The espionage art of infiltration refers to the covert insertion of intelligence agents or operatives into target organizations, institutions, or areas for the purpose of gathering information, conducting surveillance, or carrying out clandestine activities.

Confidence: The espionage art of confidence schemes, also known as confidence tricks or confidence games (also the origin of the term "con artist") involves manipulating individuals or organizations into willingly divulging sensitive information, providing access to secure areas, or carrying out actions that benefit the perpetrator. These schemes rely on building trust, exploiting psychological vulnerabilities, and creating deceptive scenarios to trick the target.

Exploitation: The espionage art of exploitation involves the strategic utilization of vulnerabilities, weaknesses, or assets within a target organization, system, or individual for the purpose of gathering intelligence, exerting influence, or achieving operational objectives.

Destruction: The espionage art of destruction involves the deliberate use of sabotage, subversion, or covert action to disrupt, damage, or neutralize enemy targets, assets, or capabilities. Unlike traditional military actions, which often involve overt displays of force, destruction in espionage is typically carried out clandestinely.

ONE

The House Is Burning Down

"We have a problem."

These are never words anyone wants to hear early on a Saturday morning, much less from the chief information officer of an international company. Though I'd traded in my gold shield for a law degree years ago, my ears were still attuned to danger.

"How bad?" I asked. My gut told me that my weekend plans would soon crash all around me. I could picture Ben on the other end of the phone. Tall and physically fit, at first glance he resembles basketball star Michael Jordan with his smoothly shaved head. His hands could probably palm a basketball, but today I imagined them resting on a keyboard.

Ben rose through the ranks from a humble beginning at the IT help desk of a small charity to the vice president and chief information officer of a company transformed into a global nongovernmental organization (NGO) supporting humanitarian work in some of the most complex environments on earth—places like Syria, Yemen, and Ukraine. He not only traveled upward through the IT department's hierarchy, but built the global IT workforce from the inside out. He knew the location of every ethernet cable and the name of every one of his hundreds of employees. Where he usually exuded

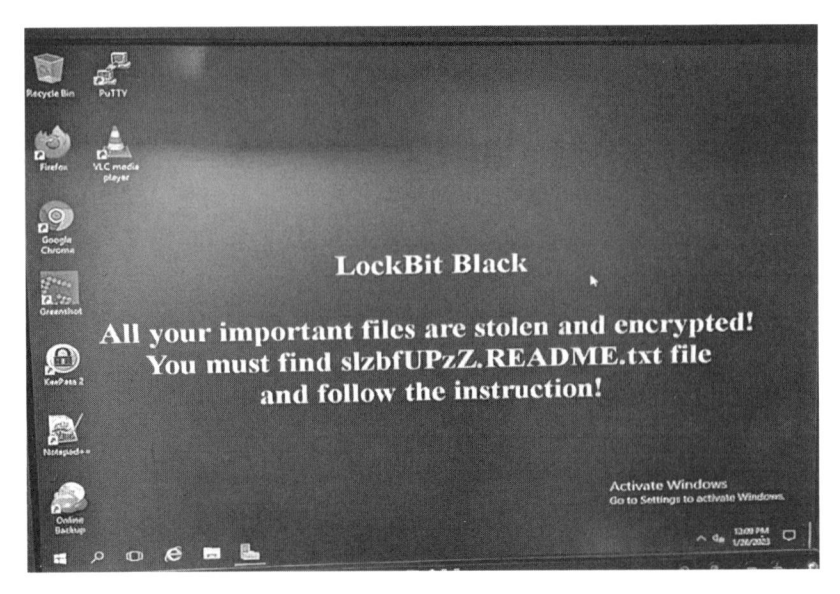

A Windows server showing a ransomware screen.

confidence and composure, he now sounded panicked. "We have a cyber event," he said, voice cracking over the phone. "I think it's ransomware."

I winced as though I'd just taken a punch to the face. "Has it spread?" Forget the weekend—in that moment, I knew I'd lose weeks if not months to the problem.

"It's *global*."

That Saturday morning in January 2022, a senior engineer in the headquarters workforce logged into the main HQ server and saw the stuff of IT nightmares:

"All your important files are stolen and encrypted!"

Terrified, he accessed the only file the attackers made available on the system, a four-page README.txt file that began with the following:

LockBit 3.0 the world's fastest and most stable ransomware from 2019~~~ >>>>> Your data is stolen and encrypted.

If you don't pay the ransom, the data will be published on our TOR darknet sites. Keep in mind that once your data appears on our leak site, it could be bought by your competitors at any second, so don't hesitate for a long time. The sooner you pay the ransom, the sooner your company will be safe.

LockBit refers to LockBit Ransomware Group, a Russian-based cybercrime syndicate that surfaced in 2019. They have distinguished themselves from other crime families with a four-stage attack methodology. They initially spend time conducting reconnaissance on an organization to discover weaknesses. Second, they exploit those deficiencies to gain a foothold in the victim's network. Next, they infiltrate deep into systems to create user accounts they control, disable security, and identify and steal critical information. Finally, they deploy their proprietary, self-propagating ransomware code, which spreads on its own to infect and encrypt as many files as possible.

According to the U.S. Department of Justice, since starting their dark web ransomware factory, LockBit and the affiliates that subscribe to their service (more on affiliate-based cybercrime later) have attacked over two thousand global victims and have extorted over $120 million in ransom payments. During the first Trump administration, they employed the tongue-in-cheek tagline Trying to Make Ransomware Great Again. In this, they succeeded—and they are not alone. Numerous other cybercrime syndicates compete with LockBit for a share of trillions of dollars that pour into the dark web. On their media site, LockBit boasts they are the "oldest ransomware affiliate program on the planet." In this statement, these no-good criminals and liars may actually be telling the truth.

Many people consider ransomware a modern threat, but criminals have launched ransomware attacks since the 1980s. And why not? Ransomware may be the perfect crime. Throughout modern history, cerebrally challenged gangsters have charged into brick-and-mortar banks with masks, loaded guns, and empty loot sacks, risking wild police chases, felony murder charges, and, at best, eventual fugitive status. As the world evolved and data transcended cash in value, the smart felons learned from spies and turned to hacking. Ransomware is akin to holding a company hostage in return for a suitcase of cash, but rather than using firearms, ransomware attackers use their keyboards.

One of the oldest known ransomware attacks occurred in 1989 when a doctor named Joseph Popp handed out twenty thousand floppy disks to AIDS researchers across the world. The disks contained his proprietary program, which used a questionnaire to analyze whether a person might contract the autoimmune disease. Those who used the program didn't know that each disk held a secret malicious program that eventually would infect computers that ran the disk. When an unsuspecting researcher turned on their computer for the ninetieth time after loading the questionnaire disk, the computer locked and displayed a message requesting between $189 and $378 for a "software lease." Security professionals began calling the sensational attack the "AIDS Trojan."

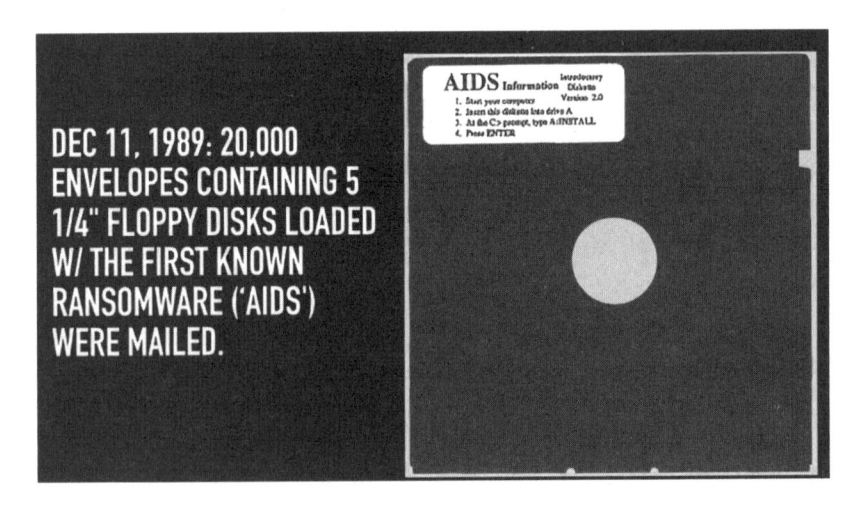

DEC 11, 1989: 20,000 ENVELOPES CONTAINING 5 1/4" FLOPPY DISKS LOADED W/ THE FIRST KNOWN RANSOMWARE ('AIDS') WERE MAILED.

Source: Courtesy David Balcar

By January 2020, when LockBit attacked my NGO client, they had adopted a new cybercrime business model called ransomware as a service (RaaS) and recruited affiliates to do their dirty work. The model copies successful software companies that provide technology, tool kits, and know-how in return for a monthly fee. But these criminals are buying access to cybercrime tools. Dark web affiliates are legions of threat actors who purchase subscriptions to off-the-shelf LockBit resources like novel malicious software (malware), email phishing templates, and even leads on human trusted insiders recruited within organizations to unlock network doors for attackers. For each successful cyberattack, the affiliate pays a 20–25 percent commission back to LockBit. This model of service-oriented cybercrime allows unsophisticated criminals with little technical skill to stake a claim in the fastest-growing business on earth.

In late February 2024, top law enforcement agencies in the U.S., UK, and Europe banded together to take down LockBit. They gave this immense operation the code name Cronos, named after the mythological Greek deity of time.

The highly secretive operation resulted in an unprecedented unraveling of LockBit. The Cronos task force dismantled thirty-two of LockBit's servers, knocked out their affiliate portal, and took control of the public website where LockBit published the information of victims who refused to pay ransoms. Law enforcement also recovered hundreds of cryptocurrency wallets (offering a chance for some victims to recover the ransoms they paid), arrested two of LockBit's threat actors in Poland and Ukraine, and issued three international arrest warrants. Finally, the task force published more than a thousand decryption keys and a universal decryption tool for anyone locked by the ransomware variant in the future.

To keep the cybercrime syndicate on their heels, the U.S. Department of State posted a $5 million reward for anyone with information about LockBit associates, and a $10 million reward for information leading to the identification or location of LockBit's leadership.[1] Threat hunters and white-hat hackers around the world have launched themselves into this bounty program like gunslingers in the old West, freshly deputized and holding a wanted poster.

Boom goes the dynamite, you think? So long, LockBit? Not so fast.

Within a week, LockBit rose from its ashes. LockBitSupp, the supposed leader of the syndicate, issued a long post crowing about LockBit's resiliency and how its backup servers had escaped the task force's reach. By July 2024, LockBit had topped the charts as the most dominant ransomware group.

* * *

The speed of destruction with which a cyberattack occurs is devastating and life altering. I know this because it's happened to me. Not just a cyberattack (that's happened too, as you'll soon see) but something just as personal.

Late one afternoon on a sunny day in early spring 1988, my best friend, Christian, and the dean of Student Services for Gonzaga High School interrupted my freshman biology class. I was asked to pack up my bag and follow Christian to where his parents picked us up and drove me home. To what was left of my home.

A couple of hours earlier, a massive fire ravaged our family home. While my brothers and I attended various schools—my father worked from his Washington, D.C., office and my mother delivered goodies cooked up by her catering company—a small fire in the basement grew to an inferno that destroyed every possession I owned. I remember staring at the empty place that had been my room at the front of the house and wondering, *What now?*

The shell-shocked feeling of watching the last curls of smoke rise from the wreckage of a family home mirrors the gut-wrenching realization that a cybercriminal has ruthlessly accessed, stolen, and destroyed data that is the lifeblood of an organization. For many of us, the data we store on our laptops is as precious as the books, clothing, keepsakes, mementos, and all the physical accoutrements collected throughout a life. Data has become the currency of our lives. It can happen to you. It can all disappear in an instant.

Fortunately, my parents had a robust fire insurance policy, but the coverage required us to list all the things we once owned. Neighbors came with legal pads to stand in our driveway and help my parents remember everything from our TV model to what kind of curtains once hung in blackened windows. If my parents hadn't planned, the cost to recover could have bankrupted us. House fires happened *to other people* in the news. They didn't burn down historic homes in sleepy Kensington, Maryland. Until they did.

Similarly, cybercriminals like LockBit know that most of us do not invest in robust cybersecurity or cyber insurance. A successful attack means immense pressure to pay a ransom to release encrypted data or repatriate critical information that the attacker has stolen and threatens to publish on the Dark Web.

The LockBit affiliate who attacked the NGO planned to extort a ransom of $5 million and claimed to have stolen three terabytes of information! If you recall the analogy from the introduction, that's equivalent to twenty-one miles of stacked paper. Over the weekend he'd essentially set fire to all that paper.

You may be asking yourself whether dark web cybercriminals, flush with millions stolen from corporations, government agencies, and even charities would ever deign to attack *you* as opposed to an NGO with terabytes of information and powerful interagency data. The answer is a resounding *yes*. Decades spent as a security strategist have brought me to a simple truth. Dark web cybercrime does not discriminate among targets. They do not care how wealthy you are or the importance of the technology you control. They know that the data each of us owns is, for that person or company, the most important commodity on earth. For that reason, an attacker only cares whether you are vulnerable. No person or company is safe or off-limits.

* * *

Ben and I had a plan. In those first moments after my phone rang and Ben struggled with what to say, we took a difficult step that ended up saving us.

After a sleepless weekend rolled into a fresh workweek, Ben and I instructed our employees to "close your laptops" and unplug from the internet, grinding to a halt all the business of the NGO. Our employees were confused by this directive—after all, not one of them had ever been told to stop working on a Monday morning.

Two days later, Ben and I put together a team that included our data protection unit and global IT team; a cybersecurity insurance carrier; data privacy attorneys in the U.S., UK, and Europe; and a cybersecurity threat-hunting company. We launched a dogfight against the LockBit attacker, closing servers and trapping him in an ever-narrowing network, seeking to pinpoint his location and flush him out. All the while, he locked computers with ransomware, compromised accounts, sought to create back doors to make us repeat customers, and stole our data.

My phone rang one evening as I sat down to dinner with my family. I never pick up when I don't recognize the caller ID, but something compelled me to tap accept on the Unknown Name, Unknown Number call. Call it a premonition.

"This is LockBit," a crisp voice said over my private cell phone. "We want to negotiate."

THINK LIKE A SPY

To understand threat actors (cybercriminals and cyber spies) you must put yourself into the mind of the attacker. Thinking like a spy means understanding the attacker's thought process before and during an attack, as well as the specific outcome they wish to achieve. Spies steal secrets clandestinely. Criminals steal data with the intent to monetize that theft directly. Both seek to launch attacks against the unwary, striking in places victims least suspect. Following each chapter in Part I, we will examine the threat actor thought process in "Think Like a Spy" sections. If these read like a handbook for the bad guys, that's intentional. It's imperative that you understand the adversary, so you will know how to beat them at their own game.

- Now is the best time in history to launch a cyberattack: (1) The dark web is here to stay, and it provides a place for cybercriminals to gather, trade, and thrive; (2) COVID-19 pandemic lockdowns in 2020 forced a flood of victims to immediately adopt new, online technologies before security could prepare; and (3) spies paved the way for criminals who sat up and took notice of the best new cyberattacks. The pandemic might be over, but security and society still haven't solved their problems.

- The dark web is part of the internet made up of an anonymous system of servers and computers spread across the globe that is redundant, difficult to locate, and provides near anonymity to those who access it correctly. It has created a haven for cybercriminals to organize into syndicates, launch attacks, collect ransoms, and thumb their noses at law enforcement.

- A prospective target's wealth, sophistication, or importance doesn't matter when choosing to launch a cyberattack. All that matters is whether the target is vulnerable. People and businesses who don't think it can happen to them make the best victims, because they never see it coming.

- The most important and valuable data to each person or organization is the information they care most about. Exploit that data correctly and victims will listen to your demands, pay ransoms, and overall dance to your tune.

- Place your targets into a pressure situation by making them frightened or concerned; placing a ticking clock on an attractive opportunity; or threatening to disclose, exploit, or destroy their data if they refuse your demands. Most victims fail to plan ahead of the pressure situation and end up trying to escape the house after you've already set it on fire.

TWO

The Cloak-and-Dagger Game

In December 2000, FBI Supervisory Special Agent Gene McClelland—the boss of the elite team of undercover Ghosts I belonged to—showed up at my apartment and briefed me on the case that would alter the course of my life. In an unprecedented investigation, I would go undercover at FBI Headquarters to catch a spy. What I didn't know going into the case was that my target, Robert Hanssen (code-named Gray Day), was Russia's best-placed mole in the U.S. intelligence community. He was also America's first cyber spy, whose penetration of FBI computer systems led to him passing on some of the most damaging information ever provided to a foreign adversary.

Hanssen, an FBI veteran, had spied for the Soviet Union and Russian Federation for twenty-two years of his decorated twenty-five-year career. In three short months, without specific training to go toe-to-toe with the spy, I learned everything about him, gained his trust, and found the smoking gun that would lead to his arrest and conviction.

Hanssen got away with his crimes for so long because he was a master at deception and a hacker in a time when the FBI computer systems had not properly secured networks from internal threats. Where he had converted his fascination with computerization into theft, I had sought to discover holes in security to strengthen defenses. It took a hacker to catch a hacker.

Our media and culture have used the term "hacker" incorrectly for decades. Most who hear the term imagine a young man in a dark basement, his face lit by a glowing screen and his hands dancing across a keyboard. Utilizing some magic that few understand, and Hollywood and television studios rarely attempt to explain, this mystical figure finally punches a single key and shouts triumphantly, "I'm in!" In real life, hacking is nothing more than the necessary evolution of espionage. As global societies moved from typewritten memos on paper to electronic messages on email, espionage units everywhere needed to evolve or disappear with all the old file cabinets and looseleaf binders.

When I chased spies across Washington, D.C., we knew to look for government employees and contractors who left their offices and drove straight to local bars. We would watch for the government badges clipped to their shirt that handily listed their name and workplace. Then we would see if a known foreign intelligence officer cozied up next to them and bought them a drink. All this fell by the wayside when society networked all our government, business, and personal computer systems. Spies no longer had to physically recruit that government worker over a dozen shots and a vodka tonic. They now do so virtually from wherever they sit in the world. It used to take a spy months or years to convince an asset to go into a government office with a microfilm camera and extract secrets. Today it takes less than an hour to compromise that same employee through an email. Modern moles have become what I call virtual trusted insiders—unsuspecting puppets with compromised accounts controlled by a spy.

The real hackers are spies who have evolved. They use the same deceptive tactics to fool a person into granting them access to all their data. So-called social engineering tactics are all the old spy tactics repackaged for modern times . . . and criminals have watched and learned from them.

To stop them, we must elevate our thinking for *all attackers*. Until everyone from the tween with her first smartphone to the largest Fortune 100 board of directors learn this premise, we will remain vulnerable to attack.

Therefore: *There are no hackers, there are only spies.*

The art of deception uses misleading tactics, misinformation, and subterfuge to manipulate adversaries, conceal true intentions, or secretly gather information. Spies like Hanssen are great liars. Robert Hanssen deceived the FBI for decades. For example, while working as a supervisory special agent tasked to audit various FBI legal attaché (LEGAT) offices, he would quietly steal the very information he reviewed, pocketing it so that he could transfer it to Russian intelligence officers via clandestine dead drops under a Virginia footbridge.

Of all the tricks in the espionage playbook, deception is the oldest and most prolific tool for a spy. In fact, the DI^{2}CED methodology runs on an engine of deception. Impersonation, Infiltration, Confidence, Exploitation, and Destruction also require deceit to accomplish its task. Obviously, to trick us into handing over secrets, a spy must first gain our trust. Hanssen could not have stolen secrets regarding the United States' nuclear warfare program and left it under a footbridge for his Soviet spymasters if the FBI did not first trust him with the information.

The great game of espionage has long focused on methods to make the unwitting or unwary trust a lie. In 1985, Ana Belen Montes began her work at the U.S. Defense Intelligence Agency as an analyst developing critical intelligence about Cuba. She rose to become the top Cuban analyst and a respected member of the broader intelligence community. She was also Cuba's top spy in the United States. In 1984, while working for the Justice Department, Montes decided that the United States had adopted unfair policies toward Central America and Cuba. Her vocal opinions attracted the notice of a Cuban spymaster, who used Montes's anti-American ideology to turn her to the dark side. Montes specifically took the job at the DIA with the ambition of spying for Cuba. She deceived and manipulated the U.S. government in her efforts to assist the tiny country south of Florida. Montes escaped detection by never removing any information from work. Instead, she memorized classified information and typed it up once she got home. She would then wait for her Cuban spymasters to send shortwave radio instructions to arrange clandestine meets, where she would hand over the secrets on encrypted disks. And she did this for thirty-six years, until the FBI finally arrested her in 2021.

Similarly, what made Hanssen a great spy was his ability to spot flaws in security and exploit them by deceiving those who trusted him. I spent a career catching spies by understanding weaknesses in security and watching for those, like Hanssen, who sought to capitalize on them. In many ways, our backgrounds as hackers made me particularly adept at foiling Hanssen, like two sides of the same coin. But even spy hunters and cybersecurity experts can find themselves tangled in clever webs of deception.

A few years ago, I received an email request to speak from the Hillsong Church in Cape Town, South Africa. The pastor reached out to me directly and requested that I tell the story of how I caught Robert Hanssen and asked if I could incorporate a faith-based theme into the speech. After surviving the most unique and complex case the FBI had ever run catapulted my public speaking career, hearing from the pastor of a large congregation was not unusual.

The pastor had seen the movie *Breach* and believed that my message would resonate with the congregation of his megachurch. We discussed this over email, and I asked him to give me a call to finalize the engagement. Over the phone, the pastor sounded educated and knowledgeable, and he knew sufficient details about Hillsong to satisfy the "verify first, trust later" mentality beat into me by the FBI. We settled on a keynote topic, signed a contract for my full speaker fee, and agreed on first-class airfare to Cape Town.

I purchased a $10,000 first-class ticket from United and began preparing my keynote. Hours later, I heard from the pastor's associate in Hillsong's finance department. She needed me to immediately send $5,000 that they would escrow with the South African authorities to ensure that I would not seek asylum in their country. My alarm bells began ringing. I called the South African embassy in Washington, D.C., and asked about the escrow process. I was told it didn't exist. I called Hillsong and spoke to one of the pastor's aides—they'd never heard of me. I used databases available to me as an investigator and reverse-searched the Cape Town phone number of the man I had spoken to numerous times. I scrutinized the email address—a valid Gmail address—but not one with the Hillsong domain. I seethed inside with anger and embarrassment. Fortunately, United refunded me the first-class ticket, and I sent one final email to the fake pastor, instructing him to pound sand. I've told this story countless times as an example that no one is safe from cyberattacks, especially individuals who subscribe to an *it-can't-happen-to-me* mindset.

The Hillsong attack began with an email that hooked my interest and allowed the pretend pastor to slowly draw me into his scheme. Like a fisherman coaxing a big catch slowly into his boat, the cybercriminal reeled me in with promises of a first-class trip to a grand stage at my full speaker's fee. The methodical scheme did not require malicious software deployed through an attractive link or clever attachment. Instead, the deception relied on careful *social engineering* to convince me to believe the lie.

I recall an investigation I conducted in which employees at a company received numerous emails purportedly from the marketing team of an online conference many of them had attended. The carefully crafted emails met all the espionage criteria: crisp logos, correct branding, no grammatical errors or misspellings. They also promised a reward: the conference organizers wished to send a physical gift to the home address of every virtual attendee. By clicking the "trusted" link, an attendee could select one of three gifts from a "secure" website: a Yeti mug, a branded backpack, or a light-up Minecraft sword. Minecraft was a huge part of the zeitgeist of the time. The blocky building game had taken youth culture by storm, and every kid with access to a device played it. Many parents too.

The employees, desiring a gift, immediately recognized the conference logo from having spotted it in person the week before. As a result, most employees clicked through. Some even discussed the gifts on their Slack channel and over intercompany email. Most chose the sword.

When an employee clicked through, a mock website opened that installed malware on their computer. This false website, built to look exactly like the virtual conference website, is called a landing page. The malicious code scans the victim's computer, searches for flaws like outdated or missing patches to applications or the operating system, and selects the perfect attack to compromise the machine. Worst of all, landing page code does not typically trigger notifications to the user from basic cybersecurity tools.*

Unsurprisingly, no one received their Minecraft swords. Instead, whoever clicked through received a grinning skull locked onto their screen and a notice from criminal attackers that "all your information now belongs to us."

How had the bad guys planned the attack? They scoured LinkedIn and Facebook for conference announcements and built their email target lists from the individuals that liked thank-you posts from conference marketers. The registration fields (Name/Address/Age/etc.) that the attackers set up were dummy fields, but they were also potential avenues to gather additional information about employees. Personally identifiable information (PII) sells well on the dark web, it turns out. Depending on the category of PII, cybercriminals can make anywhere from hundreds to thousands of dollars selling your most critical information on dark web marketplaces.

Emails like the one from the Hillsong pastor that target individuals using trusted information to hook the victim are called spear phishing emails. In contrast, the constant garbage emails we receive daily in bulk are called phishing attacks, spam attacks, or bulk-email attacks. Most of these come from lists containing millions of emails bought for about a hundred dollars from dark web marketplaces. Here are a few examples of the subjects of four email phishing attacks I recently deleted, but there are thousands of others of all shapes and sizes:

---

* Cybercriminals similarly use drive-by download attacks, in which a victim visits a website that infects their computer through a web browser security vulnerability. This often happens when we click on suspicious links on clickbait websites or visit sites displaying pornography.

Your UPS package has shipped! Click here to track it.

We've noticed unauthorized access to your Wells Fargo bank account. Click to confirm whether it was you.

Sams Club Shipment: 🛒 Final Attempt To Contact

_J.o.h.n_Deere Mower_ You have won an John Deere Mower!!

The body of each email contains some sort of [CLICK HERE] message that entices the victim. For the most part, we can identify these sorts of emails and quickly send them to the trash. But not always. Some emails blur the line between the spray-and-pray garbage and the more nefarious spear phishing emails, like the one I highlighted in the Hillsong story above.

One way we are trained to identify a legitimate email from a phishing trap is to look at the address of the sender. But criminals also are aware of this defense and have developed savvy methods to fool us. Imagine you receive an email from service@amazon.com that includes a [CLICK HERE] button to track your latest order. You might quickly check the email address to make certain it's actually from "amazon.com." But can you tell the difference between the two email addresses below? Hint: one is real and the other fake.

1. service@amazon.com

2. service@amazon.com

I couldn't tell either. The middle "a" in the second example "amazon" is typed in Cyrillic (which would map to the "F" key on a U.S. keyboard). They are different but look exactly the same. An attacker registered the domain amazon.com with a Cyrillic "a," and all the traffic directed there from his mass mailing campaign led to compromised systems.

Sometimes the attackers add a dash of personality. During the pandemic, my friend Patrick called me because his Microsoft Windows laptop suddenly rebooted into a locked screen with red text on a black background:

!!!!IMPORTANT INFORMATION!!!!

Your files are encrypted with RSA-2048 and AES-128 Ciphers

Restoring of your files is only possible with the private key and decrypt program, which is our secret.

The instructions went on to explain how to download the Tor Browser so that my friend could access a specific .onion address. The web address led to a dark web site created by the attackers, where my buddy could pay in Bitcoin for a decryption key.

We disconnected his laptop from the internet, shut it down, and discussed what had happened before the computer rebooted. My friend had come across an email from UPS.com telling him that his package was on its way and accompanied by a handy tracking link. Like most of us, Patrick expected a shipment and trusted the email in his inbox. I should also say that Patrick is no dummy. He's an engineer who develops landing gear for a major airline. When we looked at his laptop, I think he felt more ashamed for getting outsmarted than upset at the loss of his data.

An extraordinary number of people have lost data to countless variations of this precise attack during the pandemic. According to F5's Phishing and Fraud Report, in 2020, at the time my buddy clicked on the UPS email, phishing attacks rose 220 percent compared to the prior yearly average. Bad guys knew that people locked in their homes anxiously awaited packages delivered to their door and were more likely to click on tracking links.

Patrick had a good backup sitting in a locked drawer. He backs up his computer to an external hard drive every week and disconnects the backup afterward. Since many ransomware attacks also target any connected backups, it's better to unplug them when the backup completes. In cybersecurity parlance we call this *air-gapping*. We restored his system from backup, installed better cybersecurity software with endpoint monitoring and ransomware protection, and saved the thousands of pictures of his kids that help build a lifetime of memories.

One of the most nefarious phishing attacks happened in the first few months of 2025 when the United States was assaulted by a wave of cyber scams dressed up as toll notices—fast, convincing, and deadly effective. I got a text that looked like it came straight from the United States East Coast electronic toll collection system "E-ZPass." The text included urgent language, familiar branding, and a threat of DMV involvement if I didn't pay in twelve hours. It was slick. But something didn't feel right.

> The Toll Roads Notice of Toll Evasion: You have an unpaid toll bill on your account. To avoid late fees, pay within 12 hours or the late fees will be increased and reported to the DMV.
>
> https://thetollroad.com-emxq.xin/us
>
> (Please reply Y, then exit the text message and open it again to activate the link, or copy the link to your Safari browser and open it)
>
> The Toll Roads team wishes you a great day!

Scam toll roads notice text. Clicking the link led to a fake $5 charge and a cyberattack.

Turns out this was a phishing scam that's hit millions of phones. Cybercriminals—possibly tied to Chinese syndicates—faked real toll systems and used the $5 charge as bait. Click the link, and you're rerouted to a polished fake site that siphons off your credit card info, log-ins, and personal data. Cybersecurity company Trend Micro reported a 900 percent spike in toll scams in 2025 alone, and with AI generating sharper, more believable lures, it's getting harder to tell real from fake.

If phishing resembles a spray-and-pray drive-by attack, spear phishing is like trying to avoid John Wick after you just killed his dog. You'd never see him coming. Spear phishing relies on target reconnaissance. An attacker will learn a great deal of information about a specific employee or groups of employees at a target organization before crafting an email that hooks them. Spies have perfected this art, and criminals have learned from them. These email attacks are difficult to identify among the hundreds of emails we scroll through each day, particularly as our jobs continue to disassociate themselves from in-person office work into a new generation of hybrid and remote work.

The COVID-19 pandemic created a powder keg for spies and criminals to launch attacks. In fact, the greatest numbers of cyberattacks in history happened between 2020 and 2023—more than the prior ten years combined—as society puzzled out how to emerge from within various lockdowns and transition to so-called hybrid-first environments. This feeding frenzy bloated the dark web from a niche environment of ransomware attacks and Wikileaks revelations to a monstrous continent of pirates, gangs, crime families, and every other sort of ne'er-do-well.

In 2020, Russian spies compromised the Hillary Clinton campaign through spear phishing emails. These attacks were likely intended to compromise campaigns in the 2022 congressional and 2024 presidential elections. Throughout 2021, U.S. election officials in at least nine states received fraudulent emails purportedly from trusted vendors with invoice attachments requesting payment. The emails also contained links to malicious websites that steal log-in credentials. In March 2022, the FBI's Cyber Division warned that cyber spies had launched an invoice-themed phishing campaign to steal the credentials of federal, state, and local election officials. We've long known that foreign government spies have sought to steal information from election campaigns. I'm reminded of the adage "You can't teach an old dog new tricks." Cyberattackers only need to revise their methods when we fail to learn the lessons of the past.

Studies of breaches in cybersecurity are a bit of a mixed bag because they rely on broad reporting from organizations and individuals who suffer breaches. The FBI's Internet Crime Complaint Center (the IC3) has some of the best data on the number, type, and cost of cyberattacks, but even this is incomplete because it relies on information volunteered to the agency—and not everyone wants to speak to the FBI.

Spear phishing email remains the top conduit for spies and cybercriminals to steal the data that is the currency of our lives. Over 90 percent of successful targeted attacks start with email and rely on fooling a person, not a machine. If we want to make the world safe from cyberattacks, people are the new enterprise we must defend. Understanding how spies deceive by catching our interest, showing us what we want to see, and using a kernel of truth to believe their lie is the most important first step in the process of becoming a spy hunter.

THINK LIKE A SPY

- Of all the tricks in the espionage playbook, deception is the oldest, most prolific, and most critical. The art of deception uses misleading tactics, misinformation, and subterfuge to manipulate adversaries, conceal true intentions, or secretly gather information.

- Trust is the most valuable commodity on earth. Gain a victim's trust and they will happily hand over the data that is the currency of their lives. In today's data-driven society of networked information, modern spies use the same old deceptive tradecraft used in the cloak-and-dagger age of espionage. So-called social engineering tactics are all the old spy tactics repackaged for modern times.

- Most targets volunteer all the information necessary to create a perfect social engineering attack. Social media provides a cornucopia of information about vacation plans, work events, spending habits, and hobbies for future victims of cybercrime. The best lie relies on a kernel of truth. People who broadcast too much about their lives online gift wrap those truths for criminals to exploit.

- The best way to deceive a person into becoming a victim is through an email. Billions of emails are sent every day—this has made society complacent and willing to trust. The best method to win that trust and hook a target is through a spear phishing email. Spear phishing relies on crafting an email communication that is personal and relatable to the specific victim. Craft it well, and they will never see the wasp hidden in the honey.

THREE

Deception: How an Email Launched a War

"This is LockBit." I couldn't place the accent behind the voice, but my European wife probably could. I motioned her over and turned on the speaker. "We want to negotiate," the voice continued. "Our ransomware groups have attacked your servers a couple days ago. You can type in Google LockBit and you will find our website and there we have left information about companies that we have hacked."

Juliana listened intently.

"Where did you get this number?" I asked. Since that first call from Ben, the LockBit ransomware group had seeded itself through the NGO's networks, managing to slip across virtual private network (VPN) connections to infect distant offices before Ben and I gave the order to shut the company down. That the attacker called me on my personal cell phone spiked my adrenaline. They must have penetrated deep into the NGO's Headquarters data server to steal an executive-level phone list. I was a spy hunter who felt very much like prey.

"We have everything," he continued. "Before we encrypted your network, we were able to take a big amount of data from your systems." He paused, probably for effect. "Total data taken is almost three terabytes! Pay us five million dollars or we will post all your information on our blog."

"Hold on," I said, and muted the phone.

"He's Russian," Juliana said. "I'm certain of it."

Juliana grew up in East Germany, along the German-Polish border behind Russia's Iron Curtain. She learned Russian until age twelve, when the Wall fell and Russia retreated. During college she studied in Minsk and Saint Petersburg to deepen her understanding of the language. She could identify the subtle inflections in the attacker's voice that told her where the person came from.

"He's trying to sound European," she explained, "but he's doing a poor job of it." She nodded to herself. "He's Russian. From-Russia Russian."

This was a critical detail. I knew that Russia protects their cyber-criminals if they focus solely on Western countries. In turn, criminals take great care to avoid attacking allied targets. As an example, they often program their malware to search for and avoid attacking targets that use a Cyrillic language keyboard. If you are a criminal in one of the countries friendly to Russia, you don't want to mistakenly hit a target that will bring the Russian Federal Security Service (the successor agency to the Soviet-era KGB) knocking on your door.

"I was just informed from our storage administrator that your organization was scheduled for a post on our blog today," Mr. LockBit continued. "Luckily you picked up my phone call. Your price of five million reflects the size of your organization and the sensitivity and size of your data breach."

I glanced at my wife and held a finger to my lips, then unmuted the phone. "We are a charity," I said. "We don't have five million dollars. Will you settle for three hundred thousand?"

I pulled the number out of thin air. We had no intention of settling. Since first learning of the attack, Ben and I had hired a top-tier cybersecurity company, which had worked around the clock with the Global IT team to begin installing their endpoint detection sensor on every computer and server the company owned. With over two thousand employees, this would take weeks. I needed to stall.

"Three hundred thousand is impossible! You better start talking proactive on fixing this issue or we won't hesitate to publish all your dirty secrets on our blog."

"I will need to see proof that you actually have our data," I said. "I'd like to see a file tree of what you claim to have."

Another few beats. "Usually, we do not provide any details for the attack at all, but considering your cooperation and the ransom amount we demand, we will give you a directory structure listing if that is something you really need."

"We do," I insisted. And that was true. In any ransom case, you always ask for a sign of life. Did LockBit really have our data or were they bluffing?

"We have been reviewing the data as well, especially your financials," he said in that same smug voice. "It seems that you are even more worthy than what you show on website. We cannot accept such a low counteroffer. However, we are open to a discount and willing to offer you ten percent if you settle payment until end of upcoming week. This is the maximum we can wait before taking any further action."

I knew about LockBit and had read their terms of service posted on their dark web blog.

They boasted of "ethical guidelines" that claimed to avoid targeting health-care, education, charitable, or social service organizations. I had an idea to switch tactics and learn everything I could about the attack.

"You realize we are a nonprofit charity," I protested. "I've read your rules, and it seems you state that you do not attack charities. Why did you attack us?"

I imagined him thinking on the other end of the line. Mr. LockBit's best strategy was to stay quiet and stick to his script. But I knew that attackers love to boast. For many of them, the thrill of the deception is the best reward.

"You are providing help to insurgents in Ukraine," he said arrogantly. "We are doing our part to help the war effort."

Shit. It was one thing to negotiate with a clinical attacker seeking money, but dealing with ideology of any sort was a messier game. The Russian threat actor had targeted us because of the humanitarian work the NGO performed within the most destroyed areas of Ukraine in the aftermath of Russia's 2022 invasion. Only a few years earlier, an attack from Russian intelligence on the NGO would've meant deploying their physical units to disrupt our operations. Today, a destructive cybercrime syndicate can strike any company with a ransomware attack from thousands of miles away that cripples the NGO's systems. Not only that, but they boasted that they'd done their patriotic duty as part of the war effort.

"We are working to come to a higher number," I said, continuing to stall. "We're going to need your help to get there."

"We are here to help," he said with a hint of understanding. "You have one week."

The line disconnected. I shared a sad smile with my wife and headed for my home office and a day of calls and work. So much for weekend plans.

* * *

I got to work with Ben and our third-party cybersecurity threat-hunting team to race against the clock to discover everything about the LockBit attack before our week expired. We learned from forensic work that the LockBit attacker had somehow compromised the account of a senior IT administrator and used the enormous privileges of that account to cause mayhem. We didn't know precisely *how* the attackers had turned a trusted IT employee into a virtual spy, but we suspected it had started with an email. We knew *when* the attack had begun because we could see from network traffic precisely when the IT administrator's account was compromised. Unfortunately, at this early stage we barely knew the *what*—which is why I'd asked for a file tree of all the potential data they claimed to have stolen. But we did know the *why*. That was a start.

LockBit's claim that they do not attack nonprofits, charities, or hospitals is a self-aggrandizing lie. LockBit recently demanded an $800,000 ransom from Saint Anthony Hospital in Chicago, Illinois, after ruthlessly locking them with ransomware. A year earlier, a LockBit affiliate brought computer systems at the Hospital for Sick Children (SickKids) in Toronto to its knees. The group also extorted a $10 million ransom from the Centre Hospitalier Sud Francilien in France. We couldn't rely on some semblance of ethics by a ransomware group known to ruthlessly attack any organization that showed weakness. There is no honor among thieves.

* * *

Russian cybercriminals like LockBit are not pioneers in attacking organizations that provide aid to Ukraine. Russia's intelligence operatives paved the way when, in February 2022, Russian military forces marched into Ukraine from Russia, Belarus, and Crimea. This invasion capped eight years of often violent confrontation between the Ukrainian army against Russian separatist forces along the country's eastern borders. The total military and civilian death toll for the armed conflict has (according to many reports) exceeded half a million people. Russia's aggression against Ukraine was one of the first armed conflicts that paired kinetic attacks (tanks, bullets, missiles, mortars, and drones) with equally disruptive cyberattacks.

As early as March 2014, when Russia first annexed Crimea, the hostile country pummeled Ukrainian computer networks with a widespread distributed denial of service (DDoS) attack. A DDoS (pronounced *dee-dos*) attack floods a server with enough information requests to overwhelm it and prevent it from normal communications. Imagine trying to tune in to news in Ukraine's capital, Kyiv, and seeing only static as Russian cyberthreat actors created virtual traffic jams to hide their invasion of Crimea. Less than a year later, Russian intelligence launched what many call the most devastating spear phishing attack of all time.

I last visited Kyiv in the spring of 2023. The April sky sprinkled rain across streets, parks, cafés, and military checkpoints in an asynchronous pattern that would, at unpredictable moments, turn into a deluge. I walked the quiet streets, eyeing the numerous closed stores and hurrying past the watchful eyes of armed soldiers behind sandbags and barricades. An air-raid alert app on my phone helped maintain my vigilance against potential rocket attacks and pointed me toward nearby shelters. Each time a MiG fighter lifted off from nearby military airstrips in Belarus, my phone would emit a shocking siren followed by a recorded message from Star Wars' own Mark Hamill, sounding very Jedi Master as he implored, "Attention! Air raid alert. Proceed to the nearest shelter. Don't be careless. Your overconfidence is your weakness."

Never one to disobey Luke Skywalker, I would descend to an underground shelter or huddle in the chilly metro tunnels carved beneath the city until the air raid would lift, with Hamill's parting words loud and clear. "The alert is over. May the Force be with you."

The winter's chill lingered long into April. As I bundled myself inside a jacket, wool scarf, hat, and gloves, I tried to imagine a Kyiv held fast in December's wintery grip. The Russians know cold. They thrive in winter and weaponized it during World War II against Nazi forces who foolishly marched on Moscow as the snow fell. They used it against Ukraine decades later in a cyberattack that shocked the world.

Two days before Christmas on December 23, 2015, an operator at a power control center in western Ukraine had plans to organize his office and leave for the day. His bemused expression must have turned to shock as the cursor, hovering like a haunted planchette on a Ouija board, slid over to toggles controlling substations in the Ivano-Frankivsk Oblast, a region in west Ukraine that borders Romania to the south, with a population of about 1.3 million people.

He stood powerless as the cursor shut down power substations and threw thousands of Oblast residents into the dark and cold. The operator finally pressed past his bewilderment and leapt for the mouse, seeking to wrest control from a ghost in the machine that continued to shut down substations one by one. As he tried to stop the destruction, his screen logged out of the control panel. When he attempted to sign back in, his password didn't work. The attackers had stolen his account and replaced him with a virtual trusted insider.

Spies had carefully probed and tested Ukrainian security for months, learning to reconnoiter networks, understand the names and identities of employees and operators, and test and compromise user accounts. The attack was one of the most sophisticated deceptive takeovers of critical infrastructure in history and began, simply, with an email.

The prior spring, threat actors sent emails to IT staff of various power-distribution companies throughout Ukraine. The deceptive emails contained a poisoned Microsoft Word document that looked like a routine business attachment. When an administrator opened the document, a popup asked them to enable macros. If they did, a program called BlackEnergy3 quietly opened a back door to corporate networks for the spies.

Those who play the great game of espionage have incredible patience. The spies who compromised Ukraine's power grid spent months carefully drifting through network systems, quietly overcoming user accounts and creating spies within the machines that granted increasing levels of access. Eventually they hijacked VPN accounts used by grid workers to remotely access supervisory control and data acquisition (SCADA) networks that manage the flow of power. These industrial control systems are the holy grail for spies, terrorists, and criminals who prey upon critical infrastructure systems (more on that in chapters 12 and 13).

The attackers used their elevated access—achieved by sending simple deceptive emails—to rewrite firmware code at various substations that would lock out operators when they tried to take back control of the substations. They also altered the backup power systems for some of the control centers to not only cut power but make certain the operators responsible for restoring power could do little more than twiddle their thumbs in the dark.

But wait—there's more! Copying the DDoS attack from a year earlier, thousands of prank calls that researchers have since traced to Moscow dark web call centers flooded servers in Ukraine just as the lights went out. This prevented hundreds of thousands of legitimate callers from reaching support to say that they had lost power in the dead of winter.

After six tense hours of dedicated work by Ukrainian cybersecurity to identify and excise corrupted code, accounts, and malware, most of the substations came back online. The fear that such an attack could happen again is far more difficult to erase.

To stop threat actors, we need to learn to trust nothing online and verify everything. Be suspicious of every email or social media contact, especially those that contain a link or attachment. I receive so many spear phishing emails (everyone wants to compromise the security guy) that I've completely stopped clicking links and verify every attachment by calling or texting the person who sent it to me. Instead of clicking links, close the email and go directly to the web page of the company that purportedly sent the email. In other words, learn to be an email archaeologist. But not the kind who carefully brushes dinosaur remains. Carry a whip and wear a fedora like my childhood hero Indiana Jones. Hunt for the trap in every email like your life depends on it. Because it may.

* * *

"I've got an idea!" I stormed into my colleague David's office with a crumpled Excel printout in my hand. David led our data protection unit, which was created months before the NGO suffered its first cyberattack—and just in time. David and Ben had first come up with the plan to shut down all our systems if ransomware began to infect them.

Ben and David looked up from a small, three-seater conference table tucked into a corner of David's office. The computer in front of them occupied the last sliver of open real estate among piled manuals and printouts, a coffee carafe long gone cold, and various contraptions and accoutrements to feed David's expensive tea habit.

I slid into the chair beside them and swept a pile of manuals onto the floor. Both men flinched as the heavy tomes thumped against the carpet. Little sleep and constant work had made us all jumpy.

"I hope it's a good one," David said in a measured demeanor that never slipped. Sometimes his analytical mind seemed to defy emotion. "The idea, I mean."

"Maybe." I smoothed the Excel workbook I'd printed onto the table. "I did have to do math." Ben and David shared a look. "I'm good at math," I insisted. "Look at this."

The ten-page document was a printout of the file tree Mr. LockBit had sent us after our phone call. Our attacker had claimed to have stolen three terabytes of information as well as a file tree detailing his haul. Essentially, the document boasted that LockBit had not just taken an immense amount of data, but *all* of our data. If true, they had taken every byte of data from the entire Headquarters server. This had the entire executive team's hair on fire as we analyzed all the personally identifiable information in that massive dataset, including passports, home addresses and phone numbers, payroll and human resources information, programmatic information including confidential intellectual property, employee lists, and so much more. LockBit had doused the NGO in gasoline by stealing our information. Publishing it on their dark web message boards would be like lighting a match and throwing it at us.

"We've been looking at this for days," Ben groaned. "It's just a file list."

"Right," I said. "But it's not what's listed, but *how much* is in here." David sat up straight, eyes wide. I could sense his mind working.

I glanced at Ben and said, "Our systems are slow. It takes forever to download a single document. How long would it take to download *three terabytes* of information."

They understood immediately. A quick test on our server could tell us precisely how long it took to download a single file of, say, one gigabyte. It didn't take a math prodigy to calculate the time it would take to download three thousand times that amount of data. The answer would be measured in weeks, not hours.

My years in law enforcement left me with a simple axiom: Criminals are lazy. If they weren't, they'd get day jobs. A criminal will do as little work as possible to land the biggest payout possible, much like someone aiming to meet a job's minimum requirements without reaching toward what my FBI squad called the "kick-ass line."

Our forensics had told us the dwell time the LockBit attacker had lurked in our system before punching the launch code and detonating his ransomware payload. We knew this by subtracting the time LockBit first compromised our IT administrator's account from the moment the ransomware began. By defining the attacker's dwell time in our system, we knew exactly how much time he had to extract our information. It wasn't long.

"It's hours, not weeks," Ben said. "He can't have taken more than a gig, maybe less."

Just 1 gigabyte of data, or 1,024 megabytes—about the size of a typical movie download.

"Can you figure it out?" I asked.

They got to work. If I was right, we would know how much data LockBit had actually stolen. While still not the *what* of the attack, this information would possibly allow us to call their bluff and avoid a costly ransom. The idea—and the intelligence it might provide us—energized me. I'm not much of a gambler, but I've learned from plenty of games of pitch at the family card table that sometimes, even when you don't have the best hand, you need to bet high and call their bluff.

THINK LIKE A SPY

- The top three ways to compromise the account of a victim are: (1) purchasing usernames and passwords on the dark web; (2) taking advantage of poor cybersecurity or unpatched computer systems; and (3) using email spear phishing attacks.

- The world loves email. More than 350 billion emails are sent and received *daily*. A small but mighty portion of these— between three and five billion—are maliciously targeting us.

- Most people aren't good enough email archaeologists and spend too little time scrutinizing emails to search for threats.

Most people fall for the 25/25 rule: 25 percent of all breaches occur because of spear phishing attacks, and one in four people (25 percent) will click on a malicious link in an email.

- A distributed denial of service (DDoS) attack floods a server with enough information requests to overwhelm it and prevent it from normal communications, essentially slowing data to a crawl or stopping its movement along networks or the internet altogether. A DDoS attack can be used in combination with another cyberattack to overburden cybersecurity, causing chaos, or as a sleight of hand to hide the more promising spear phishing attack.

- Criminals might be lazy, but patience pays. The most successful attacks for the biggest paydays occur after weeks to months researching targets to craft the perfect spear phishing email. Maintaining persistence inside compromised network systems means more compromised accounts, supplying a wealth of data to steal, encrypt, and destroy, creating pressure situations that will make victims pay.

- To stop cybercrime, internet users must learn to trust nothing online and verify everything. Just as criminals are lazy, victims are complacent. They should treat every email or social media contact like a viper that might strike—especially emails that contain a link or attachment. Instead of closing emails and visiting the web page of the company that purportedly sent the email, a spy's future victim will click a link for the sake of expediency.

FOUR

Impersonation: How to Skip School

During my four years at Gonzaga College High School, which was steps away from the U.S. Capitol, I skipped school only once. I'd scored tickets for my friend Chris and me to see the irreverent and infamous DC101 radio program *The Greaseman*. If I wanted to experience the show, I would have to successfully impersonate my parents *and* beat Gonzaga's "multifactor identification procedure." I spent hours practicing the forging of my father's signature and eventually I could re-create it down to every whorl. I even punctuated it with a forceful tap of the pen to make a period after the "Jr.," just like I'd seen him do. The day before the show, I drafted a document in my father's penmanship that could have fooled an old East German border agent, explaining that I was sick. The next day, moments after leaving our respective houses, Chris and I untucked our shirts, threw unnecessary schoolbags in the back of his car, and rushed to see the show.

The next morning proved critical. Gonzaga had instituted an identity-verification procedure for my graduating class (great job, class of 1991) after they'd discovered that too many of us had skipped and forged absence notes from unwary parents. After verifying the signature on the note, student services would call the student's home number to confirm the absence. To trick this multifactor identification, I convinced my soon-to-be aunt to join the scheme. My parents had invited my uncle and his fiancée to stay with us while they worked in D.C. and prepared for their wedding. On my sixteenth birthday, Harry and Stephanie had written in my card: "Happy Birthday, This card is a clue—you need one. Use it well." By clue they meant that my safe, straitlaced, and cautious nature made me clueless. It was time to cash in that clue and let out my inner rebel. It didn't take much convincing to get Stephanie to agree to wait by the phone and pretend to be my mother, Vivian O'Neill. Operation Greaseman was my first successful covert operation.

This story is like any number of business email compromise (BEC) schemes. An attacker impersonates a trusted individual and uses a carefully crafted email communication to entice the mark to do something they shouldn't. Back then, the forged note represented an "email" communication. That it appeared to have come from my father authenticated the sender. My aunt tricked student services into thinking the forged "email" was valid by impersonating my mother. This allowed me to defeat Gonzaga's multifactor authentication and get away with a morning spent lounging in a DC101 Barcalounger steps from a shock jock instead of bustling to classes. The perfect crime.

Modern attacks that leverage cutting-edge technology—such as business email compromise and artificial intelligence deepfakes—have their origins in tools long used by spies (more on deepfakes in chapter 5). Throughout history, clandestine operatives have used disguise and impersonation tactics to walk into secure buildings, fool targets into believing their lies, and steal generations of information without a firing a single shot. At the end of the day, most impersonation attacks are just variations of my high school hack modernized for a world dominated by email.

Impersonation upgrades the deceptive practice of spear phishing to the most devious levels. The psychology behind impersonation often leaves a victim feeling a lot like a best friend or trusted colleague just backstabbed them. For this reason, impostor attacks (sometimes called CEO or CFO fraud attacks because scammers often pose as these executives to coerce employees to wire money fraudulently) are some of the most prevalent and costly cyberattacks on earth. The FBI's Internet

Crime Complaint Center (IC3) has given BEC the title of the most damaging and prominent internet crime scam for the past four years. The numbers bear this out. From 2019 to 2024, BEC went from costing organizations $26 billion to more than $55 billion.[1]

Impostor attacks are typically financial in nature and target individuals and companies of all levels of complexity. At the heart of an impostor attack, criminals impersonate someone who is either trusted or in a position of authority, and then convince a victim to wire or send funds to an account the attacker controls. The impersonation typically begins with email, although attackers have stolen millions with a phone call or a chat sent in Microsoft Teams or Zoom. Many of the victims fall for basic email impostor scams like invoices sent from a favorite big-box store or from a utility company. Others are wrapped in more complex schemes that layer impostors from multiple sources, each adding to the deception by building on a kernel of trust. The best way to attack a mega corporation? Seek out the weakest link. Most cyberattacks compromise people by gaining their trust and turning it against them. The difference between a cyberattack and an old-fashioned espionage recruitment is in how the human target is accessed. Threat actors compromise people through computers. People are always the weakest link in a security system.

The grandest impostor attacks to date have targeted mega companies Google and Facebook, both known for investing millions in cybersecurity. Massive companies have an Achilles' heel, because their financial departments routinely process thousands of transactions, invoices, and payments every day. A Lithuanian man by the name of Evaldas Rimasauskas knew this and decided to make his fortune as an impostor. Rimasauskas and his conspirators researched Facebook and Google and noted that many business transactions were with the Taiwanese company Quanta Computer. For two years, the impostors sent carefully crafted emails from impersonated Quanta accounts to the tech giants. The clever emails included invoices, letters, and even contracts that Facebook and Google paid because they trusted communications from Quanta. In all, Rimasauskas stole over $100 million from the companies, all deposited in "drop" bank accounts in Lithuania, Slovakia, Hong Kong, and other countries. Drop bank accounts are typically created by stealing an innocent person's identity and using it to open a legitimate bank account that the criminal controls. Once the victim of the impostor crime sends money to the drop bank account, believing they are transferring it legitimately, the criminal moves the money to dark web pay centers before law enforcement catches wind of the scheme. Rimasauskas successfully impersonated Quanta for two years before authorities finally arrested him in 2017.

In 2015, tech giant Ubiquiti Networks suffered another costly impersonation attack—and one of the most common. Attackers impersonated both the company's CEO and attorney and sent clever emails paired with phone calls to Ubiquiti's Hong Kong subsidiary. Posing as the CEO, the attackers directed the newly promoted chief accounting officer (CAO) to make several financial transfers to finalize a highly confidential acquisition. Over the next seventeen days, the subsidiary transferred over $46 million through fourteen wire transfers from Hong Kong to accounts in Russia, China, Poland, and Hungary. Ubiquiti first learned of the scheme when the FBI contacted them to suggest that the large amount of money transferred out of Ubiquiti's Hong Kong business unit may have been fraud. The FBI routinely monitors large money transfers, particularly in Hong Kong, where global criminals establish many of the drop accounts that receive stolen funds. That was fortunate for Ubiquiti. Had the FBI not warned the company, which at the time was seeking to go public, the now former CAO might have continued transferring funds.

Much closer to my Maryland home, a grand jury indicted three Maryland residents in 2021 for conspiracy to commit wire fraud, money laundering, and identity theft. For two years, the coconspirators executed a sprawling business email compromise scam that tricked companies into sending money to drop bank accounts they controlled. Casting a wide victim net, mastering impersonation, and careful planning led to $2.3 million of successful fraud against numerous organizations in multiple states. Each Maryland attack followed a similar pattern. In one, the fraudsters created a false email account spoofed to look like it belonged to the owner of a furniture distributor in Florida. Posing as the boss, they sent emails to the furniture distributor's controller and directed him to send a wire transfer to a drop account at Bank of America. The email fooled the controller, who believed it came from the boss. The fraudsters took care to research the furniture distributor, discovered how the company uses signatures on their email communications, and made the fake email look like an expertly forged document.

Even municipalities, government organizations, and entire cities have fallen prey to impersonation crime. In 2022, a cybercriminal compromised a Portland, Oregon, Housing Bureau email account and used a BEC attack to divert a $1.4 million payment for costs related to the construction of an affordable-housing project to the attacker's account. A year earlier, Peterborough, New Hampshire, a town of seven thousand residents, was tricked into sending $2.3 million to a criminal account located overseas. Criminals used forged documents and compromised email addresses to impersonate the school district and request payment of funds from the town. By the time law enforcement investigated the attack, cybercriminals had already converted the funds to cryptocurrency and escaped in their digital getaway car.

Impersonation thrives on the impersonal, strange as it seems. The disaggregated way we conduct business in our new hybrid workforce world has made it especially easy for criminals to fool colleagues who may have never met face-to-face. The interconnected global economy and evaporation of borders in cyberspace makes detecting impostors even more difficult. To protect ourselves, the rules of engagement for communication, particularly email, must evolve. We must make it more difficult for attackers to use email. We must treat our digital communications with the importance of a physical letter, written on looseleaf and delivered lovingly through the mail with a wax seal pressed by a signet ring. But the problem is, we are too lazy, pressed for time, or distracted to do so. Defeating this grandest of cybercrimes requires, at a minimum, email archaeology. Scrutiny of all internet messaging, especially email, is the first step to protecting yourself from losing a potential fortune to cybercrime. Establishing second and third levels of verification for every financial transaction is just as critical.

But even added layers of security are not always perfect. As I began work on this chapter, I received a rather mundane email from PayPal, a company I have long used for everything from online payments for various companies like eBay and Amazon to receiving payments for sales of my books on my website. I had taken a break from writing to engage in the daily chore of email harvesting. As I separated the wheat from the chaff in my multiple inboxes, I paused on the PayPal email presenting my "2023 Tax Return Information." It was January 2024 and I had tax preparation on my mind. The report would help me close out the year.

I automatically conducted my version of email archaeology: checked the logo, scanned for correct grammar and spelling, examined the email address to verify a good domain (or so I thought), and noticed the handy link to open the report. Maybe my desire to get back to writing this book distracted me. Or perhaps I felt in a rush because a mountain of other work had piled up. Or, more likely, I suffered from a momentary lapse of my rigid controls. In other words: Laziness subsumed me. I clicked through to my PayPal account page and entered my username and password. I then received the prompt for my two-factor authentication, which handily popped up on my phone as a text with six digits.

I entered five of the numbers before my inner spy hunter slapped me across the face. Something on the page looked off. Something you'd almost need a magnifying glass to notice. The continue button under the "Enter Your Code" prompt had square corners. Every button on PayPal's *actual* website has rounded corners. No hard edges for PayPal.

I jerked my hands away from the keyboard as if scorched by a hot pan. A couple of deep breaths later, I felt prepared to investigate the clever attack. The email address I had failed to properly scrutinize had everything but one letter. When I clicked through the handy link in the email, I arrived at a dummy site, created by cybercriminals to trap me. Like a mouse after cheese, I blindly walked onto the wooden frame, mindless of the heavy bar ready to snap my neck from overhead. I entered my username and password and pressed send. The delay between entering my credentials and the next screen that asked for my two-factor code should have clued me in. Instead, I pulled at the cheese.

Scam PayPal login screen.

    Somewhere on the dark web, an attacker had the true log-in page for a PayPal account open and waiting for me. When I entered my username and password in their dark web website, the system rang an alert. He might have watched as my username and password appeared on his screen and then rushed to enter them into the legitimate PayPal log-in. This triggered PayPal's *actual* two-factor authentication prompt—which sent a text message to the phone in my possession. They just needed my full two-factor authentication code to spring the trap. Blithefully unaware, I'd entered five of the six required code numbers into the criminal's fake website before coming to my senses. I have thousands of dollars in my PayPal account, and the account is connected to my bank and credit cards. An attacker with full access could have made purchases, withdrawn funds, and transferred my hard-earned money, all because I momentarily slacked off.

    I closed the browser and opened a new window to log into the proper PayPal site and change my password. I had to hurry because I'd given them five of the six two-factor authentication code numbers they needed to take over my account. The sixth number they would need but that I had wisely not given them was a three. That meant, if they tried to brute force the final number by entering the five digits they knew and guessing the sixth, starting with a one, they would access my account in three tries. Once they entered that fatal number three, they'd change my password and lock me out of my account while they drained my money. Thankfully, my own security acumen had beat the cyber criminal's intrusion attempt, but barely. Another few seconds of my naivete would've been the difference between getting back to writing this chapter and handing over the keys to my PayPal account to an attacker lurking on the dark web. If I had only relied on the password, I'd be significantly poorer. Although the second method of authentication isn't foolproof, the added step gave me much-needed time.

While the PayPal attack might look like a typical spear phishing impersonation attack, it included several next-level additions, including a tech support number. The email and the criminal impostor website each had a 1-800 number for me to call for help. After closing the fake web page, I called the number and reached a polite female voice from "account services." She was "happy to help me access my account."

Impersonation attacks through email spear phishing are suddenly so successful and difficult to spot because artificial intelligence (AI) has changed so much about cybercrime. Indeed, AI may be the most transformative innovation since January 1, 1983, the birthday of the internet. AI has led to incredible transformations in how we research, write, learn, develop, code, and problem solve. Prompt engineering—writing questions for neural networks to solve, like the most famous AI, ChatGPT—is replacing basic coding classes in colleges and will be a required skill for many professions of the future.

AI can already create novel programming code, write articles and stories, conduct research, and produce any image a human mind can dream up, and many that defy imagination. AI out-predicted the best pollsters in the run-up to the 2024 U.S. presidential election, has beaten chess grand masters, passed a Wharton MBA exam, and outshined human doctors in diagnosing disease in patients.[2] Thousands of AI applications have flooded the internet, bringing this inventive power to humans everywhere.

AI is revolutionizing industries by boosting efficiency and driving innovation, reshaping how businesses solve problems and engage with customers. From health care to finance and beyond, AI automates tasks, analyzes massive data, and delivers real-time insights. To keep up with demand, the AI market is skyrocketing, projected to grow to more than $400 billion by 2027, and exploding to $2 trillion by 2030, with AI software leading the charge.[3] Thousands of new AI tools are flooding markets daily, making it nearly impossible to count them all—but the total likely sits in the hundreds of thousands. In the U.S. alone, over fifteen thousand AI start-ups are driving innovation across industries, offering solutions for everything from health management and payment processing to deep learning, content creation, and data analytics.

Tech giants Google and Microsoft have integrated AI into their search engines. Numerous AI websites can generate images, write essays, correct grammar, translate languages, and create code, music, stories, and logos; it can even produce full YouTube videos. Content creators, influencers, and podcasters have adopted AI at a mad sprint, leveraging powerful applications to simulate Hollywood studios and soundstages on their smartphones. Musicians now create entire songs with unique lyrics in a second, and AI avatars have replaced actors in videos and shorts—a few text prompts can create a reimagining of the Moon landing with green aliens, all narrated in actor Morgan Freeman's deepfaked voice.

AI even crashed Super Bowl LIX. As the Philadelphia Eagles crushed the Kansas City Chiefs 40 to 22, a wave of AI-generated ads from Google, Meta, Salesforce, GoDaddy, and OpenAI took center stage. About half a dozen primetime spots blended human storytelling with algorithmic creativity. The public response was mixed, but overall leaned positive. As more viewers become accustomed to AI-generated content, skepticism appears to be declining. And with AI playing such a visible role during one of the most-watched broadcasts in the world, it's clear the technology is moving further into the mainstream.

And the hijinks! Memes starring Trump, Putin, Biden, Obama, both Clintons, Musk, and Zuckerberg, to name a few, flooded the

2024 presidential election in the United States. My favorite meme of the election was crafted by AI artist Ari K (@arikuschnir) on the AI platform Kling. The fifty-seven-second video took the artist three hours to produce, but it was worth the time. In a lighthearted series of scenes that imagine a Trump–Biden lunch at the White House, Presidents Trump and Biden romp across America doing iconic things, like two old friends crossing off a long bucket list, all set to the 1975 song "Why Can't We Be Friends?" If only real life were so collegial!

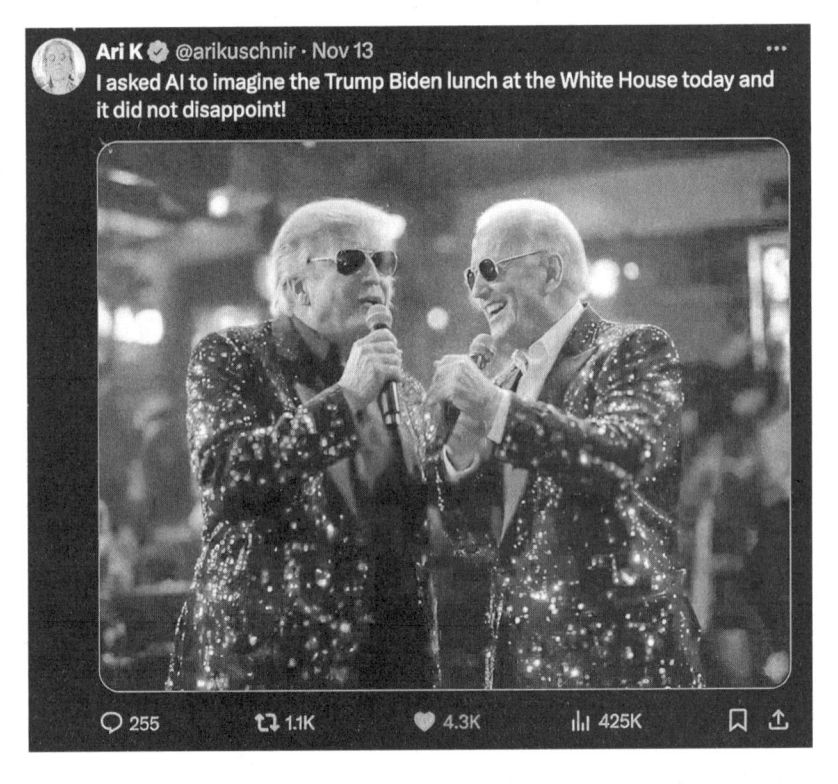

https://x.com/arikuschnir/status/1856739100222718261.

While content creators are using AI to rewrite history (or at least retell it with a comedic twist), militaries are leveraging the same technology to reshape strategies and tools on the battlefield. In September 2023, an AI fighter pilot took on a human in a live dogfight using the modified F-16 X-62A VISTA ("Variable In-Flight Simulator Test Aircraft").[4] While the Air Force is tight-lipped about the outcome, this builds on AI's earlier 5–0 drubbing of a human pilot in a simulated showdown. The AI demonstrated precision and reaction times that far outpaced its human counterpart—all while following strict safety and ethical standards. If *Top Gun*'s Maverick were watching, he'd probably be googling "AI pilot hacks" right about now.

And it's not just in the skies—AI-driven warfare is playing out on the ground too. In Ukraine, tens of thousands of low-cost, nimble drones are turning the battlefield into a high-tech chessboard, often doubling as guided explosives in a cat-and-mouse game of drones versus counter drones.[5] Warfare is evolving, with electronic and autonomous systems taking center stage. At this pace, we might need to start asking if Skynet is hiring—because the future of war is looking a little too much like *Terminator* for comfort.

AI has also dominated the spoken word. In May 2022, I sat with my family in the National Air and Space Museum's Steven F. Udvar-Hazy Center's Airbus IMAX Theater to watch the Hollywood blockbuster *Top Gun: Maverick*. I sat forward in my seat when Val Kilmer, reprising his role as Iceman, stood up and spoke two emotional lines of dialogue. Throat cancer had led to a tracheotomy that left Kilmer unable to speak. Voice synthesis company Sonantic used AI technology to sample hours of Kilmer's archived voice to develop a clone that could speak the two lines. It only takes an AI program a few seconds to clone a voice that will say anything you type. With a bit more studio time, AI can read your favorite book in Snoop Dogg's voice or answer your phone as Arnold "the Terminator" Schwarzenegger.

Voice technology has revolutionized global communication by breaking down language barriers. During a recent visit to Germany, Juliana left me alone with her father—an intimidating prospect given that he speaks no English, and my German is barely conversational. For years, the language gap had kept us at arm's length. But armed with courage from the large German beers he brought up from the cellar, I decided to give conversation a shot, with a little help from Google Translate on my phone. The app filled in the blanks in my vocabulary, and when he spoke too quickly, I used the voice dictation feature to keep up. Now, I've upgraded to the ChatGPT app, which translates his German into English in real time and even responds in a natural-sounding male voice. For the first time, I feel like we're having real conversations—not just navigating around a barrier but breaking it down entirely.

I can sense your inner spy hunter perking up, and congratulations if you've begun to make the connection between AI and impersonation cybercrime. Your future self will thank you for asking pertinent questions such as: What happens when you can't trust the face in front of you? What happens when the person you think you know was created solely to secretly gain your trust? What if that impostor has expertly played the role of someone you love? What if that impostor has played the role of *you*?

THINK LIKE A SPY

- Modern attacks that leverage cutting-edge technology like artificial intelligence deepfakes, business email compromise, cell phone smishing (text message) attacks, virtual meeting compromises, among others, have their origins in tools long used by spies. In fact, espionage attacks are easier today than at any prior time in the history of clandestine crime. Criminals that study the past succeed in the attacks of the future.

- Impersonation upgrades the deceptive practice of spear phishing to the most devious levels. The psychology behind impersonation relies on making the victim trust implicitly in the attacker. Impostor attacks are some of the most prevalent and costly cyberattacks on earth.

- At the heart of an impostor attack, a criminal impersonates someone who is either trusted or in a position of authority, and then convinces the target to make what they think is a legitimate transfer of money into the attacker's control. Typical attacks consist of the following: (1) researching the target; (2) establishing deceit through a perfect disguise; (3) gaining the victim's trust; (4) creating a pressure situation; and (5) executing the crime.

- Impersonation attacks typically begin with an email, but attackers have stolen millions with a phone call, a text message, social media chats, or through conferencing applications like Microsoft Teams or Zoom.

- Impersonation thrives on the impersonal. The disaggregated way we conduct business in our new hybrid workforce world has made it easier for criminals to fool colleagues who may have never met face-to-face.

- To perfect impersonation attacks, criminals may steal a person's voice from many sources, including social media posts, YouTube videos, corporate videos, and even a victim's voicemail recording.

- Impersonation attacks through email spear phishing are suddenly so successful and difficult to spot because AI has changed everything about cybercrime. Mass-market artificial intelligence has irrevocably changed the way we trust each other and has provided incredible tools to criminals who rely on impersonation. In this world of suddenly ubiquitous deepfakes, trust has become an uncertain commodity.

FIVE

Impersonation: Deepfakes

On what should have been a typical Friday afternoon, Jennifer DeStefano received a frantic phone call from her fifteen-year-old daughter, Brie. Jennifer had almost let the unknown number go to voicemail, but remembering that her daughter and husband were in northern Arizona training for ski races, she was on alert should an emergency occur. She took the call.

"Mom!" her daughter sobbed. "Mom, I messed up."

Jennifer stayed calm and asked what had happened. She next heard a man's voice, grating and harsh, through the speaker. "Put your head back, lie down."

What began as concern for a daughter racing in a high-risk sport escalated into panic.

"Mom, these bad men have me," Brie's voice pleaded. "Help me, help me!"

A man's voice replaced Brie's on the phone, then spoke directly to Jennifer. "Listen here. I have your daughter, you tell anyone, you call the cops, I am going to pump her stomach so full of drugs, I am going to have my way with her, drop her in Mexico, and you'll never see her again!"

Jennifer heard her daughter's bawling in the background, farther away this time. "Help me, Mom. Please help me!"

The man demanded a ransom of one million dollars. When Jennifer became distraught, saying that she didn't have that much money, he lowered it to fifty thousand dollars in cash. Shaking with fear, Jennifer put the phone on mute and screamed for help. She was at her younger daughter's rehearsal at a dance studio. Soon other moms surrounded her. Jennifer kept the kidnapper on the phone and kept talking while she had her friend call 911 and her younger daughter dial her husband, who was supposed to be skiing with Brie.

The mother who had called 911 reported that the police were familiar with an AI scam that could replicate a loved one's voice. Jennifer allowed herself a moment of hope but didn't pause the whirlwind of action she demanded of her friends and daughter.

Jennifer alternated between talking to police on the friend's phone and frantically negotiating with the kidnappers. A mother knows her daughter's voice, and Jennifer was certain that *her child* cried and pleaded for her help.

While Jennifer's younger daughter, Aubrey, began calling and texting Brie, her father, brothers, or anyone who could help determine what had happened to Brie, Jennifer asked the kidnapper for wiring instructions and routing numbers for the ransom.

"Oh no," the kidnapper protested. "That's traceable. That's not how this is going to go down." He paused. "We are going to come pick you up."

"What?!" Jennifer shouted. Already shocked at the turn of events and terrified for her daughter, this latest demand threw her further off-kilter.

"You will agree to being picked up in a white van," the man's voice continued, "with a bag over your head so you don't know where we are taking you. You better have all fifty thousand in cash, otherwise both you and your daughter are dead!" Jennifer choked back panic. "If you don't agree to this, you will never see your daughter again!" the man screamed.

Stall him until the police get here, Jennifer thought. She once again muted the phone while he continued to ramble demands over her speaker. Before the police (or a white van) arrived, Aubrey reached her father, who rushed to locate Brie. Jennifer's husband confirmed that their daughter was safe, resting safely in bed—that, no, she wasn't being held against her will.

Huh?

Jennifer couldn't believe Brie was safe until she heard her daughter's voice. She listened to her daughter tell her, repeatedly, that she was really Brie, she was safe, and nothing had happened.

Jennifer's mind whirled between terror and relief. Relief finally won out, and fury settled into the place where terror had reigned. Jennifer unmuted her phone and lashed out at the kidnapper, declaring him the lowest of the low. Doggedly, the kidnapper continued to threaten to kill Jennifer's daughter. Jennifer promised to do everything in her power to stop them so they could not harm others with their terrible scheme. She finally hung up on the false kidnappers and collapsed to the floor in tears.

Jennifer didn't pay the ransom, but the horror of the manufactured phone call continues to haunt her. Every single day. In her June 13, 2023, testimony to the U.S. Senate regarding abuses of artificial intelligence, she stated, "AI is revolutionizing and unraveling the very foundation of our social fabric by creating doubt and fear in what was once never questioned, the sound of a loved one's voice."[1]

For thousands of people every year, impersonation scams destroy fortunes, empty life savings, and erode trust in society. AI deepfakes have made separating scams from reality nearly impossible.

Deepfakes—electronic impersonations of a trusted person's voice or image—are radically changing how we trust what we see and hear. They cause financial damage as well as prey upon our emotional well-being.

When my daughter Hannah was six years old, I took her to the International Spy Museum in Washington, D.C. The museum had a Soviet Union exhibit dressed in dark red hues and shadows. An enormous desk dominated one wall of the exhibit under the crimson flag of the Union of Soviet Socialist Republics. Glued to the desk was a dim glass lamp, some mock papers in Cyrillic letters, and a clunky rotary phone. My inquisitive daughter picked up the receiver and asked me, "What is this, Daddy?" In that moment, I understood something that all parents eventually experience: the fast-marching beat of technology. How each older generation struggles to keep up while each newer one fails to have a visual vocabulary of the past. My generation instigated the journey away from broadcast television through Blockbuster movie rentals into cable TV. My children's generation, meanwhile, has eschewed cable for a broadband internet connection and a YouTube account.

Movies now release directly to homes at the same time they hit the silver screen. Instead of driving a van full of kids to the movie theater and dropping a hundred dollars on popcorn and buckets of soda, we can pay twenty dollars or less to stream a new movie in our living room. We can pause for a bathroom break and never miss a scene.

Speaking of stay-at-home entertainment, museums have created virtual reality art exhibits that allow users to "walk through" exhibits at home on their couches. Artists and performers such as the Weeknd, Ariana Grande, and Snoop Dogg host live concerts in virtual constructs. In a virtual world where anyone can look any way they wish, how can we trust that the person across the virtual conference table is who they say they are?

Attackers are adopting deepfake technology for espionage, breaches, and scams. In laymen's terms, they are getting to us by showing up as . . . well . . . us. And who wouldn't trust someone who looks and sounds like us? World-famous podcaster Joe Rogan's voice was perfectly mimicked by an AI start-up company that deepfaked a Joe Rogan podcast in which the influencer announced his intention to sponsor a hockey team "made up entirely of chimps." Enterprising content generators have deepfaked Arnold Schwarzenegger's face and voice, and they have replaced Rose in *Titanic* and Dr. Evil in *Austin Powers* with the Governator's voice and face. Want a bedtime story read to you by your favorite movie star? AI developer ElevenLabs's Reader App allows you to do that, by a growing list of celebrity icons including James Dean, Burt Reynolds, Judy Garland, and Sir Laurence Olivier—none of whom are alive! I'm holding out for AI Christopher Walken to read my favorite horror stories.

Deepfakes are also a threat to whom we trust on all stages, from politicians to our favorite entertainers. In April 2020, an activist group named Extinction Rebellion released a video of the Belgium prime minister Sophie Wilmès asserting that COVID-19, Ebola, swine flu, and other diseases are caused by the "exploitation and destruction by humans of our natural environment." The video caused great consternation, not because of the content, but because Wilmès never said *any* of it. The activist group had used deepfake technology to synchronize a replacement speech over video taken from a prior national address. Past global elections have already seen constant misinformation spread throughout social media and laundered to news sites. Today, political activists, conspiracy theorists, and spies use deepfakes to sway public opinion, manipulate politics, and potentially change votes.

In late March 2023, days before President Donald Trump's arraignment in New York City for allegedly falsifying business records, images of the president took the internet by storm. The detailed pictures showed him running from a horde of police officers, getting gang-tackled by officers in riot gear, crying on the witness stand, and lifting weights in a prison yard dressed in an orange jumpsuit. Some of the images were shared over five million times and created mass confusion as to whether President Trump had reported to the courthouse ahead of his April 5 arraignment date. Various provocateurs, including a Netherlands-based investigative journalist, created the pictures using AI image generators like Midjourney.com's text-to-image synthesis model.

Around the same time, a video clip of President Joe Biden caught on a hot mic made the rounds. The grainy audio features Biden speaking in private about the collapse of two major banks that had caused uncertainty and turmoil in the banking system. The president had just spoken publicly to assure Americans that his administration would take steps to ensure that the banking system remained stable. The clip, released just after Biden's formal remarks, undermined his work to calm fears of a large-scale bank collapse.

"All the money is gone," Biden can be heard saying in the clip. "A collapse is imminent." Biden also goes on to claim he will use the full force of the media to calm the public and, in expected Biden fashion, mumbles a few sentences incomprehensibly.

While numerous language and speech experts quickly debunked the clip as a fake—the pitch was too low for a human voice—the clever deepfake impersonation of the president rang alarm bells and could have led to unnecessary runs on banks throughout the country, leading to failures similar to Silicon Valley Bank's earlier that month.

On Monday, January 22, 2024, the day before the New Hampshire primary elections in the United States, numerous New Hampshire residents picked up a call from Kathy Sullivan's personal cell phone. Sullivan ran a campaign to convince New Hampshire Democrats to write in Biden's name in the primary after the Joseph R. Biden campaign decided not to run in the New Hampshire primary election. The robocall sounded a lot like the president.

"What a bunch of malarkey," President Joe Biden's recorded message began. "It's important that you save your vote for the November election. We will need your help voting up and down the ticket. Voting this Tuesday only enables the Republicans in their quest to elect Donald Trump again. Your vote makes a difference in November, *not this Tuesday.*"

The robocall sounded almost exactly like President Biden, except that it wasn't. The clever deepfake confused voters and may have reduced turnout in New Hampshire. The concern over voter suppression was so dire that the New Hampshire Department of Justice launched an investigation. The attorney general's office identified and indicted numerous parties behind the deepfake, including political consultant Steve Kramer and Lingo Telecom, the voice service provider that distributed the deepfake robocalls through "spoofed" phone numbers.[2] Fraudsters and criminals will often deliberately change (aka "spoof") a phone number to hide their identity or make the target believe the call or text comes from a trusted source.

Not to be left out, the Federal Communications Commission negotiated a $1 million fine with Lingo Telecom and has fined Kramer $6 million for his part in the deceptive robocall. Kramer also got hit with thirteen misdemeanor counts of impersonation of a candidate and thirteen felony counts of voter suppression in New Hampshire. The FCC then built a bulwark against future political deepfake robocalls. On February 2, 2024, it issued a Declaratory Ruling defining calls made with AI-generated voices as "artificial" and therefore a violation of the Telephone Consumer Protection Act (TCPA).[3] The ruling makes voice-cloning deepfake technology used in both political and criminal robocall scams that target consumers illegal. So the next time you receive a call from Morgan Freeman or Keanu Reeves asking you to turn over your life savings to a cryptocurrency investment, hang up and report it to the state attorney general. You might help catch a criminal.*

In late January 2024, pornographic images of superstar Taylor Swift exploded across the social media site X (formerly Twitter). For nearly the entire day (until X removed the images and prohibited further posting or sharing), at least a dozen images of Swift in numerous objectifying acts were shared and viewed about forty-seven million times. The most frequently shared images depicted Swift naked or partially clad in a football cheerleader's outfit, covered in red (blood or paint) and performing pornographic acts on and with deepfaked football players.

While X might not have reacted swiftly, the megastar's fans leapt into action. Using the hashtag #ProtectTaylorSwift, a legion of Swifties flooded X with positive images of the musician and reported any accounts sharing the deepfake pictures. The event caused such an uproar that the White House called it "alarming," and generative AI companies like OpenAI's Dall-E 3 and Microsoft took steps to ensure that their platforms prohibited the creation of such images.

Criminal cyberattackers have also developed their own large language model (LLM) AIs to draft unique spear phishing emails with perfect grammar and spelling, launch persuasive BEC attacks, write novel malicious code, and spread disinformation. Meta, Facebook's parent company, may have just helped them achieve their goal. A powerful AI model named Llama that Facebook developed was posted to

---

* For more tips on avoiding the robocall impersonation traps, see The Spy Hunter Tool Kit on page 267.

4chan and distributed publicly across the internet. Sophisticated cybercrime syndicates converted the formerly benign AI to darker purposes. Spies are probably already deploying deepfakes, generated by their own AIs, to gain entrance to high-security-clearance areas, as if bringing scenes from *Mission Impossible* to real life.

In December 2021, Chinese investigators arrested a group of tax scammers who defrauded countless citizens out of 500 million yuan (about $76.2 million) by sending fake tax invoices from a registered shell corporation. To succeed, the cybercriminals had to bypass a government-run identity verification facial-recognition system that the State Taxation Administration uses to track payments and prevent tax evasion. They purchased identities and high-definition photographs of targeted individuals through dark web marketplaces before using AI to turn the photographs into video avatars that blinked, nodded, and opened their mouths. This fooled the video verification system and allowed the criminals access to the Tax Administration network.

Since 2021, the continuous explosion of AI has brought on even more expressive and realistic video avatars, with the creation of avatars that do and say whatever the user commands. Free AI websites will swap the face of your target onto an already animated avatar. The best software stitches the images together so perfectly that even a forensic expert would have a hard time seeing the fake. Premium AI sites sit behind a minimal paywall. For a small monthly fee, users can create entire video scenarios and export video limited only by their imagination and skill at injecting the right prompts to the AI engine (aka "casting spells"). As you might imagine, everyone from criminals to political activists and even pornographers have taken advantage of this technology.

It's one thing to trick an image-verification system, but what happens when criminals use an avatar to fool a person? Imagine you work in the finance department of a Hong Kong multinational corporation, secure at your desk behind high glass overlooking the cityscape below. One evening, an alert pops up on your monitor, and you open an email from the CFO in the United Kingdom. He invites you to a video conference meeting to discuss a secret transaction that he says must be carried out as soon as possible.

You join a meeting already in process. The CFO is there, as are other employees you recognize. There are also several individuals you don't recognize, outsiders who are introduced as the other party to the critical financial transaction that you're being asked to facilitate. Each of the people in the meeting, beginning with the CFO, introduce themselves. Finally, it's your turn. You give your name and title and pause, wondering whether you should have listed a hobby or some other fact about yourself. You realize that the high-powered meeting has you frazzled, and you clamp your mouth shut to keep your foot out of it.

The CFO cuts the meeting short after abruptly giving you orders to transfer millions to a specific bank account. You stare at the empty screen for a moment before clicking the button to leave the meeting. *What just happened?* Hands shaking, you process the transaction—the first of many—and wire the funds.

Over the next week, you make fourteen additional transfers to five separate Hong Kong–based bank accounts for a total of 200 million HK. That tickle in your stomach has grown to an ulcer before you finally gather the courage to call headquarters and ask to speak with the CFO directly. The CFO has never heard of you.

This hypothetical story isn't actually hypothetical. It happened in January 2024 and cost a multinational corporation (MNC) over $25 million before the employee stopped sending wires to dark web drop accounts. Police investigated and learned that cybercriminals had used deepfake technology to create digital avatars of the CFO and employees by mining publicly available video and audio clips. When the MNC employee joined the video conference, he thought he saw colleagues and partners. What his lying eyes did not see were puppets controlled by cybercriminals who typed whatever they wanted their impostors to say.

Companies have lost millions to impersonation attacks like the one that fooled a junior finance person at the Hong Kong MNC, and more are on the way. A recent threat intelligence report published in January 2025 by BlackBerry projects that AI deepfake scams will cause financial losses amounting to more than $40 billion to individuals and companies by 2027. We've entered the age of synthetic deception—where every voice can be forged, every face can be faked, and trust is the new battleground.

On a recent meeting through Zoom, I asked all the attendees to humor me in a counterintelligence exercise. When I said *Go*, we all shook our heads and hands vigorously in front of their cameras. It looked ridiculous, but proved to me that no one on the call was an AI deepfake. Current AI avatars tend to look forward and, although they blink and move deceptively like humans, they don't move their hands much and certainly don't wiggle wildly on command. (Let's hope they're not reading this book to pick up new cues.)

Closer to home, it cost me less than an hour and five dollars to make a small argument with my wife exponentially worse. We all have little spats with those we love. Some minor disagreement is magnified by external factors like a bad day at work or someone cutting you off in traffic. Sometimes you can't help it. One evening Juliana and I fell into just this sort of marital trap around the kitchen sink. I can't remember what we argued about, and had I left it alone, the whole event would've disappeared. But I felt I was in the right, wanted an apology, and decided I would manufacture one.

I scrolled through my photo collection and found a fun picture of Juliana, smiling at the camera and holding an oversize beer stein in her hand. The excellent image quality, straight-into-the-camera face profile, and her beautiful smile made the image a perfect choice. The fact that a dark beer filled the glass in her hand was a bonus.

It took a few minutes to upload a sound sample from a recent voicemail from Juliana on my phone into an AI emulator. It took a few more minutes to process the photo into an AI animation application. In less time than it took to write these paragraphs, I had an animated Juliana avatar, smiling at the camera, blinking occasionally, and poised to deliver a rousing speech—or anything I wanted her to say. And she said a lot! I carefully typed the most impressive, expressive, and dramatic apology I have ever heard (and I suspect ever will hear), and it all came out of her avatar's mouth. With kind eyes, the avatar swung the beer glass merrily and apologized for all she was worth.

My handiwork so impressed me that I felt the need to share it (husbands everywhere, I implore you not to make a similar mistake). I showed it to my entire family, who were fooled and confused by the uncharacteristic apology. One day, Juliana will forgive me, but I will not hold my breath.

THINK LIKE A SPY

- The pandemic thrust us into a society where technology bridges human interaction and has replaced face-to-face connection for most aspects of our lives. During COVID-19 lockdowns, we adopted technologies that simulated a quality of life lost when we stopped meeting each other in person. Distributed workforces continued after the pandemic ended. Not since the Industrial Revolution has the way we work changed so radically—today, more of the global economy works from home than ever before.

- AI has a dark side. Deepfakes, AI-generated videos, images, or sounds are clever manipulations designed to appear real, turning every online interaction into a battleground of deception. It's alarmingly easy to create an AI impostor avatar to gain a target's trust. These deepfakes not only undermine our ability to trust what we see and hear, but they also cause financial damage and prey upon our emotional well-being.

- Creating deepfake avatars that do and say whatever the user commands takes little time and less skill. For a small monthly fee, a criminal can use numerous AI websites to create videos that impersonate trusted people and use those avatars to coerce, beguile, and convince family, friends, colleagues, and associates to send large sums of money to their attacker.

- Don't make a deepfake avatar of your spouse or partner. It is a terrible idea, even for a spy.

SIX

Infiltration: The Trojan Horse

A few days had passed since LockBit had called my personal phone number. Since then, the usually sleepy little NGO buzzed more than a kicked hornet's nest. Shutting down all business hadn't pleased the board of directors, and a whisper of recriminations hummed from the executive team.

Jill stormed down the NGO's IT corridor, fists clenched at her sides, ready for a fight. I understood her frustration and anger. A similar rage filled me when the false Hillsong pastor had tricked me into thinking I'd have an all-expense-paid trip to Cape Town several years earlier. No one enjoys learning that a criminal got the better of them or temporarily made them a puppet. Jill's credentials—her authenticated username and password—had been stolen by LockBit and turned against the organization, and I could see how she wore feelings of self-recrimination on her sleeve.

I stopped her with a soft word. Her dark eyes, framed by a shoulder-length haircut and bangs that draped her eyebrows, shifted from glare to plea. I hadn't known her long, but I knew she never backed down from a fight.

"It isn't your fault," I said for what might have been the ninth time over the past few days. I'd told the same to the CEO and a board member who had blamed Jill for the breach. But knowing didn't make

Jill feel any less used. This was a case where bad luck and poor timing intersected. Where some of our colleagues leapt to blame her for incompetence, I saw circumstance. Jill was the victim of a clever attacker who pinpointed the perfect time to strike.

"If I'd only finished the update on Friday," she said, groaning, "none of this would have happened."

Jill had spent much of the Friday before LockBit infiltrated the NGO's Headquarters server attempting to install an update (sometimes called a "patch") to an outward-facing IT help desk system. The help desk allowed employees, from their workstations across the globe, to log in to a system through the internet and change or recover their passwords. Most companies deploy automated systems like this. You use a similar one every time you change your password for your favorite website or email account.

Organizations, vendors, and software developers issue patches and updates for a variety of reasons. Some provide improvements to operating systems, like the next version of Windows or MacOS, some remove bugs from your favorite video game. The most important updates solve problems and patch identified flaws in security. When we fail to update, we are leaving a window cracked for an attacker to slip through. Criminals know that potential victims are slow to update and patch. For that reason, the moment a company like the service desk vendor issues a security update, threat actors race to exploit the flaw before the vendor's customers install the patch—which is what can happen to you if you sleep on critical updates.

The service desk software vendor had issued a patch the morning of the NGO attack. Jill's attempts to install the patch on the help desk server had required hours of the vendor's tech support, which kept her late in the office and ultimately proved fruitless. She decided to let it go until Monday, when she could return with fresh eyes. She was partially right in saying none of this would've happened had she finished the update that evening, because come Monday, the LockBit attacker had used drive-by malicious software to scan for vulnerabilities and lucked on the unpatched help desk. LockBit's infiltration followed quickly.

While Jill spent a weekend frustrated over the service desk vendor's tricky software, LockBit exploited the vulnerability she had been unable to patch. In 99 percent of other cases, she would have solved it on Monday. But it came down to this one instance.

The NGO was not alone in LockBit's incursion. A month before the global threat actor slipped into the NGO's networks through the service desk back door, LockBit used a similar approach to throw the U.S. Treasury bond market into momentary chaos. On November 8, 2023, Industrial Commercial Bank of China (ICBC) Financial Services, the sole Chinese bank authorized to clear securities in the United States with assets of over $5.7 trillion, issued a notice that their "systems were disrupted." Disrupted was an understatement. LockBit had exploited a known critical update to the Citrix NetScaler product suite, a tool ICBC (and many organizations) use to make websites and online services faster, more reliable, and safer to use, and (ironically) to protect against cyberthreats. Citrix had issued a critical patch to the tool on October 10, but as you might surmise, ICBC did not immediately follow Citrix's advice.

LockBit used this vulnerability to circumvent ICBC's multifactor authentication and to access the bank's internal network remotely. They soon launched a ransomware attack against ICBC that disrupted critical financial operations and disconnected ICBC's market makers, brokerages, and partner banks, impacting ICBC's ability to execute Treasury trades. Unable to clear the sudden trade backlog electronically, ICBC sent the settlement details of the trades across Manhattan on a USB stick in the hands of a courier. The attack sent shockwaves through the $26 trillion U.S. Treasury market, shaking its stability. The latest NGO attack was only a minor asset in LockBit's greater ransomware portfolio, though an important victim no less.

The NGO was struck as soon as Jill left the office that Friday evening. The service desk vulnerability allowed LockBit to request a memory dump from the service desk server using basic Windows PowerShell commands.

C:\windows\System32\rundll32.exe
C:\windows\System32\comsvcs.dll,
MiniDump 688
C:\windows\AppCompat\log5.txt full

The first two commands, part of the Windows operating system, revealed the identity of the last person to log in to the service desk engine: Jill. The log5.text command then spit out Jill's username and password. Unfortunately, the NGO had not configured the server for two-factor authentication, a second step after the password to verify credentials. All the attacker had to do was enter the username and password, and he controlled her account in the NGO's network.

Since Jill was a network administrator, anyone with access to her account could create new accounts, reset passwords, elevate security privileges, and exude a demigod-like domain over the data network. Over the next two days, LockBit used Jill's credentials to create its own superuser account. These superuser keys allowed LockBit to sift through the main HQ server like a beachcomber carefully looking for a gold watch.

"They were waiting for us," I explained to Jill in the hallway. "Sitting there on the internet, watching for an opportunity. It's not your fault the vendor's patch was a nightmare to configure." I shrugged. "I couldn't have installed it."

This lightened her up a bit. "You're a consultant."

"And you're the superbright network engineer. Go engineer the problem."

She nodded, back straightening. "I'm going to find Mr. LockBit attacker wherever he's hiding."

"Just stop him before he gets to the administrative server," I said.

"Why?"

"It'll be a real crisis if Josiah can't make this month's coffee order."

She mockingly rolled her eyes before jogging down the hall to her office. She wasn't a mole like Robert Hanssen, who had volunteered his services to the Soviet Union for decades. Rather, she had been victimized, compromised, and turned against the organization without her knowledge or consent. She'd been infiltrated.

* * *

Infiltration is a tale as old as time, and no story captures its grandiosity as does the Trojan horse myth. In traditional retellings of the story, Paris, son of the Trojan king, eloped with Helen, the wife of Sparta's king. In retaliation, the Greeks launched a war against Troy. The ten-year war concluded with a clever ruse: The Greeks pretended to withdraw, leaving behind a large wooden horse containing a hidden raiding party. When the Trojans brought the horse into their city, the hidden Greeks emerged, opened the gates, and brutally sacked Troy.

After the destruction of Troy, no one would've thought twice about opening their gates to effigies anymore. But spies are brilliant at repackaging old techniques for a modern audience, even going so far as to rely on myths for inspiration. Ransomware relies on infiltration, and spies have perfected the art. A few years before LockBit infiltrated the NGO, another Trojan horse story led to one of the most damaging cyberespionage attacks of the twenty-first century.

In late March 2020, SolarWinds, a software company based in Texas that provides system management tools for network and infrastructure monitoring for approximately three hundred thousand customers worldwide, issued a routine update to its popular Orion software.

It noted: "This release includes bug fixes, increased stability, and performance improvements."

About eighteen thousand customers downloaded and installed the update, a critical protocol in any cybersecurity checklist. Best practices require that people and organizations patch quickly, before attackers can launch attacks. In this case, the reverse turned out to be true.

Nine months after SolarWinds' update, one of the company's key customers identified an internal crisis. On December 8, 2020, the cybersecurity company FireEye announced that a foreign intelligence unit, presumed to be Russian, had stolen their Red Team tool kit.

Red Teams are white-hat hackers who test cybersecurity by seeking to penetrate (or "pentest") their systems. The best way to expose flaws in security like the NGO's unpatched help desk is often to hire a white hat to have a go before the black hats sniff out the problem.

Within five days of investigating the issue, FireEye determined that state-sponsored attackers had compromised the company through a supply chain attack. FireEye contacted the FBI, detailed their investigation in a report, and called SolarWinds to warn them that their Orion software had become a Trojan horse. The world would later learn that Russian spies had quietly infiltrated SolarWinds in September 2019 to covertly gather intel. They analyzed SolarWinds for months, until they found a way to inject malicious code into an update SolarWinds planned to push out to the Orion software installed by their customers.

Then the crafty spies laid low for months, ensuring that no one had noticed their quiet reconnaissance, before returning in February 2020 to launch their Trojan horse attack. This time, they came armed with back-door code that snuck into the Orion update before it was published and certified by the SolarWinds team. The attacker's earlier reconnaissance had paid off. They had learned that the development team verifies their updates, signs, and seals them before they go out to customers. In late March 2020, the spies infiltrated the code while SolarWinds' developers had checked it out of the metaphorical library and swapped SolarWinds' certified update for their malware just before developers returned the "book."

"The tradecraft was phenomenal," Adam Meyers, vice president of threat intelligence for CrowdStrike, the cyber forensics team SolarWinds hired to investigate the attack, told NPR in an interview. "The code was elegant and innovative. This was the craziest fucking thing I'd ever seen."[1]

On March 26, 2020, SolarWinds sent out Orion software updates that Russian spies had artfully manipulated. In other words, they wheeled a Trojan horse named Sunburst right out in front of SolarWinds' customers. Recall that all the spy tactics in DI²CED rely on the base ingredient of deceit. Infiltration follows suit. Russian intelligence deceived SolarWinds' customers into believing that the update could be trusted. The customers could not know that spies hid within the update, waiting like Greeks within the horse. Once pulled through the gates, they leapt out and struck.

"Eighteen thousand was our best estimate of who may have downloaded the code between March and June of 2020," Sudhakar Ramakrishna, SolarWinds' president and CEO, said.

For eight months, Russian spies infiltrated and analyzed those customers of SolarWinds that had wheeled the horse through the gates. Not one of these customers, including top U.S. government agencies, knew that cloaked figures had infiltrated and sacked data networks across the globe. Embarrassingly, one of those agencies was the Cybersecurity and Infrastructure Security Agency (CISA), an office at the Department of Homeland Security tasked with protecting U.S. computer networks from cyberattacks. If the Russian spies had not gotten greedy and decided to try to compromise a cybersecurity threat-hunting group, their unprecedented attack may have lasted years instead of months. But greed often clouds judgment. Within hours of FireEye's December 13 rejection and burning of the Trojan horse at their gates, SolarWinds rushed to issue an alert and a patch to address the security vulnerability.

SolarWinds deserves credit for their prompt action, but it was still eight months too late. The eighteen thousand potentially compromised government agencies and businesses also included the Department of Homeland Security; the Departments of State, Commerce, and Treasury; NIH; the Department of Energy; and the National Nuclear Security Administration, which maintains the United States' nuclear weapons stockpile. In addition, numerous Fortune 500 companies, including Microsoft, Intel, and Cisco, hospitals, local governments, power companies, and medical, educational, and financial institutions, were possibly compromised. I stress *possibly* because, while Russian spies had the *ability* to compromise any organization that wheeled a Trojan horse into their data systems, they did not have the time, capacity, or manpower to compromise *every* breached organization. Each attack required the spies to deftly exploit code to steal information without triggering alerts from cybersecurity soldiers manning the walls.

"It's really your worst nightmare," Tim Brown, vice president of security at SolarWinds told NPR. "You feel a kind of horror. This had the potential to affect thousands of customers; this had the potential to do a great deal of harm."[2]

What is most concerning about the SolarWinds espionage attack is not what we know now, but what the future will reveal. Espionage survives for decades and spans government administrations. Spies play the long game, often stealing intelligence that they may not activate for a generation. One can presume that Russia primarily attacked SolarWinds to compromise the government agencies, even if it took time. Frighteningly, the level of access afforded to Russian SVR spies by the Sunburst Trojan would have allowed Russian intelligence not only to steal data, but to destroy it or alter it. Or, still more nefarious, spies could have left behind quiet code like a ticking time bomb, to be activated with destructive results.

Such an attack by Russia is not unprecedented.

In 2017, Russian military intelligence launched a destructive ransomware attack against the world called NotPetya, using a similar Trojan horse. In this case, spies comprised a software update mechanism built into an accounting program used by firms working with the Ukrainian government. Computers infected with the accounting program reached out to other networked computers and spread the malware. Nearly one hundred thousand computer systems fell victim to NotPetya, including systems in both Ukraine and Russia, throughout Europe and North America, and as far away as Australia.

A career in counterintelligence and national security has taught me a few valuable lessons. The first is that if an attack works, spies will continue to leverage the attack until security stops it. The second is that criminals have become adept at emulating spies, particularly when it comes to launching ransomware attacks. Cryptography is like a secret code language used to keep information safe and private. It involves techniques for scrambling messages in such a way that only the intended recipient can unscramble and understand them, even if someone else intercepts them. The most secure computer systems, likely including your own, leverage encryption to protect data.

Of course, criminals have turned encryption to the dark side to ensure a payday after infiltrating compromised systems. Ransomware *uses against us* many of the same variants of encryption technology *that protects us*. Successful attacks fund cybercrime syndicate innovation. Cybercrime syndicates established R&D departments that experiment and research ways to corrupt data, from finding flaws in operating systems to installing command-and-control servers that would allow the attacker to talk to and even control the victim machine. Still, ransomware remained on the fringe until another medical industry attack sensationalized the crime in the media and around the world.

In February 2016, ransomware crippled the networks of Hollywood Presbyterian Medical Center (HPMC) in Southern California. Back then, HPMC had 424 beds and more than 500 doctors who cared for over 16,000 patients. As the attack unfolded, doctors and nurses could not send emails, couldn't receive blood test results, or transmit X-ray images. Instead of updating digital records, already exhausted nurses had to write patient information on pads of paper. My mother was a nurse in the 1970s and '80s and would come home with vital readings scrawled in pen on the back of her arms. I can imagine the nurses at HPMC wearily leaving the hospital with the equivalent of a sleeve of ink from wrist to elbow.

The hospital's systems were compromised by a ransomware variant called Locky, which encrypts data and holds it hostage until a key is purchased with Bitcoin. Cryptocurrency operates independently of a central authority, like a bank or government. It's based on a technology called blockchain, which securely records all transactions. Unlike traditional currency, it's decentralized, meaning no single entity controls it. People can use cryptocurrencies to buy goods and services online, and some see them as investments because their value can change rapidly, like stocks.

Blockchain is like a digital ledger or recordkeeping system that stores information across a network of computers. With cryptocurrency, instead of one central authority controlling blockchain, like a bank, everyone on the network has a copy of the ledger. Whenever a new transaction occurs, it gets added to the ledger as a "block," which is then linked to previous transactions, forming a chain of blocks—hence the name blockchain. This way, it creates a transparent, secure, and presumably tamperproof way to track transactions.

Ransomware attacks have grown because tracing transactions on the blockchain gives law enforcement a major headache. Despite blockchain's security features, its decentralized nature inadvertently created a dark web economy based on crypto.

Back at HPMC, security professionals sought to understand how the infiltration began and where it spread. Locky typically worms its way in through a malware-laced Word document disguised as an invoice. In those early days before cybersecurity solutions like endpoint detection and response (EDR) and zero trust became the gold standard, malware inserted into a macro in a Trojan Word document could bring down an organization.

The HPMC president and CEO declared an internal emergency that stalled emergency room systems and forced the transfer of patients to other hospitals. The attack stressed medical staff and impacted the hospital through negative reviews and reputational harm. After a week of futilely fighting the attack, the hospital eventually paid 40 Bitcoin to free their data, then equivalent to $17,000.

Some of the best analysis companies routinely track the damage ransomware causes and predict how serious the crime will grow in the future. Cybersecurity Ventures is a company that conducts research for the global cyber economy and provides some of the most cited and trusted data in the information security industry. They claim to track over one hundred ransomware dark web gangs and variants each quarter to inform their research. And the results are grim. The company recently predicted that the global cost of ransomware will hit $57 billion by the end of 2025, exceed $70 billion in 2026 and will skyrocket to $265 billion by 2031. These numbers are based on a historical 30 percent year-over-year increase in damages to organizations infiltrated by ransomware over the last decade. They also predict that by 2031, if cybersecurity doesn't defeat dark web and espionage threat actors, ransomware will infiltrate and infect a business, consumer, or device every two seconds—up from one every eleven seconds in 2021.

Another analysis company that focuses on blockchain and cryptocurrency in over seventy countries is Chainalysis. Chainalysis's 2023 annual crime report demonstrated that global ransomware payments exceeded $1.1 billion in 2023.[3] Compare that with the $42 billion estimated for 2024, and it's clear: ransomware isn't just rising—it's skyrocketing.

Paying a ransom is only a small part of the incredible cost to recover from a ransomware infiltration. Some businesses never recover. Actions such as investigating attacks, building cybersecurity to prevent future ransomware, and handling reputational fallout when customers and shareholders discover a breach can cost an organization millions of dollars. In 2022, Lincoln College, a liberal arts school in Illinois, finally closed its doors after 157 years. The college had survived a major fire in 1912, the Spanish flu, the Great Depression, both world wars, and the 2008 financial crisis. The final straw that broke its back was a ransomware attack in December 2021 that made it impossible for the school to recruit and retain students and fundraise.[4]

To add insult to injury, cybercrime syndicates know that data is valuable. Stolen data can be sold on dark web marketplaces for a premium. As security companies developed excellent backup systems that are outside an attacker's reach, the bad guys turned to extortion. Today, criminals will immediately begin to disclose stolen data on the dark web, often bit by bit as a timer counts down, unless the victim pays the ransom quickly.

As spies perfected the art of infiltration since Sparta left a giant horse in front of Troy, so criminals mastered ransomware. In the years since Russian intelligence showed the world how a Greek myth could lead to one of history's most damaging infiltration attacks, criminals, to borrow one of their phrases, "Made ransomware great again."

* * *

Hunting LockBit through the NGO's systems became an endless task. To discover where the attacker lurked, Ben, Jill, and their IT peers had to understand the NGO's data both systemically and intrinsically. This was no small task. To start, they had to understand the detailed operation of the NGO's networks, not only in the United States, but through connections to other countries. Each of those pools of data required protection, authentication, patching, understanding vulnerabilities, and analysis of the data that flows back and forth. In the world of cybersecurity, we call this holy grail *context*.

Ben squeezed the bridge of his nose and rubbed tired eyes. I suspected he might have a headache coming on and could sympathize. I'd had plenty in the last week. Jill looked a bit frazzled, hair out of place as though she'd slept in her office. I knew that the organization's global IT workforce had pushed themselves to exhaustion to lay the groundwork that would eventually kick LockBit from our networks. To get that particular train to the station, Ben's team had to lay the tracks. The distance was formidable.

We huddled outside the executive conference room on the second floor of the NGO's small offices in Washington, D.C. I didn't like coming here and had long-since given up downtown traffic and inside-the-Beltway pomposity for a more chill suburban existence. But Ben and I had a report to give to the full executive team. As my old mentor at DLA Piper used to say about difficult situations where one must do whatever is necessary, even if it's undesirable, "Needs must when the devil drives."

"Let's go through it again." I waved at the closed door to the conference room. We could hear low murmurs through the thick wood. "Remember," I cautioned. "Less is more."

Ben placed his glasses back on his nose. "We know how the attacker got in, where he landed, and the exploit he used, but we don't know where he is."

"We will." Jill's confidence made me smile. "We've installed an endpoint security sensor on all our servers and most of our employee computers."

"So far we've cleaned and restored fourteen hundred and twenty-three computer systems out of roughly two thousand," Ben said. "We've cleaned artifacts off about one hundred twenty systems."

By artifacts, I knew that Ben meant foreign code that included ransomware (both triggered and dormant), beacons the attacker could use to reconnect with our network, and system alert footprints that showed what LockBit had sought to compromise as they quietly infiltrated. By cleaning and securing our systems, we eliminated LockBit's hiding spots. Imagine our data systems as a vast network of pipes, some old and rusty, some leaking, others smashed by LockBit. Ben cut off the water flow, replaced the broken pipes with pristine copper, and reinforced weaknesses to block new infiltration paths. As Ben and Jill removed the corrupted pipes, they forced LockBit to retreat until the trap finally closed around them.

"We also restored our servers to a backup image taken prior to the earliest evidence of threat actor activity." Jill wrinkled her nose. "That took forever but at least we know that the servers are completely clean." She sighed. "We also took down the help desk server that was the initial point of attack."

"When this is all said and done, we will look for a different vendor," Ben added.

Jill pounded a fist into her palm. "One that connects seamlessly with our system and doesn't take forty-eight hours to patch!"

I threw a thumb behind me at the closed door. "We'll make sure they know that this is a complicated effort, but that we are moving fast." I paused. "You know . . . it's one thing to boot LockBit from our systems. It's another to say what they stole."

"First things first," Ben said. "The secret of getting ahead is getting started. The secret of getting started is breaking your complex, overwhelming tasks into small manageable tasks, and then starting on the first one."

I raised an eyebrow. "Einstein?"

Ben smiled. "Mark Twain."

The door opened and I peered at anxious faces that would not relax until we led them from the center of a firestorm. Days of effort and sleepless nights lay ahead, but by working the plan we had in place we'd emerge from the crisis. One step at a time.

THINK LIKE A SPY

- Organizations are slow to respond to attacks. If an attack works, criminals will keep using the attack until security finds a way to prevent it.

- Intelligence units develop the best attacks. Spies play the long game and seek to infiltrate organizations to quietly steal information for as long as possible without being noticed.

- Criminals have become adept at emulating spies, particularly when it comes to launching ransomware attacks.

- The dark web engine runs on blockchain and cryptocurrency.

- Blockchain is like a decentralized digital ledger storing information across a network of computers. Unlike centralized systems, everyone in the network possesses a copy of the ledger. Transactions are added as "blocks" linked to previous ones, forming an immutable chain. This fosters transparency, security, and ostensibly tamperproof transaction tracking.

- Cryptocurrency is digital money operating independently of banks or governments, utilizing blockchain technology for secure transaction records. Unlike traditional currency, it's decentralized, with no single controlling entity.

- Ransomware attacks have grown because tracking cryptocurrency transactions through blockchain is difficult for law enforcement.

- The best ransomware attacks model espionage: (1) use deception practices like spear phishing emails, reconnaissance, and

Trojan horses to slip past the gates; (2) quietly lurk in systems undetected until a critical mass of networks are compromised by ransomware; (3) trigger the attack when the victim's guard is down (Fridays before a holiday weekend are best).

- Context in cybersecurity refers to understanding the environment in which a system operates, including its specific threats, vulnerabilities, and the behavior of users and adversaries. Contextual information is critical for effectively identifying and responding to cyberthreats.

SEVEN

Infiltration: Indomitable Weeds

At the FBI Academy, my instructors drilled many truths into me, including this timeless one: *Nothing comes without a cost, and if it seems too good to be true, it probably is.* The best spies use a combination of espionage tools to infiltrate and steal secrets. Cybercriminals, modeling their betters, deploy all the best deceptive practices to perfect ransomware infiltration. Sadly, Camille was not forearmed or forewarned about these threats.

Camille worked in the department of finance in the Paris office of a company that produced and sold high-end textiles to garment manufacturers around the world. She spent much of her day reviewing vendor agreements, processing vendor invoices, and holding the company's outside partners accountable for their work. She enjoyed her job but marveled at the sheer number of invoices she had to process daily for the multinational corporation. Still, she knew that even a small cog in a big engine had an important role to play. She could never have known how important until she met Guillaume.

An invoice from a vendor she recognized by name caught her attention, demanding payment for catering services provided for the Parisian company's customer sales kickoff events. Camille knew that the marketing team loved hosting SKO events and that many top-tier customers attended, but although the invoice amount seemed in line with expectations, she didn't recognize the event. Fortunately, at the bottom of the invoice, she saw a Paris number to call.

Guillaume, a representative, answered on the second ring. Camille appreciated his polite tone, excellent French, and detailed knowledge of the workings of her company, especially information about the event she couldn't initially recall. He listed the managers from marketing who had hired his company's services and the dates of each event they had catered. All of this sounded correct to Camille, who would later admit that it was his cheerful, resonant voice that won her over. They'd even exchange emails when Guillaume suggested they meet for a drink that evening.

Guillaume detailed a new payment portal that his company had invested in to quickly process payments. Camille agreed to give the system a try. After all, if she didn't like the way it functioned, she could always revert to sending a hard check in the mail. He directed Camille to his company's website and then to a *connexion de paiement* link. She clicked the link and scanned instructions to download and install the vendor's proprietary payment application. They chatted about Camille's favorite café near the office as the small application installed. After tinkering with the app for a short while, she decided that it would not suit their payment controls and closed it. She promised to send the check by mail. In turn, Guillaume promised to meet her that night at the café Camille had mentioned.

Camille hung up, pleased by the conversation. As she daydreamed what the man with the soothing voice might look like, the "voice" used the remote access Trojan Camille had unknowingly installed to compromise her computer.

A remote access Trojan (aka "RAT") is malware that cybercriminals use to gain unauthorized access to a computer or network from a remote location. Once installed on a victim's device, an attacker and his gang of criminal colleagues can quietly infiltrate the victim's network.

That evening, as Camille waited alone for a Guillaume who would never arrive, the cybercrime syndicate named Royal Ransomware executed an attack that locked all the computers they'd spent the day infiltrating and crippled the company.

Camille's story is hardly an anomaly. Perhaps because of the expertly demonstrated infiltration attack against SolarWinds, or more probably because of the dissociation imposed on society by COVID-19 pandemic lockdowns in 2020, 2021 became the Year of Ransomware. The largest publicly disclosed ransom paid to date happened earlier that year when CNA Financial Corporation, a U.S. insurance company based in Chicago, paid $40 million to attackers.* On March 21, CNA announced that a sophisticated cybersecurity attack caused a network disruption and impacted CNA systems. The attackers demanded a $60 million ransom after tricking a CNA employee into downloading and executing a fake browser update. The attackers, later revealed to be a group called Phoenix, then lurked in CNA's systems for two weeks and quietly escalated their privileges—meaning they took control of user accounts and created their own virtual trusted insider accounts that had the ability to access highly confidential data. Phoenix brought down approximately fifteen thousand systems. While at it, they grabbed personally identifying information including Social Security numbers of over seventy-five thousand people and dumped it into their cloud account. The FBI miraculously worked with the cloud storage platform Phoenix used to repatriate the data before Phoenix could move it to their dark web servers and use it to extort CNA. But it didn't end there. Phoenix had encrypted large swaths of CNA's data, so much that the largest U.S. insurance company was forced to haggle with Phoenix. After a round of negotiations, CNA paid Phoenix $40 million for the decryption key to CNA's data.

---

* The Dark Angels cybercrime syndicate has likely shattered CNA Financials' record for the largest ransomware payout. According to Zscaler's ThreatLabz, an undisclosed victim paid a staggering $75 million to this cybercrime group in 2024. Dark Angels first appeared in 2022 and has since gained notoriety for its highly targeted attacks, including the 2023 breach of Johnson Controls, where they reportedly stole 27 terabytes of data and demanded $51 million in cryptocurrency (there is no evidence Johnson Controls paid). Unlike other ransomware groups, Dark Angels selects its victims carefully, stealing vast amounts of data—often 10 to 100 terabytes—and avoiding indiscriminate attacks. Their operations, including a data leak site ominously named Dunghill, highlight a dangerous new evolution in ransomware strategy. See "Threat-Labz 2024_Ransomware Report," https://www.zscaler.com/resources/industry-reports/threatlabz-ransomware-report.pdf.

Two months later, JBS Foods, the world's largest meat producer, shut down their operations in the United States, Canada, and Australia after suffering a crippling ransomware attack. If you're a dedicated carnivore, there's a good chance you've eaten meat prepared by JBS, which processes most of the beef, poultry, and pork from around the world. Vegans rejoiced and carnivores cried into their beers as cattle slaughter halted in the United States and meat prices skyrocketed before Memorial Day Weekend grill fests. Australia and Canada spent a meat-deprived week waiting for JBS to restore normal operations.

The FBI launched an investigation into the who, what, and how of the ransomware attack and learned that a notorious Russian cybercriminal group named REvil (pronounced "R-evil," like "are-evil") was behind it. REvil had made a name for itself by building a ransomware-as-a-service model like LockBit's affiliate program. Prior to the attack, REvil had made the news and came onto the FBI's cybercrime radar because they targeted celebrities and politicians. Their scheme involved data mining compromising information about the wealthy or famous and then issuing a press release demanding payment within a certain time. If the celebrity or politician failed to pay, REvil would publish the information on their dark web site, Happy Blog. In one of the most public examples, they threatened to publish "dirty laundry" that would embarrass then-President Trump which they claimed to have stolen from a law firm. They requested $42 million from the president to keep the information off the website. When Trump refused to pay, REvil published 169 emails that mentioned Trump to their dark web message boards. Fortunately for the president, the emails had not been weaponized by the attackers. Instead, REvil appeared to have searched for any mention of "Trump" and lumped those emails (many of which used "trump" as a verb) together in one data dump.

REvil's extortion against a U.S. president might not have borne fruit, but they hit the jackpot against the meat industry. JBS had a secure, encrypted backup of its data and used it to begin to restore operations at certain plants. While cybersecurity consultants examined JBS's systems like terriers rooting out rats, other consultants negotiated the ransom demand with REvil. On June 9, despite the FBI's misgivings, JBS took the most expeditious route out of the crisis and paid an $11 million ransom. A forensic analysis demonstrated to the company's satisfaction that no customer, supplier, or employee data was compromised in the attack.

The REvil case was a momentous blow in the land of cyberattacks, but the largest fight of 2021 ransomware attacks occurred on Friday, July 2, of that year. Have you noticed a trend when it comes to cyberattacks? Attackers love to launch these on Fridays, particularly before holiday weekends.

Kaseya is a multinational company, headquartered in Dublin, Ireland, and Miami, Florida, that provides software services to over forty thousand organizations worldwide. One of Kaseya's most popular software solutions is a virtual system administrator (VSA) network and endpoint remote management tool used by many managed service providers, who then provide the tool to the customers they service. A VSA is an automated software agent that oversees computer systems and networks in virtualized or cloud-based setups. Endpoints, meanwhile, refer to the devices and technology that are entry points for humans to access secure data. In cybersecurity, an endpoint is like the bouncer at a digital club. He stands guard at the entrance of your digital world, checking IDs (or in this case, verifying permissions), and making sure only the invited guests get in—keeping out the cybercriminals who try to crash the party, not to mention those intrusive Trojan horses. Endpoints might include computers in a dentist's office or cash registers at a supermarket, or your very own smartphone, tablet, or laptop. Kaseya, as the digital bouncer for numerous companies, was and remains a critical player in the global IT supply chain—precisely the kind of target a cybercriminal would want to compromise.

Our old pals in REvil had warmed up on JBS Foods and had studied the Russian intelligence infiltration of SolarWinds the year before. In a startlingly similar attack, REvil compromised Kaseya, not to steal from Kaseya, but from all the companies that licensed Kaseya's VSA. I've often wondered if Russian intelligence officers, much like SolarWinds, moonlighted at REvil to score some extra cash. If forced to, I'd bet on black.

In September 2023, the U.S. Department of Justice indicted nine cybercriminals (eight from Russia and one Ukraine) for their part in the notorious Conti Ransomware gang. Conti had spent years holding numerous organizations—especially hospitals—for ransom and collected over $100 million in payments.[1] Despite multimillion-dollar rewards, the criminals remain at large and untouchable—as long as they stay in Russia under the protective arm of intelligence services. National security strategists like me have long known that Russia does not consider ransomware attacks against Western countries a crime. There is ample evidence that Russian cybercrime syndicates work as surge contractors for Russian intelligence services when critical foreign espionage infiltrations are required, and it stands to reason that intelligence service comrades would share in the largesse from criminal attacks on the other side of the coin.

On that Friday in July, Kaseya began receiving a flood of calls from upset customers who reported ransomware attacks linked to the Kaseya VSA. REvil managed to exploit a zero-day (aka "novel") vulnerability within the VSA software that allowed them to bypass authentication and execute ransomware. In other words, the cybercriminals found a previously unknown vulnerability in Kaseya's software and leveraged the vulnerability on day 0, or the day before the flaw became known to Kaseya and could be patched.

REvil shook down each of Kaseya's customers locked with ransomware for between $50,000 and $5 million. In a devilishly clever twist, REvil offered to sell Kaseya a universal decryption key for $70 million. As the customers fell to ransomware and angry shouts reached Kaseya, massive pressure built for the company to pay REvil in order to stop the bleeding. Kaseya could presumably pay $70 million for a Monopoly get-out-of-jail-free card they could pass to each of their compromised customers. While Kaseya deliberated, REvil posted the following:

> Your files are encrypted, and currently unavailable. You can check it: all files on your system has extension csruj. By the way, everything is possible to recover (restore), but you need to follow our instructions. Otherwise, you cant return your data (NEVER)

Its just a business. We absolutely do not care about you and your deals, except getting benefits. If we do not do our work and liabilities—nobody will not cooperate with us. Its not in our interests. If you will not cooperate with our service—for us, its does not matter. But you will lose your time and data, cause just we have the private key. In practice—time is much more valuable than money.

Kaseya swiftly sent messages to customers advising them to shut down their locally installed VSA servers. It also shut down its cloud-based VSA servers and called in consultant cybersecurity support. On July 3, Kaseya released a tool to customers that could detect indicators of compromise (like breadcrumbs left behind by cybercriminals) and warn ahead of time that REvil might be lurking. On July 11, 2021, Kaseya issued a patch to correct the zero-day vulnerability. According to Kaseya, approximately fifteen hundred worldwide customers suffered the REvil ransomware attack.

It would take another ten days to fully resolve the situation. While Kaseya steadfastly refused to pay, the FBI descended on the dark web to hunt down REvil and their nefarious servers. Cyber investigators seized a decryption key from REvil that victims of the ransomware attack could use to restore their scrambled data.

Kaseya's speed in responding to REvil's attack suggested that the Miami company also learned lessons from the earlier Russian espionage against SolarWinds. REvil, on the other hand, continued to run scared. On January 14, 2022 (another Friday), Russia's Federal Security Service (FSB) raided more than two dozen residences in Moscow, Saint Petersburg, and elsewhere, and arrested fourteen members of REvil. During the raids, which the Federal Security Service published on YouTube, the FSB seized millions in cash, luxury cars, and cryptocurrency wallets.[2] The arrest was the brainchild of a diplomatic White House–Kremlin experts' group on ransomware. The United States and Russia began communicating about the problem in June 2021 after the Russian cybercrime attacks on JBS, Kaseya, and Colonial Pipeline. (We'll get to Colonial Pipeline and critical infrastructure attacks in chapters 12 and 13.)

You might ask yourself why the FBI, Russian FSB, or other global law enforcement agencies don't simply stomp out all the cybercrime syndicates like gardeners pulling weeds. They do. At least, they try. But bad guys have backups too. Within months of the joint United States–Russia takedown, REvil's ransomware variant weed had made its way back onto the lawn.

In a White House press briefing regarding the arrests, not a single reporter thought to ask about SolarWinds.

* * *

In mid-2024, I stood on a spectacular stage in the Aria Hotel and Casino's West Convention Center in Las Vegas, Nevada. I love speaking in Vegas. Not because I enjoy gambling (I did enough of that with my safety in the FBI), but because everything in Vegas is supersize and awe-inspiring. Grand stages, big audiences, and tremendous productions make stepping foot on any stage an outsize rush.

On the Aria Hotel and Casino stage, I looked at the expectant crowd and asked, "What do a casino, a pharmacy, and a field of weeds have in common?"

This was not an opening joke to rival the *three guys walk into a bar* series of comedy. This was a story about ALPHV (pronounced "Alph Five") and their Scattered Spider affiliates, two cybercrime syndicates that made the news in 2023 for all the wrong reasons.

If I'd walked onto the Aria stage in September 2023, the experience would have been far less pleasant. For roughly ten days, starting on September 11, 2023, everything at MGM-managed resorts in Las Vegas, including the Aria, fell into pandemonium. Thousands of slot machines stopped working, and exuberant gamblers couldn't collect their electronic winnings or use their room key cards. Guests who accessed their rooms couldn't charge purchases, use hotel phones, or watch TV. ATMs refused to dispense cash, the reservation system failed, and websites went offline, causing long check-in lines and shuttle transfers to other hotels. Some hotels stocked elevators with water bottles just in case guests got trapped. Grand Vegas casinos resorted to handwritten receipts for casino winnings, as if thrust fifty years into the past.

MGM Resorts International is a big player in the Vegas scene. The company manages some of the key properties, including the Aria, Bellagio, Cosmopolitan, Excalibur, Luxor, Mandalay Bay, MGM Grand Las Vegas, and New York-New York hotels. According to some reports, the global company lost $8.4 million in revenue each day from the beginning of the attack until September 20, when they announced that their hotels and casinos were "operating normally." It gets worse for them. By October 5, the company provided an update revealing that cybercriminals may have stolen certain guest information, including names, contact information, gender, date of birth, and driver's license, passport, and even Social Security numbers—everything and more an attacker would need to steal an identity. In the aftermath, lawyers have brought multiple class-action lawsuits against MGM, alleging that the company failed to protect personally identifiable information of thousands of customers.

This attack was made possible when ALPHV and Scattered Spider conspired to launch a Vegas casino heist that rivals the movie *Ocean's Eleven*. Scattered Spider is an elusive newcomer to the cybercrime business that specializes in social engineering through telephone calls (aka "vishing"). Much like REvil and LockBit, Russian-speaking ALPHV (sometimes called BlackCat—dark web crime syndicates often rebrand themselves) runs a ransomware-as-a-service business. Scattered Spider is believed to be one of the affiliates of ALPHV. Unfortunately for Las Vegas and MGM, Scattered Spider's silver tongue and ALPHV's data infiltration skills complemented each other perfectly.

Scattered Spider began with careful reconnaissance of the resort chain. A review of LinkedIn revealed potential MGM employees who had systems administrative access to the network. A huge hurdle that the Spider/ALPHV team had to overcome was MGM's use of the cybersecurity company Okta to protect user accounts with multifactor authentication. Recall that MFA adds an extra layer of security by requiring users to verify their identity using additional factors such as a one-time passcode sent to their mobile device. Okta automates what they call identity-driven security that turns basic MFA protocols up to eleven. To compromise MGM employees with super-administrative permissions, Scattered Spider had to trick other MGM employees into letting them in. The Okta safeguard would not allow them to simply guess a password or buy one off the dark web.

That's where things get clever. Scattered Spider threat actors with silver tongues used their social media investigations to impersonate the targeted employees. Pretending to be an employee who had their account locked, they called the MGM IT help desk and asked for both a password reset and a new MFA code. According to a former MGM employee, to pass help desk protocols, the employee must know basic information including name, employee identification number, date of birth, and other things any proficient background investigator can find after a few hours of online searching. Scattered Spider had a few advantages. They are fluent in English, knew detailed information about the employee they impersonated, and had likely read Okta's August 2023 warning about this exact attack. The warning, meant to protect customers like MGM, gave Scattered Spider a road map for how to breach security.

Allow me to beat the patch drum once again. Spies and criminals and all manner of attackers know that organizations are slow to patch, update, and fix vulnerabilities. Bad actors actively monitor patches and updates for the entire information technology supply chain, from operating systems to security applications like Okta. According to a 2023 study by Statista, it takes companies worldwide between 88 and 208 days to patch cyber vulnerabilities.[3] On average, high-severity problems are fixed within 82 days. Low-severity vulnerabilities? Nearly 10 months. The LockBit attackers that turned Jill into a virtual trusted insider compromised the NGO within 24 hours of learning about a vulnerability. How many attacks do you think they can achieve if they have 82 days to plan! Take a moment to consider how long it takes you to update your smartphone or the operating system on your PC or tablet. Would you feel safe during an 82-day waiting period?

Once Scattered Spider got their virtual foot in the door, ALPHV took over. According to their blog posts, the cybercrime group quietly infiltrated MGM's internal networks across several MGM-managed Vegas casino hotels. MGM's cybersecurity caught wind of the compromise and promptly shut down infected systems, seeking to prevent the damage from spreading. This added to the chaos as internal networks, built to trust each other in a cohesive system, went offline. To make matters worse, once ALPHV learned of MGM's defensive actions, they triggered a ransomware attack and threatened to publish stolen information as well as notify Troy Hunt of HaveIBeenPwned.com if MGM failed to negotiate satisfactorily.

Have you ever wondered if your username and password has been lost in a data breach? Any data breach? The website www.HaveIBeenPwned.com is a great way to check. The organization collects data from countless data breaches and publishes the names of websites and organization that have been pwned (or in video-game slang "owned," i.e., ruthlessly defeated) by cyberattacks. MGM was definitely pwned to the tune of approximately $100 million.

Take a deep breath and then try the usernames of your most important accounts on Troy's website. I'll bet at least one of them has been compromised and is available for sale on the dark web.

The FBI got involved and set out to hunt the cybercriminals. Investigators from the FBI, Europol, and law enforcement agencies in Germany, Spain, the United Kingdom, Australia, and elsewhere collaborated to punish ALPHV, shut down their servers, and send them scurrying to the deepest corners of the dark web. The FBI then data mined ALPHV's servers for decryption keys that would release victims from ransomware attacks.

Don't pop the champagne yet.

Remember the analogy about weeds? By February 2024, ALPHV and their affiliates had launched an incredibly disruptive ransomware attack on UnitedHealth Group's Change Healthcare business unit, a company that connects payers, providers, and patients in the health and pharmacy space. When you bring your prescription to a pharmacy, Change Healthcare routes the claim to a claim reviewer, who ultimately decides whether a patient's prescription will be covered by insurance. Interrupt this process, and the pharmacy has no method to confirm that insurance will pay. This forces a patient standing with her prescription to decide whether to pay hundreds of dollars out of her own wallet or go without medications.

On February 21, 2024, the health-care attack impacted more than 90 percent of the United States' seventy thousand pharmacies. They had trouble filling prescriptions electronically or checking a patient's eligibility for treatment. Providers were also unable to submit claims and receive reimbursements from insurers, all of which placed the health-care industry into crisis. Like the MGM attack, ALPHV also stole patient data for the purpose of extorting Change Healthcare into paying a ransom.

If you lived in the United States in February or March of 2024 and needed a prescription filled, you had ALPHV to thank when the pharmacist gave you a blank stare. The cost for Change Healthcare, after class-action lawsuits for potential data exfiltration, Biden administration investigations, reputational damage, and a $22 million ransom payment, that resulted in no data recovery, has eclipsed MGM's $100 million losses. On an earnings call related to the first quarter financial report for 2024, UnitedHealth CEO Andrew Witty told analysts that the cybercrime was "straight out an attack on the U.S. health system and designed to create maximum damage." Witty's forceful comment may have been an understatement. By October 2024, UnitedHealth estimated $2.77 billion in total financial losses from the cyberattack.[4] For American citizens, it could be worse. In an April 22, 2024, press release, UnitedHealth admitted that "based on initial targeted data sampling to date, the company has found files containing protected health information or personally identifiable information, which could cover a substantial proportion of people in America."

In earlier chapters we discussed the importance of quickly learning the who, what, how, and why of a cyberattack. ALPHV spent little time boasting that they had launched the attack. This gave UnitedHealth the *who*. Why? Because ALPHV knew that by extorting potentially stolen personal health data for millions of customers,

UnitedHealth would pay a ransom. And they did. We recently learned the *how* when Witty testified before Congress.

On February 12, 2024, criminals exploited compromised credentials (stolen username and password) to access Change Healthcare's Citrix portal, the application that allows remote access to desktops. ALPHV then moved laterally within the network and exfiltrated data. If you can believe a gang of thieves, ALPHV claims to have stolen 6 terabytes of data. Change Healthcare has admitted that between February 17 and February 20, "a substantial quantity of data had been exfiltrated."[5] The compromised data potentially included a wide range of sensitive information including health insurance details, comprehensive medical records, financial data related to health-care services, personal identification information, and even medical diagnoses. All told, the ransomware attack exposed the personal health information of 190 million people.

The cybercrime syndicate lurked in Change Healthcare's systems for nine days before triggering their ransomware attack on February 21. Immediately upon discovering the attack, UnitedHealth disconnected from Change Healthcare's data centers to contain the attack. Sound familiar? This was the same "close all your laptops" tactic that I took with the NGO upon learning about the attack, and it was just as disruptive. Multifactor authentication was another eerily similar problem. Change Healthcare's Citrix portal did not have multifactor authentication turned on. All ALPHV needed to gain access was the stolen username and password. I'll keep beating this drum. If you haven't already, mark your place, set the book down for a moment, and turn on multifactor authentication for *every single one* of your accounts.

The FBI and other global investigative agencies routinely descend into the dark web to, in the wise words of Dwayne "the Rock" Johnson, "layeth the smack down" on cybercriminals. While they're successful in antagonizing and disrupting criminal gangs, the total defeat of them remains an aspiration. ALPHV keeps taking punches and manages to get back to its feet, reemerging with such names as BlackCat,

BlackMatter, and Darkside. Operating as Darkside, ALPHV was responsible for one of the most notable critical infrastructure attacks in history (stay tuned for chapter 12).

Chasing cybercriminals has required the same level of effort and has imposed similar frustrations as cornering intelligence officers. Criminals have deployed infiltration to extract data that they then exploit against organizations of all sizes and people like me and you. And they aren't going away. Just as the FBI aspires to catch the criminals, we need to learn to stop them. Otherwise, you'll be asking law enforcement to clean up the mess after the weeds have overrun your garden.

THINK LIKE A SPY

- In the realm of cybercrime, remote access Trojans (commonly referred to as RATs) stand as indispensable tools for infiltrating and controlling target systems. These insidious pieces of malware empower cybercriminals to breach computers and networks from afar, evading detection and exploiting vulnerabilities with ease. Once embedded within a victim's device, RATs grant the operator unfettered access, enabling them to sift through valuable data, manipulate system functions, and extract sensitive information without arousing suspicion.

- The Friday before holiday weekends theme for cyberattacks is strategic and calculated, aiming to intensify pressure and induce panic as employees face the prospect of sacrificing their cherished downtime to combat an unfolding crisis. Whether it's the allure of cocktails by the beach or gatherings with friends and family, the desire for relaxation becomes a distant dream as individuals find themselves tethered to their keyboards, grappling with the relentless onslaught of cyber assaults.

- Virtual system administrators (VSAs) are digital guardians deployed within virtualized or cloud-based infrastructures, tirelessly configuring, monitoring, and safeguarding computer systems and networks. Acting as automated or remotely managed software agents, they undertake tasks such as patching software, updating systems, managing user access, and enforcing security protocols, all without the need for physical presence or human intervention.

- Endpoints serve as the gatekeepers of your digital domain, comprising all devices and technologies that provide entry points for human interaction with secure data. In the realm of cybersecurity, an endpoint functions like a vigilant bouncer stationed at the entrance to a digital club. With the task of verifying permissions (much like checking IDs at a club door), it ensures that only authorized guests gain access while thwarting the attempts of cybercriminals seeking unauthorized entry.

- A zero-day vulnerability refers to a previously unknown weakness exploited on day 0, just before it's disclosed and fixed. These vulnerabilities are exploited in zero-day attacks, which target undisclosed software weaknesses for maximum impact. These attacks breach systems, steal data, and create chaos with precision and stealth. Mastering such exploits requires thorough research and precise execution.

- Indicators of compromise (IOCs) serve as the breadcrumbs left behind by cybercriminals and can guide a threat hunter's pursuit through the digital wilderness. These subtle cues, whether anomalous network behaviors or unusual file activities, offer critical insights into the presence of threats lurking within secure data systems. Threat hunters meticulously analyze IOCs to uncover hidden dangers and neutralize them before they strike.

- Cybercriminals are not without their own defenses in the realm of cybersecurity. Employing redundant systems, backup servers, and various other tactics, they possess the ability to regenerate like resilient weeds even after being dealt significant blows by law enforcement efforts.

EIGHT

Confidence: "I Want to Believe"

The espionage art of confidence schemes, also known as "confidence tricks" or "confidence games," uses an undercover disguise to manipulate individuals or organizations into willingly divulging sensitive information, providing access to secure areas, or carrying out actions that benefit the attacker. These schemes—as detailed in the story of Mary, below—rely on building trust, exploiting psychological vulnerabilities, and creating deceptive scenarios to misguide the target. They also take advantage of pressure situations like exploiting loneliness or the need for human connection.

When I operated as a counterintelligence and counterterrorism investigative specialist, I could follow a target from sunup to sundown and try to learn everything about them. I'd identify every person they met, even if just through a stolen glance. I'd begin a database of all the places and things they prefer. Parks or shopping malls? Coffee or tea? Fancy restaurants or the local food truck? The target might've seen me multiple times throughout the day, but each time, their eyes slid past someone unremarkable and unimpressionable—an impostor blending into the background like a chameleon on a stone wall. I, in turn, had the confidence to stand there.

Okay, sometimes I used multiple disguises—from fake glasses to beards—in order to fit any given situation. In other words, to work undercover. I had costumes neatly folded in my back-seat kit: bike delivery guy, college student, office businessman, a homeless person. I could transform from a bright socialite to a dreary office worker in mere moments to blend into the day-to-day machinations of society and make a target believe I was someone else.

Mary lived alone in a condo just outside of Tampa, Florida. Years earlier, her husband had died of cancer, and Mary, at sixty-one, wasn't yet ready to throw in the towel on finding a new partner. She had tried Match.com and a few other dating sites but hadn't found the right connection. Her social life thrived with her friends and at her local church.

When the pandemic struck and in-person hangouts weren't possible, Facebook became Mary's window to the world. Just when the monotony of her four walls began to press in on her, something exciting happened. A person she did not know began liking her Facebook posts. A digging exploration showed that he was a little older than she, successful in that he ran his own construction business, and he was widowed, religious, and lonely—all learned from reading through his Facebook profile. Their mutual likes on each other's pages became short comments that soon moved to Messenger, followed by an exchange of email addresses. Jonathan had moved from Southern Europe to Southern California, right outside of San Diego. He had built a successful remodeling business and suffered the same frustrations and concerns she did over the pandemic. The lockdowns had stifled his business and made it difficult to retain employees or pay his bills.

Emails transitioned to personal cell-phone conversations. Jonathan had a faint British accent that excited Mary. They spoke of shared faith, frustrations over the climate, the state of the world, and politics. They bonded over sad stories about the spouses they had lost and told each other that they were ready to date again. They exchanged photos over text. There was Jonathan sitting on a lonely beach, backdropped by a brilliant setting sun. There he was leaning against a wall in a crisp shirt, sleeves rolled up on tan arms and a smile on his face. Jonathan laughing into his phone camera as he tried to take a selfie.

Each email became more romantic than the last. They became desperate to meet but blamed the lockdown on their forced separation. Each agreed that the pandemic made it too unsafe to fly. Still, they communicated with each other every day, and Mary spoke to Jonathan more often than her sister in Michigan. She had fallen deeply for a man she'd never met in person.

Love turned to requisition when Jonathan asked for a $10,000 loan so he could make a payment to a vendor for his remodeling business. He assured Mary that the client would pay as soon as he finished the job. The loan would bridge him in the meantime, and he would pay Mary back in a few days, with interest. The unusual request gave Mary pause, but she began to rationalize the favor. She could trust Jonathan. He had shared so much of himself, and they'd created a connection. Mary never thought she'd find love again. A few days later, Jonathan asked for additional funds: $5,000 to pay his lawyer. He explained that the vendor had walked away from the worksite after he paid them (with Mary's money), and now he needed to take them to court. Mary sent another transfer from her checking account and then a third, for another $10,000, when Jonathan could not pay the mortgage on his home.

When Mary became upset with him over the repeated requests for money, Jonathan promised to fly out immediately to see her. He would risk COVID-19, travel to her, and stay in a hotel for ten days to make sure he was safe. His being there would prove that his commitment to her was secure. Mary sent him money for the airfare and for the hotel. He sent her a dozen roses in return.

It's no surprise that Jonathan never arrived. She didn't hear from him for two days and became frantic. When he finally did call her back, he cried on the phone. On his way to the airport, a truck had sideswiped his BMW. EMTs had pulled him from his shattered car and taken him to the hospital. He needed money for surgery immediately—$20,000 should cover it. It's no surprise either that Mary paid this time too.

Eventually, Mary's sister flew down from Michigan and showed her a daytime talk show clip on YouTube in which a guest cried to the host about how a lover had defrauded her. The parallel between the YouTube story and Mary's was eerily clear. Mary and her sister conducted online research. They ran Jonathan's pictures through a Google Image search and found a social media account for a completely different person. Mary realized that she didn't know Jonathan's address—had never even video chatted with him—and though they'd talked about religion for countless hours, she'd never learned what church he attended. Stunned at her own ignorance, Mary reported Jonathan to the police. Jonathan, who was really a nineteen-year-old cybercriminal working out of a Minsk cybercafé, had stolen nearly $200,000 by the time the law got involved. He was identified but never prosecuted. Belarus does not typically extradite cybercriminals to the United States.

In Romance Fraud, a subcategory that Mary's story falls under, cybercriminals disproportionately target women and elderly victims. Monica Whitty, a cyber-relationship psychologist at Queen's University Belfast, explained in her book *Truth, Lies and Trust on the Internet* that computer-mediated relationships can sometimes become stronger and more intimate than physical relationships. The computer serves as a mediator that spares us the distractions of face-to-face interaction, which allows a criminal to control how they present themselves and create an idealized avatar that commands more trust and closeness than their true selves. Whitty opined that written text can be stronger in reinforcing intimacy than a single face-to-face interaction, because a victim can read the written text repeatedly.

The psychological theory of confirmation bias explains how an educated person like Mary could completely fall for "Jonathan's" cyber scam. When we fall in love, we naturally bias our decisions to find truth in what our partner says rather than pick apart their words to seek out lies. Desperation will strengthen the bias toward belief, particularly, as it did for Mary, when the money given to "Jonathan" added up to a catastrophic amount. The cybercriminal in Mary's story gained her confidence by exploiting her loneliness and presenting a persona that she admired. He then reeled her in a little at a time until she wanted so desperately to believe (confirm) the romantic connection was true, she influenced her natural skepticism.

Remember Camille and Guillaume from chapter 7? Or the pastor at Hillsong who nearly fooled me? Confirmation bias played a role in both cases. Guillaume played the role of a trusted partner with precision and added the spice of a potential romance to set the trap. The impostor pastor exploited my desire to cross off a bucket list destination and to present a unique keynote to a grand audience. In those impersonation schemes, the attacker leverages confirmation bias to, in the words of my favorite fictional FBI agent, Fox Mulder, make the mark "want to believe" the lie.

But what's the difference between impersonation schemes, such as the PayPal attack against me in chapter 4, and confidence schemes? The essential one is time. Impostor schemes are quick hits in which a criminal plays a role, tricks the target, and runs away with the prize. Confidence schemes, like the one that trapped Mary, are slow burns that build and grow. They are relationships between two people that slowly gain trust, affection, and even love. They make us *want to believe* the lie.

Generative AI has made it easier for cybercriminals using confidence schemes to access victim's lives. In the past, attackers like the one who fooled Mary would use stock photos or mine pictures from an unsuspecting person's public social media account. A few minutes of research with a reverse image lookup on Google or Bing could defeat this attack by identifying the images as borrowed or stolen from an entirely different person. AI applications like ChatGPT, Dall-E 3, or Midjourney (my three favorites) can create in seconds any image you dream up. Below is a picture of Jonathan I created in ChatGPT 4.0 using the following prompt:

A fit and trim elderly man in his late 60s leaning against a wall in a crisp shirt, sleeves rolled up on tan arms, and a smile on his face.

A reverse image search of this picture would find only the unique version used to create a social media avatar account. With a few additional prompts, the criminal would have numerous other images to send in texts. Identifying deepfakes is difficult, but not impossible. There are practical ways to identify these AI-generated deceptions.

An image created in ChatGPT 4.0's image generator.

By paying attention to subtle details, using detection tools, and verifying context, you can often spot a fake before it causes harm. Below are some of the best methods to detect deepfakes:*

1. Check for unnatural blinking or eye movement (in videos).

2. Observe lighting and shadow mismatches.

3. Listen for robotic or mismatched audio (in videos).

4. Use AI detection tools for added confidence.

5. Trust your gut—when something feels off, dig deeper.

If this seems complicated (after all, who wants to scrutinize every image we receive), fortunately there is technological hope on the

---

* For a comprehensive checklist to identifying deepfakes, check out The Spy Hunter Tool Kit's Top Ten Tips to Avoid Romance Fraud Scams on page 268.

horizon. Researchers at New York University's Tandon School of Engineering are throwing us a lifeline in the battle against deepfakes with an inventive new detection method. Chinmay Hegde and his team have rolled out challenge-response systems designed to unmask real-time deepfake audio and video. Think of it as CAPTCHA on steroids—rapidly analyzing quick, quirky tasks like exaggerated facial expressions or whispering a sentence. Easy for humans, downright frustrating for AI. The results? Impressive. Both machine learning models and human evaluators are already scoring big in exposing these digital impostors.

This sort of research doesn't just stop at promising results—it envisions practical applications that could silently work in the background as a "deepfake scanner." Integrated into video conferencing platforms, social media apps, or smartphones, it could seamlessly analyze audio and video streams for manipulation, flagging potential fakes without disrupting conversations. By combining simple challenges with randomized or layered tasks, these tools offer a scalable, proactive defense against increasingly sneaky AI-generated fakes. As the technology continues to advance, these systems could become the digital bodyguards we didn't know we needed, keeping our online interactions real—and keeping the fakes out.

These scanners are increasingly necessary. As we've seen in chapter 5 on impersonation, video deepfakes of our "Jonathan" are capable of not only sending quick messages across text but Zooming with Mary or connecting through a quick FaceTime or Google Meet. The depth of the scam is only limited by the imagination of the attacker.

The statistics are sobering. During the height of the pandemic in 2021, when loneliness was in great supply, twenty-four thousand victims across the United States reported losing approximately $1 billion to romance scams.[1] These numbers have risen steadily as cybercriminals have become more adept at their undercover spycraft. The Federal Trade Commission (FTC) lists romance scams as the largest FTC fraud category.[2] More than a third of the reports to the FTC by people who claimed to have lost their money to an online suitor said the scam began on Facebook (23 percent) or Instagram (13 percent).

In taverns, bars, and pubs across history, the pickup line lives on as a courtship ritual. While a good conversation starter might make us groan, the intent is to elicit a smile, appear witty to a prospective date, or spark up a conversation with a stranger. They range from the uberconfident: *Well, here I am. What are your other two wishes?* Intellectual flattery: *I must be in a museum because you truly are a work of art.* To simply lame: *Are you a parking ticket? Because you've got FINE written all over you.*

Criminals employ their own icebreakers in confidence schemes. The FTC pored over eight million romance fraud reports and put together a list of the greatest hits. Here they are in order, and you'll note that, unlike pickup lines, these are neither cute nor witty:

1. I or someone close to me is sick, hurt, or in jail.

2. I can teach you how to invest.

3. I'm in the military far away.

4. I need help with an important delivery.

5. We've never met but let's talk about marriage.

6. I've come into some money.

7. I'm on an oil rig.

8. You can trust me with your private pictures.

Loneliness and isolation are the primary ingredients attracting professional romance scammers. During the COVID-19 pandemic, lockdowns drove more people online than at any other time in history. Facebook, Instagram, X (then Twitter), virtual reality, dating sites, and a host of other social media outlets became the primary way isolated individuals shared experiences, met others from afar, and engaged in social interactions. Criminals inserted themselves into the mix with abandon and preyed upon the isolation.

Of course, the pandemic ended, and while criminals pivoted to other attacks, romance fraud continues to trap unwary victims. By the end of 2023, romance fraud in the United States, tracked by the FTC and FBI IC3, resulted in $1.14 billion in losses in criminal theft from more than sixty-four thousand victims.[3]* As society emerged from global lockdowns to return to attending concerts, church gatherings, sports outings, and all the other ways we connect as humans, technologically enhanced romance became less important. But the desire to improve our financial situation never ends, and criminals cooked up another perfect scheme. "I can teach you how to invest" became the go-to pickup line for cybercriminals.

THINK LIKE A SPY

- Confidence schemes, or "confidence tricks," involve using deception and manipulation to gain sensitive information, access secure areas, or influence actions. They rely on trust-building, exploiting psychological vulnerabilities, and creating deceptive scenarios. They often exploit pressure situations, such as loneliness or the need for human connection.

- Confirmation bias: Confidence schemes rely on making the target want to believe that something is true so deeply that they rationalize ways to make it true in their mind.

- Romance fraud is a global crime disproportionately targeting women and elderly victims. Unlike broader confidence

---

*For more information see my Top Ten Tips to Avoid Romance Fraud Scams in The Spy Hunter Tool Kit on page 268.

schemes, it focuses on making the target fall in love rather than just believing in something untrue. Loneliness and isolation are key factors attracting professional romance scammers.

- When engaging a target in a confidence scheme, the attacker will have countless excuses for not meeting in person. These will include delays, accidents, canceled flights, and personal crises—all of which are used as an excuse to extract more money from the target.

- One way that potential victims can identify confidence schemes is to use reverse lookup tools to identify false images and pictures taken from stock photos or mined from social media accounts. One method a scammer may use to defeat this defense is to create a series of unique images with generative AI. These images can become the basis for social media accounts based on a thematic avatar.

- Resources like Deepfake Detector (https://deepfakedetector.ai) and Is It AI? (https://isitai.com/ai-image-detector/) are free online applications that allow users to upload videos, audio clips, or images to determine whether the source material was generated by AI. These tools can assist a potential victim in identifying deepfakes.

- Computer-mediated relationships can surpass physical ones in strength and intimacy. The computer acts as a mediator, eliminating the distractions of face-to-face interaction. Criminals exploit this by controlling their presentation and creating idealized avatars, fostering trust and closeness. Written text can reinforce intimacy more effectively than a single face-to-face interaction, as victims can revisit it repeatedly.

- The difference between impostor and confidence schemes is time. Impostor schemes are quick hits where the scammer plays a role, tricks the target, and runs away with the prize. Confidence schemes are relationships that build and grow. They make us *want to believe* the lie.

The poster in Fox Mulder's FBIHQ office in the TV series *The X-Files*.

NINE

Confidence: Question Everything

In my second year at Auburn University, I considered law as a possible career choice and excitedly accepted an invitation from my uncle to work with him over the summer. My uncle John Gemelli (aka Johnny G.) leads a thriving family law practice in Queens in New York City. He's a larger-than-life Italian and the last person you'd ever want to get into an argument with. His often wild, unpredictable, and wisecracking practice in New York puts the best legal sitcoms to shame. And my uncle is the real King of Queens.

I pointed my Jeep Wrangler north and drove from Auburn in Alabama to Rockaway Beach, New York. When I arrived at my uncle's apartment, I didn't find him, but a note waiting for me, scrawled in his unmistakable penmanship.

> Welcome to New York, the best city in the world! I'll be back tomorrow. Make yourself at home, don't break anything, don't talk to strangers, be nice to the old ladies downstairs. Don't let anyone sell you the Brooklyn Bridge or Marla Maples's underwear!

I had to look up Marla Maples. At only nineteen years old, how was I to know that she was an actress and model who had an infamous affair with Donald Trump in 1992 while the future president was married to Ivana Trump? Later that year, the Trumps would divorce over the affair, and Maples would become Trump's second wife.

I couldn't find any documented evidence of a confidence scam selling an unwitting nineteen-year-old or any other person Marla Maples's unmentionables, but there are countless such finance-related scams throughout history (including "selling" the Brooklyn Bridge to unwary immigrants). My uncle's snarky warning was excellent advice for a Southerner who found himself alone in the big city, which had all the confidence schemes one could fall prey to.

In the annals of history, few confidence schemes are as iconic as the audacious swindle orchestrated by Victor Lustig in 1925—the sale of the Eiffel Tower. With brazen, cunning charm, Lustig capitalized on the gullibility of his marks and the allure of one of Paris's most prestigious landmarks. Posing as a government official, Lustig convinced a group of scrap-metal dealers that the Eiffel Tower was slated for demolition due to financial burdens. In a stroke of genius, he convinced them to "purchase" the monument for a fraction of its worth, promising lucrative returns from the metal's resale. By the time his victims realized the hoax, Lustig had vanished into the shadows, leaving a legacy of deception and intrigue that still echoes through the corridors of con artistry today.

Charles Ponzi may have orchestrated the most famous confidence fraud though. His eponymous Ponzi scheme of 1919 has become synonymous with fraudulent investment operations. Promising extravagant returns through a loophole in international postal reply coupons, Ponzi captivated investors with the allure of easy money. Like a modern-day alchemist, he spun tales of wealth from thin air, captivating the dreams of countless individuals seeking financial fortune. However, behind the facade of prosperity lay a house of cards destined to collapse. A Ponzi scheme pays returns to earlier investors using the capital of new ones, rather than any actual profit, and they eventually fail. So did Ponzi's, leaving shattered dreams and financial ruin in its wake. His has become a cautionary tale, a testament to the seductive power of greed and the enduring allure of get-rich-quick schemes.

More recently, fellow cybersecurity keynote speaker Frank Abagnale used a knack for impersonation and forgery to embark on a whirlwind spree of scams that captivated the imagination of the public. Posing as an airline pilot, doctor, and lawyer, among other professions, he effortlessly slipped into roles of authority, exploiting the trust of unsuspecting individuals and institutions. His exploits, chronicled in the memoir and film *Catch Me if You Can*, serve as a testament to the vulnerability of human trust. Or maybe it's the susceptibility of people who recognize that something is too good to be true but still wish to believe.

* * *

Edward enjoyed his retirement among the bustling streets and whispers of history in London, England. At seventy-five, with silver hair and a twinkle in his eye, he spent his days leisurely strolling through the city he loved, relishing the memories of years gone by. He'd lost his wife some years earlier, and his daughter had married an American, with whom she moved across the Atlantic. They brought Edward's two grandchildren to visit each year at Christmas, but, other than that, he had no family time.

One autumn morning, as Edward sipped his tea and perused the morning paper, a message pinged on his phone—an innocent text simply saying "Hello?"

On a lark, Edward keyed his own response: "How are you?" In seconds, the polite stranger replied and, after a bit of confusion, apologized for texting the wrong number.

"Apology accepted," Edward responded. "It's nice to make your acquaintance."

Over the next few weeks, Edward sipped his tea each morning and corresponded with Karthi, a gentleman in Belgium who ran an investment company. Occasionally, they talked on the phone, where Edward enjoyed Karthi's educated, polished demeanor, and sometimes laughed at Karthi's slightly odd accent. They spoke of many things, from current European Union politics to their families (Karthi also had a child who had moved to America). Edward explained that he'd retired after a career as a steelworker and lived off a fine pension as well as his own SIPP account (Self-Invested Personal Pension). An investment guru, Karthi knew a good deal about retirement savings and was fond of offering advice to the retiree.

A month later, Edward's new friend invited him into a brand-new investment opportunity. For only £1,000, Edward could "dip his toe" in the water of Karthi's foray into cryptocurrency. Edward knew little about the new cyber currency but had heard how many young people had made fortunes from it. While Edward had no need of a fortune in his final days, he wished to please his new friend, so he transferred £1,000 from his London bank account to Bergstromm & Billings, the finance company where Karthi worked.

Two weeks later, Karthi directed Edward to scrutinize Edward's account through the secure portal at the Bergstromm website. On the iPad his daughter had given him the previous Christmas to "keep in touch," Edward gasped. His £1,000 had grown to £1,333, a 30 percent return on investment!

"How is this possible?" he asked Karthi.

"Cryptocurrency is different," Karthi explained. "It does not follow the traditional channels of currency." He added grandly, "Now, imagine had you placed ten thousand quid under my care."

And so Edward did. Over the next month he transferred most of his SIPP to Bergstromm and then found a way to begin moving his steelworker's pension. A tickle made him wonder whether placing all his eggs in one basket was wise, but each time he tapped his iPad to open the Bergstromm portal, his eyes widened. He'd already doubled his pension. Next Christmas he planned to surprise his daughter and family with an extravagant holiday trip for the entire family.

As Christmas approached, Edward called Karthi and asked to make a withdrawal from his sizable accounts. When he received no answer, he sent a text, followed by an email. When Karthi had still not responded days later, Edward feared something had happed to his friend. He called the main number for Bergstromm and received a not-in-service message. He emailed the main office, but that did no good either. Dumbstruck, the harsh reality began to dawn upon him. The business he'd invested in was nothing more than an illusion, a facade woven by deceitful hands. His savings, nearly £300,000, which he'd painstakingly accumulated over decades, had vanished into the abyss of deception. Karthi, or whatever the man's real name was, had fattened him up like a pig for market. When Edward had given all his savings, the criminal butchered Edward and left him destitute. There are always silver linings. Edward would leave his beloved city and move into his daughter's American home. Penniless in pounds, he's now happy spending time with grandchildren that he sees every day, not just once a year at Christmas.

Pig butchering is not just a metaphor—in law enforcement, we call Edward's blunder exactly that. The criminal gains the target's confidence and draws them in carefully and consistently. Once trust is established, the new "friend" offers an exclusive financial benefit. Where romance confidence schemes stalled after the pandemic ended, investment schemes skyrocketed. By 2023, they became the most reported crime to the IC3. Pig butchering and other such crimes rose from $3.31 billion in 2022 to $4.57 billion in 2023, an increase of nearly 40 percent. Investment fraud promising cryptocurrency gains (including pig butchering) more than doubled from $2.57 billion in 2022 to $5.6 billion in 2023. They are the modern equivalent of the get-rich-quick scheme, and they entice far more people into parting with their hard-earned wealth than any Ponzi scheme or promise to sell a model's underwear. Cryptocurrency investment fraud leverages modern communication technology to exploit victims more efficiently and on a larger scale than older, traditional cons.[*]

It's one thing to trick a person out of their hard-earned cash, but once the target is deceived, how does the criminal get paid? In modern times, money is not typically exchanged by handing over a briefcase filled with stacked $100 bills. Most currency transactions are

---

[*] For more information see my Top Ten Tips to Avoid Pig Butchering Schemes in The Spy Hunter Tool Kit on page 271.

digital, and criminals have leaned on technology to prevent police from identifying them. The method criminals use to collect money after successfully deceiving a target relies on the sophistication of the bad guy.

"Karthi" used what we call a drop account, the most sophisticated method of parting a target from their savings. We will get to drop accounts, but let's begin with the basics. The entry-level cybercriminals deal in gift cards. When you purchase a gift card at a store for anything from American Express or Visa to Amazon or the popular video game Fortnite, that card becomes currency the second it leaves the cash register. Each card has a specific number and a code hidden below an ultraviolet ink and foil material that you scratch off. Both number and code are worthless until you purchase the card by exchanging cash for an activation code sent to the card issuer. In other words, you have turned your cash into the activated card.

While email is often the first vector of coercion for romance and confidence fraud, as Edward learned, a great deal of confidence fraud begins over the telephone. Criminals can purchase the same lists that telemarketers use to harass us just as we sit down for dinner or the precise moment when the first die is cast on family game night. Recently, my friend Sarah called me and asked me advice about a friend of hers who'd purchased gift cards. I held the phone away from my face for a moment so she couldn't hear my immense sigh. I knew what had happened before she even told me.

Sarah explained how her elderly friend Corrine had received a phone call the night before from her grandson. The call went something like this:

"Grandma, is that you?"
"Gregory? Where are you? I can't hear you well."
"Yes, it's me Grandma. It's Gregory. I need help. Please!"
"What's wrong, sweetheart?"
"I'm in Panama, Grandma. I got arrested!"
"Arrested! In Panama? What are you doing—"
"Forget that grandma," the voice insisted. "I need help. Right away!

There's . . . there's a police officer here. He says that if we pay him, they will let me go . . ."

The "grandson" handed the phone to the "police officer." A voice demanded five hundred dollars in cash, or the grandson would "go to prison for life." Panicked and beside herself with worry for her grandson, Corrine complained that she had no way to get five hundred dollars cash to Panama. The police officer then switched to a helpful voice and explained how she could go to the store, purchase ten $50 Visa gift cards, and read the numbers and PIN codes over the phone.

Her grandson's impending imprisonment, the shock of receiving an evening phone call, and the immediacy of the request sent Corrine to the nearest twenty-four-hour pharmacy to buy gift cards. She called the numbers in to the "police officer" over her cell phone while standing in the grocery aisle of her local CVS. The time that had elapsed from phone call to gift-card reveal was less than fifteen minutes. Once the card numbers and PIN codes were with the scammers, Corrine would never see her money again.

Level-two attackers use legitimate payment transfer companies to receive the fruits of their confidence schemes. The most popular are Western Union, MoneyGram, CashApp, and even popular peer-to-peer payment vendors like PayPal and Venmo. Once a victim sends money through these services, the criminal quickly launders the funds through bank accounts and often into cryptocurrency wallets, where the digital trail ends. Tracking stolen cryptocurrency is difficult because it uses pseudonymous addresses, decentralized systems, and advanced obfuscation methods like "mixers" (i.e., mixing stolen cryptocurrency with legitimate funds), making it hard to link transactions to real identities. Additionally, cross-border transfers and privacy-enhancing technologies further complicate law-enforcement efforts.

For all these reasons, level-three attackers with more time and resources will skip straight to cryptocurrency. Do you own cryptocurrency or have a crypto wallet or know how to purchase Bitcoin or Ethereum? Most people haven't dipped their toe into digital coins and wouldn't have the first idea how to purchase one.

In 2009, Bitcoin became available to the public for $0.00099 per Bitcoin, or about one tenth of one U.S. cent. The new currency was met with incredible skepticism. Like the city of Venice or reality TV, you loved it or hated it, with few indifferent moods in between. As a security researcher, I decided I should purchase some of this new currency—which had started being repurposed by cyberattackers even in its nascency. With one hundred dollars in my pocket, I set out to buy a digital unicorn. In those early days, the process of acquiring Bitcoin was much less streamlined and user-friendly than it is today. There were no exchanges, wallets, or services like we have now. One option was to download and install Bitcoin Core on your computer, then sync with the Bitcoin network. Alternatively, enterprising and computer-fluent "miners" could use their computer's processing power to solve complex mathematical puzzles and earn newly minted Bitcoins as a reward.

I started down the Bitcoin Road but became more frustrated with every turn. There were few established exchanges in 2009 and no user-friendly platforms. To get a coveted token, you'd have to invest in computer processors that allowed you to mine your own or trade directly with others in niche forums, which meant trusting a stranger with your money. Eventually, I had researched everything I needed to know to acquire one hundred dollars in Bitcoin but stopped just shy of parting with it. Had I followed through, my hundred would have purchased 101,010 Bitcoin, an amount that would be worth over $700 million today. We all have that one thing we would go back in time and tell ourselves to do differently. That's mine.

Even though today you can purchase Bitcoin through a simple application downloaded to your phone and securely connected to your bank account, most humans find even this complex. Unless the cybercriminal plans to walk you through the process or has the capability to hand you over to their tech support (which most cybercrime syndicates do), most who deal in attacks against single individuals (levels one and two) avoid crypto entirely.

The most sophisticated criminals smooth the way for easy money transfers by opening legitimate bank accounts created with stolen identities. These drop accounts require a next level of criminal genius because the accounts must first be opened using information purchased off the dark web. The financial confidence scheme that coerced Edward into reinvesting his pension used a combination of drop account and website spoofing. Edward believed he sent his money into a legitimate account at the fictional Bergstromm & Billings because he trusted Karthi and was swept in by the exceptional results shown on the Bergstromm website. Had Edward and Corrine known to *think like a spy*, they would never have willingly thrown their savings down the bottomless hole of the dark web.

In chapter 5, I introduced the cybersecurity concerns over the advent of generative AIs and deepfakes, whereby large learning models like ChatGPT and its siblings have changed the game for deceptive emails. AI can easily draft a perfect impersonation spear phishing email to trick the unwary. The same holds true for confidence schemes. Today, an AI can write original spear phishing emails and responses in seconds, while in the past a threat actor would require weeks of research. Generative AI can refine the attack by escalating the fictional crisis through additional emails, further coercing the target to send a Western Union wire or to go buy cryptocurrency. Remember the Hong Kong deepfake attack in chapter 5? Imagine that the Bergstromm confidence scheme executed against Edward added a video conference chat where AI avatars played the role of Begstromm "employees," each puppeted by Karthi.

I learned a lot that summer in New York City with my uncle. From Rockaway Beach to Manhattan, New York City is not a place for the faint of heart or the very gullible. My uncle taught me a few lessons that I carried forward from the family law litigation trenches to undercover work in the beating heart of Washington, D.C., the spy capital of the world. A little skepticism goes a long way. Clients don't always tell you the truth and witnesses swear to tell "the whole truth," then lie on the witness stand with a straight face. People who approach you on the NYC subway system's A train late at night aren't doing so to make friends. Having one's guard up goes a long way to recognizing a lie, identifying a scheme, and eventually for me, catching a spy.

Confidence schemes rely on trust, but defeating them requires education, skepticism verification, and instinct. Spies are adept at layering plausible lies around a nucleus of truth. A healthy amount of suspicion will save you from a spy . . . or a cyberattack. Question what you see. A phone call might hide an ulterior motive. An amazing investment offer from a person you've *never met in person* could initiate a complex confidence scam. The love of your life could be an AI deepfake. Philosopher, mathematician, and scientist René Descartes once wrote, "In order to seek truth, it is necessary once in the course of our life to doubt, as far as possible, all things." We do not uncover the truth without asking a simple question: Can I believe my lying eyes?

THINK LIKE A SPY

- Online investment fraud via confidence schemes is the fastest-growing cybercrime. These schemes resemble modern "get-rich-quick" schemes, attracting more victims than Ponzi schemes or any other deceptive promises. They lure people into parting with their hard-earned money at an alarming rate.

- A great deal of confidence fraud originates in telephone communication. Criminals often acquire lists like those used by telemarketers to target victims. Additionally, the dark web offers stolen identities, including personal cell numbers, through various marketplaces, facilitating the expansion of fraudulent activities.

- Before initiating a confidence scheme, cybercriminals conduct thorough reconnaissance. They surveil targets on social media, attempt to compromise email accounts through spear phishing, and gather information about the target's friends and family. This reconnaissance enables them to identify the most effective way to integrate themselves into the target's life and execute their fraudulent activities.

- "Pig butchering" is a financial confidence scheme where criminals gain the target's trust methodically. They offer exclusive financial benefits, often related to cryptocurrency, after establishing trust. As the victim invests more, the criminal fabricates false rates of return. Eventually, the victim loses most of their savings as the criminal transfers the funds to dark web cryptocurrency wallets.

- In financial confidence scheme attacks, criminals deploy various methods to separate victims from their money. The most basic tactic involves coercing or extorting victims into purchasing gift cards and providing the card numbers to the attacker. These cards, with hidden codes beneath scratch-off material, become valuable once activated with cash exchanged for an activation code. This basic yet effective approach capitalizes on the anonymity and ease of use of gift cards.

- Another method utilized by criminals is leveraging legitimate payment transfer companies to receive funds from their schemes. Companies like Western Union, MoneyGram, CashApp, PayPal, and Venmo are popular choices. Once victims send money through these services, criminals swiftly launder the funds through bank accounts, often funneling them into cryptocurrency wallets to obscure the digital trail and evade detection.

- More sophisticated attackers may direct compromised targets to send cryptocurrency. Despite the accessibility of purchasing Bitcoin through user-friendly apps connected to bank accounts, many individuals find cryptocurrency transactions daunting. Unless the cybercriminal offers guidance or tech support, most opt to avoid crypto-related transactions when targeting individual victims due to their complexity and the risk of exposure.

- The most advanced criminals streamline money transfers by establishing legitimate bank accounts using stolen identities. Setting up these drop accounts requires a higher level of criminal sophistication, as they first require obtaining personal information from the dark web. By utilizing these accounts, criminals can facilitate large-scale transfers with relative ease, exploiting stolen identities to cover their tracks and evade law-enforcement scrutiny.

TEN

Exploitation: Spelunking into a Nightmare

When he turned nineteen, Angelo walked into a recruitment office for the U.S. Army, planning to follow his father's and grandfather's footsteps into service to his country. Angelo planned to use the GI Bill to eventually study electrical engineering at a university, after a high school class sparked his interest in the field. He would become the first in his family to serve in the armed forces and later graduate from college.

Angelo's score on the Armed Services Vocational Aptitude Battery, particularly in math and electronics, was excellent. His army career counselor thought he'd be a great fit as an Electrical Systems Technician in the Army Corps of Engineers. The physical examination went just as smoothly since Angelo proved to be just as athletically competent as he was mentally. The problem emerged when the background check was initiated.

Unbeknownst to him (he was a young kid, after all), his credit score had sunk below 350. While the score alone did not disqualify him from gaining a security clearance, the army's report detailed red flags, including significant debt, poor debt-to-income ratio, unpaid balances, and defaults on loans. His father thought this must be a mistake and requested his free credit reports from Experian, Equifax, and TransUnion. The documents told a very different story from the life Angelo had led under his strict father's roof. According to the credit reports, Angelo had defaulted on multiple credit cards, missed payments on a loan, and abandoned multiple bank accounts. Most of the transactions had occurred in places he'd never heard of. Angelo and his father struggled to understand the extent of the damage. As targeted as it was, perhaps more worrisome was the notion that it had been going on for years.

I was the investigator tasked with trying to understand what had happened to Angelo. I discovered that an identity thief had not only stolen Angelo's personally identifiable information and exploited it but had also sold it on the dark web to others—this was a consequence that Angelo and his father hadn't thought of. Criminals had used Angelo's identity to open numerous bank accounts to move stolen funds to drop accounts. Many of these drop accounts remained open and all contributed to lowering Angelo's credit score. Too many open credit lines, even if they are not used, hurt credit scores by making the account holder look risky to lenders. In just the past year, an attacker had used Angelo's identity to open a home equity line of credit on a home in Op, Alabama, a town Angelo had never been to or even heard of. The attacker had bought the title to the home off a dark web marketplace and, after transferring the title to Angelo, the criminal had opened a line of credit in Angelo's name. The bank eventually defaulted the loan. It would take years and money he and his father did not have to slowly repair and litigate Angelo's decimated credit. Angelo did go to a community college he could afford and graduated with an electrical engineering degree. He's gainfully employed and happy with his life but often reflects on the criminal attack that robbed him of an easy path to his future.

A 2021 child identity fraud study by Javelin Strategy & Research revealed that one in fifty children were the victims of identity theft and lost $918 million to this crime.[1] Javelin's 2022 follow-up study determined that 915,000 U.S. children were victims of identity fraud and that 1.7 million had suffered an identity breach.[2] One out of every forty children in the United States has had critical identity information on the dark web for years. This number is likely even higher now, following the early 2024 National Public Data breach, which exposed over 2.9 billion Social Security numbers and pieces of personally identifiable information for sale on the dark web.

Children are an attractive target for criminal exploitation because most parents don't realize they should monitor a child's SSN and credit reports. Furthermore, most parents don't take the time to actively monitor children's use of social media, a convenient gateway that turns children into victims. By the end of 2023, Javelin's studies found that 47 percent of children victimized by identity theft and fraud also had their accounts compromised by the attacker.[3] Nearly half of the children who fell prey to identity fraud in the Javelin study were scammed by a cybercriminal after downloading a game or social media application to their phones.

Our kids love social media. Scrolling has become an art form, and applications like Snapchat and TikTok have replaced basic text and phone calls. The 2022 Javelin study found that children under the age of seven who are given access to social media applications are the cohort most likely to be victimized by identity theft. As children age, if they haven't learned cyber-safe internet behaviors early on, they are much more likely to be victimized by identity theft and fraud. Javelin's study revealed that cybercriminals are increasingly targeting social media, email, and mobile phone accounts over financial accounts. By taking over these nonfinancial accounts, cybercriminals can begin using a child's identity to fraudulently open new accounts or scam others, often going undetected for years. This highlights the urgent need for parents and guardians to monitor and guide children's online behaviors to prevent such risks.

As Angelo learned, identity fraud is also incredibly costly. Combined losses from identity fraud and similar exploitative scams have cost households an average of $42.9 billion from 2021 to 2023. But identity fraud is not the most concerning aspect of criminal exploitation of children.

The dark web is also filled with marketplaces that rob investigators of sleep and become the foundation for nightmares. Some of the largest dark web marketplaces consist of child pornography—some created through artificial intelligence image creators, others coerced through social media accounts. Many are stolen from unsuspecting victims.

* * *

My cousin's friend Halima came from a strict religious family. Her mother and father tended to smother her, but she knew that it came from a place of love. As a teenager she rebelled in small ways—staying out a little later than curfew, dressing slightly more immodestly than her parents approved of, dating a boy who came from a family that did not practice her religion. Despite these small moments of defiance, she got straight A's, excelled on her field hockey team, and crushed her opponents in debate club.

My cousin introduced me to Halima just after she turned seventeen and was seeking help with a devastating problem that she could barely speak about to friends and family. Numerous pictures of Halima in various poses, most nude, were available on the internet by googling her full name, plus the words "snapchat teen pics leaked." Halima confirmed that two years earlier she'd taken the pictures and sent them as snaps to her boyfriend. She'd thought that the Snapchat application on her phone deleted pictures as soon as she clicked send.

Halima had reported the crime to her local police department, who had advised her to wipe her phone, change all her passwords, and delete her Snapchat account. I was able to reconstruct her phone using a backup on her Apple computer and determined that Halima had fallen prey to a spear phishing attack through her Apple iCloud account. The attacker had coerced Halima into installing an application that he claimed would save money by looking through online merchants to find the best prices. Instead, the application gave the attacker access to Halima's phone, including all the photos that had uploaded to her backup on iCloud.

Halima did not know that Snapchat saved all her snaps, including the naked pictures she had sent her boyfriend, to her photo roll. A user can turn off this setting, but Halima believed that her snaps disappeared a few seconds after her boyfriend viewed them. She hadn't realized that everything created and transmitted across the internet is stored or copied in one way or another—from embarrassing emails to the most private pictures and images.

The attacker began reaching out to Halima on her public Instagram account. He demanded $10,000 or he would publish the photos "all over the internet and send them to all your friends and contacts." Almost two years later, Halima hyperventilated on the call with me when she mentioned the demand. Her fragile mental state seemed on the verge of breakdown. Her parents were equally distraught, and rightfully so. The threat to teenagers exploited by cybercriminals can be deadly.

I enlisted my friend and colleague Tom to help track down Halima's attackers and put her frantic mind at ease about the exploitive situation. Among the many titles Tom has held through more than a decade of hunting cybercriminals—threat researcher, white-hat hacker, DHS asset—he grins when I call him a dark web spelunker. When he isn't preparing special technology and using his expertise to crawl downward into the depths of the internet, he's also an ultramarathoner. His stocky frame looks more suited to dead lifts than runs averaging one hundred kilometers, but distance running is about tenacity, and Tom has it in spades.

Tom made his forays into the dark web in the 2000s as a threat researcher seeking to determine how criminals used and corrupted legitimate portions of the internet to launch attacks, trade information, and coordinate crimes. Back in the early aughts, spies and cybercriminals would embed hidden servers for their schemes right under our noses. They targeted businesses with weak security, quietly hijacking part of a server for their own purposes—imagine 10 percent of your laptop's C: drive being secretly commandeered by criminals. From small-town hardware stores to Fortune 500 companies, any vulnerable system could serve as a stepping-stone in the dark web's early evolution.

Tom was a big problem for criminals. His work to map darknet servers and create an index for law enforcement led to numerous criminal arrests in jurisdictions like Baltimore, Maryland, which had strict cybercrime laws. It also saved companies from criminal harvesting of their server space and encouraged better cybersecurity to prevent repeat attacks. Tom was instrumental in taking down the infamous Silk Road and its founder, known as the Dread Pirate Roberts, the first mass-market and largest dark web drug trade in history.

In early 2024, Tom and I met at his office to spelunk into the dark web on behalf of Halima and discover who was extorting her. Just like my caving friend, Josh, with his crawl suit and carbide lamp, Tom has his own tools and rules:

- Use a clean computer with a fresh operating system installed.

- Install the Tor Browser application to access dark web websites that use onion routing.

- Use a virtual machine to hide the Media Access Control (MAC) address of the host computer.

- Use a VPN to mask the IP address of the host computer.

- Never spelunk into the dark web from home! You don't want criminals to discover where you live. (Hence, the office.)

After each search mission, Tom completely erases his computer to destroy any artifacts or nasty surprises he might have contracted along the way. This requires him to install a fresh version of Windows or Linux each time. The Tor web browser allows anyone to brave the internet's caverns by accessing special unindexed websites on dark web servers. A virtual machine is like a computer within a computer, permitting Tom to run software and operating systems that are designed for one type of computer on a different type of computer. This hides the physical MAC address of the host computer from curious cybercriminals. Finally, virtual private networking software masks Tom's originating Internet Protocol (IP) address—the software equivalent of a MAC address. Sound complex? It is.

Tom established his credentials as an undercover cybercriminal on the dark web years ago when DHS hired him to identify drug pushers on dark web marketplaces. He uses those credentials to explore the most nefarious levels without being stabbed in the dark. But criminals and spies alike are a wary sort. Spies use deep-cover operations and subterfuge and misdirection to conceal their identities from law enforcement and spy hunters like me. Criminals use similar tradecraft to hide their identities, relying on pseudonyms to evade law enforcement. Take LockBit's leader, who operated under the alias LockBitSupp. Confident in his ability to stay anonymous, he even dangled a $10 million bounty for anyone daring enough to unmask him. The FBI finally did, revealing a Russian national named Dmitry Yuryevich Khoroshev. I doubt Khoroshev has any intention of paying the FBI the $10 million. But not because he's lacking cash; he's reportedly made $100 million in ransomware theft and extortion.[4] He *is* lacking in freedom and can no longer travel to the EU, United States, Australia, or the UK without risk of capture.

Tom practices a similar wariness during his dark web spelunking. If his cover fell away and a criminal syndicate learned his identity, his home might be visited by a hit man. There is also a dark web marketplace for assassination. Go figure.

Tom's dark web laptop is an old Dell repurposed for research. He opened Microsoft Hyper-V on a clean Windows install, creating a secure, isolated ("sandboxed") environment on his computer. This setup prevents dark web attacks from escaping the virtual machine, protecting his laptop's MAC address and ensuring any cyberattacks remain isolated, keeping us safe from discovery.

Tom then opened a version of the Tor Browser within his virtual machine and manually entered an onion address for a dark web index. Unlike the internet, where powerful indexing browsers such as Google and Bing will find virtually anything available on the surface web, the dark web reminds me of the earliest years of internet browsing. In 1990, when the first World Wide Web browser was born, few websites existed. Few enough that one could own a Yellow Pages for internet sites (I had one of them).

My old copy of the Internet Yellow Pages.

To open a particular site on the internet in 1995, you'd find it in the Yellow Pages and manually type the address in a web browser. These days, dark web marketplaces do not want to be found by law enforcement or amateur "poseurs" and danger seekers. For that reason, most .onion locations are traded and marketed on underground message boards that are difficult to join without the correct criminal bona fides. Fortunately, I have Tom.

The first .onion site Tom opened led us to a dark web links directory: http://y4dbl7qzgnzxurelfpzmz4zfm7zqdt3t7ljru27█████
████████.onion/

Tom chuckled as the Tor Browser in Hyper-V flickered and alerts began popping up from his cybersecurity software. "This is a trap," he said. "Right now, the onion site is bombarding my machine with malicious software. That's why you don't play around here."

I examined the innocuous but polished "dark web directory" site. It listed numerous links to dark web marketplaces—everything from hackers for hire to drugs, stolen email addresses and accounts, and even passports and identification cards from virtually anyplace in the world.

Tom indicated a text paragraph that invited us to enter our email and click on a link to "show you how to navigate the Dark Web." He shook his head. "Click there and it's like clicking a spear phishing email."

"Another trap."

"Exactly. As you'll see, it's not easy maneuvering around here." Tom tapped a rhythm on his temple. "It takes a lot of practice and know-how to discover the worst kinds of things."

Tom showed me sites where enterprising criminals learn from each other. We scanned PDF instructions on how to ship cocaine. "Hide it in coffee beans," Tom said. "The dogs can't sniff it." Or paper tabs of acid. "They place them between the pages of a book and then ship the book through U.S. media mail."

We found instructions for manufacturing your own ghost gun (an untraceable firearm assembled from parts or kits, often lacking a serial number and not requiring background checks) with a personal 3-D printer, and for setting up a criminal cryptocurrency wallet. We explored mercenary websites where enterprising cyberattackers, terrorists, and spies showcased their acumen in breaking security. Offerings included hacking email, passwords, PayPal accounts, cell phones ("valid to invade any mobile device that has a SIM card"), messenger applications, and colleges and universities to "change your grades." Attackers for hire made grand offerings to compromise and steal social media accounts, one with the tagline to "connect more with fans online."

We found a marketplace to purchase stolen $2,000 prepaid Visa gift cards for a tenth of the cost. All transactions paid in Bitcoin.

Counterfeit passports and identification cards cost significantly more at the "Original Counterfeiting Center." I questioned whether any such fake passport would fool a customs agent, but the site promised that each was fully registered in the relevant government database. Of course, trusting a criminal is a little like hoping to knock over all the pins at a carnival game. Succeeding at this requires more luck than skill, and most of the time the carnival barker keeps your money.

Exploitation: Spelunking into a Nightmare | 141

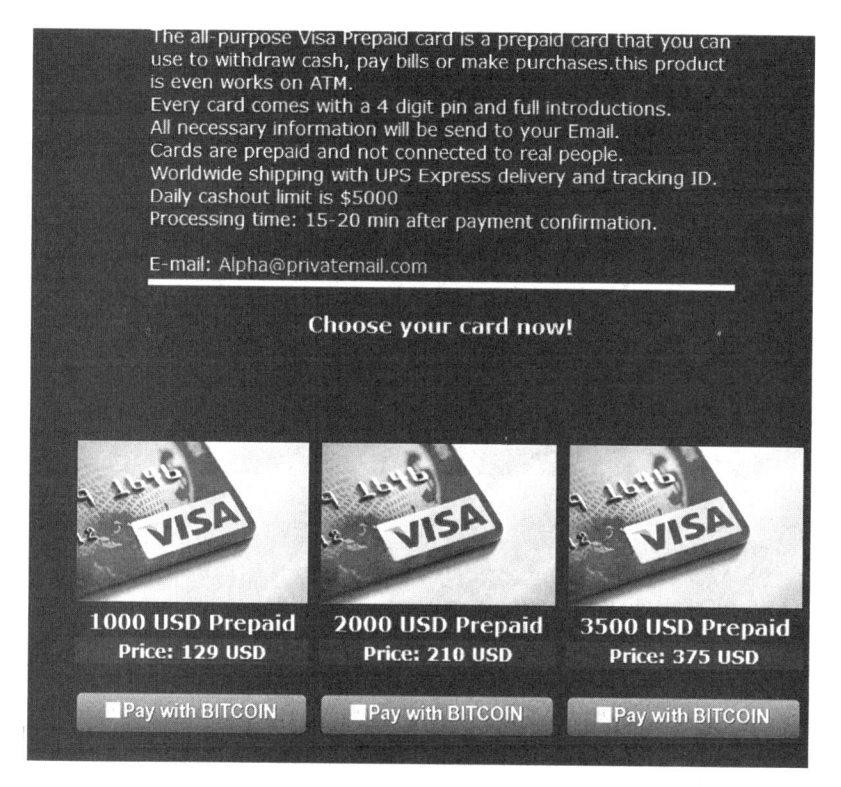

> The all-purpose Visa Prepaid card is a prepaid card that you can use to withdraw cash, pay bills or make purchases. this product is even works on ATM.
> Every card comes with a 4 digit pin and full introductions.
> All necessary information will be send to your Email.
> Cards are prepaid and not connected to real people.
> Worldwide shipping with UPS Express delivery and tracking ID.
> Daily cashout limit is $5000
> Processing time: 15-20 min after payment confirmation.
>
> E-mail: Alpha@privatemail.com
>
> **Choose your card now!**
>
> | 1000 USD Prepaid | 2000 USD Prepaid | 3500 USD Prepaid |
> |---|---|---|
> | Price: 129 USD | Price: 210 USD | Price: 375 USD |
> | ■ Pay with BITCOIN | ■ Pay with BITCOIN | ■ Pay with BITCOIN |

Dark web marketplace snapshot of stolen prepaid Visa gift cards.

Wherever we traveled, a drug marketplace would sprout up and offer countless colorful wares to sell. In one such marketplace, intrepid buyers could risk their digital wallets on various offerings from ecstasy to opioids. Planning a weekend rave? One thousand Jigsaw ecstasy pills cost only $229.00.

Tom couldn't help throwing them into his cart and clicking the purchase button. When I threw him a look, he shrugged. "I'm curious whether the transaction will actually go through, or if this is one of those sites that just steals your money." I was dumbfounded. "I'm not actually going to buy it!" he clarified. "What am I gonna do with a thousand freaking pills?"

While small in terms of the total internet, the dark web is mighty.

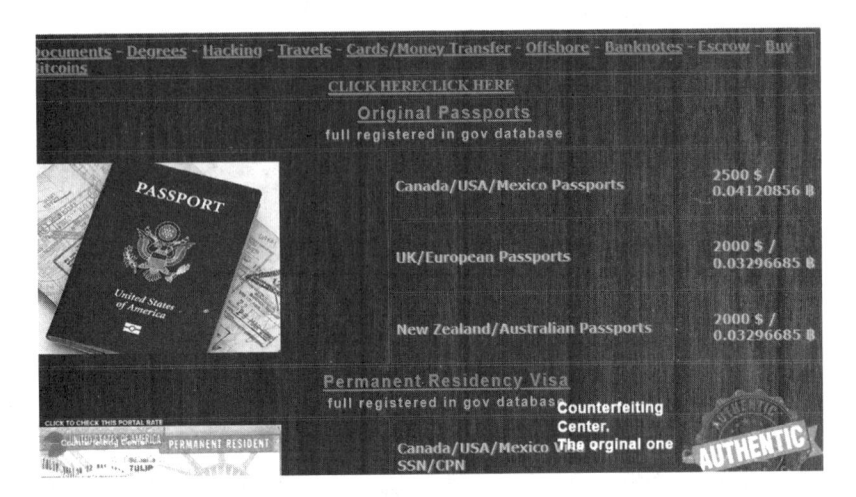

Marketplace snapshot of dark web counterfeit passports and identification cards.

Every flavor of data is for sale in those depths, from customer and financial, to operations and intellectual property. The dark web has been good to evil.

In addition to pills, guns, hitmen, espionage, cyberattacks, and malicious software tool kits, the dark web is host to some truly depraved and macabre storefronts. Tom swung by the Body Parts Bazaar, a clearinghouse for organ sales that targets the world's most desperate patients. There are roughly ten thousand illegal organ transplant surgeries every year. Sensing my dread, Tom sat and folded his hands below his chest and told a story. "This mortician who owned a funeral home in North Carolina made a fortune," he said. "She would cremate empty cardboard boxes and sell the corpses she kept through her personal dark web marketplace." He paused for effect. "Imagine being at a funeral where Aunt Tilly is supposed to be in an urn on the altar, when really she's being carved up in some North Carolina back room and shipped out for parts."

His story didn't ease me.

"It gets worse," Tom sighed. "A marketplace exists to purchase Russian girls—cash on delivery." He shook his head. "We aren't going to even try to land on those sites. But I've seen them. They offer in-

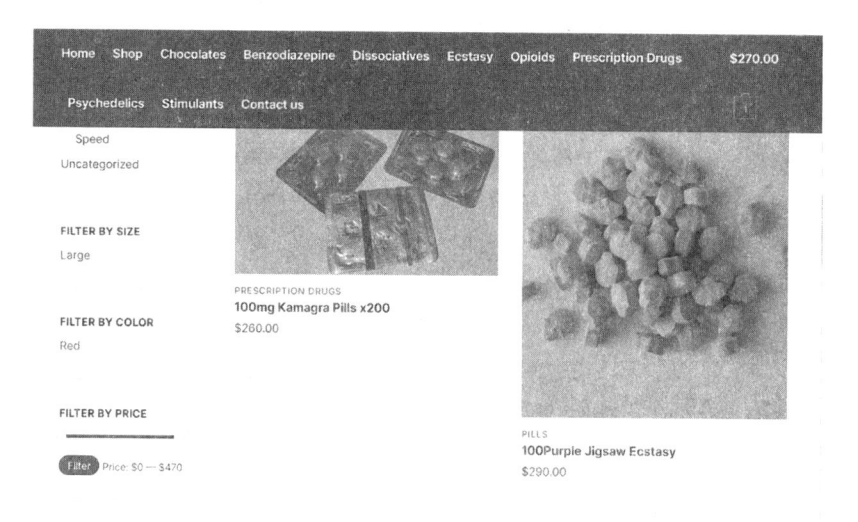

Marketplace snapshot of dark web illegal drugs for sale.

structions on building a soundproof basement dungeon to keep them quiet."

I had to ask, morbidly curious. "How do they, um, deliver the . . ."

He waved off the rest of my question, saving me from saying it out loud. "You pay half up front and then the rest at the exchange. They will arrange to meet you at a hotel where they drop off the girl. Some of this stuff you can't unsee."

"What else?" I asked.

He thought before speaking. "I suspect we are about to go there to find out who is blackmailing Halima," Tom grumbled. "Child pornography is everywhere. The obscener, the bigger the nightmare for people like you and me."

Tom's mention of Halima had ended the macabre tour. It was time to get to work. For many victims of cybercrime, the most frightening aspect is the sense of powerlessness over the theft of data. For Halima, this was even more personal. She had been exploited and did not know why or by whom. We aimed to answer those questions.

We had extracted metadata from Halima and her attacker's chat history on Instagram. She had abandoned the old account, but the attacker continued to harass her there. When we logged on as Halima, we found plenty of information that led us to the attacker's IP addresses—located in Moldova, which we immediately reported to the FBI. I would later tell Halima that she should not hold her breath over hopes for an extradition and trial in the United States. Most of this sort of crime goes unpunished, unfortunately.

Knowing the attacker's location, we found Halima's photos on a Russian server listing "sexy teen pictures" for sale. Clicking through the link would expose thumbnail poses of Halima naked in her bathroom mirror, cell phone in one hand. It would also trigger malicious software to begin a takeover of the visiting computer. Tom's virtual machine crashed, and we had to wipe, install, and start over twice before we'd even gathered enough information. Countless other teen girls had their images listed for sale on the same dark web site, each sourced by name and nationality and the number of pictures and/or videos available for each.

While we couldn't scrub pictures from a Moldovan-based cybercrime group, we did reach out to Google, Bing, Safari, and other search engines and asked them to remove indexing to the surface web versions of these websites. Halima was underage in the pictures and therefore a child sexual exploitation victim. The major search engines are responsive to requests to remove child sexual abuse material (CSAM) from their platforms and index servers. Microsoft, Google, and Apple (among others) have committed to fighting CSAM online and preventing their platforms from creating, storing, or distributing this vile material. While they claim to devote significant resources to detecting CSAM, they tend to tilt at windmills. For that reason, it is imperative that humans who identify CSAM report it. Sadly, despite efforts by technology giants, the prevalence of child sexual exploitation online remains outrageously high.

Statistics related to CSAM are particularly alarming. According to an Interpol report, more than 60 percent of sexual exploitation victims were prepubescent and 65 percent of victims were girls, although the most severe abuse images predominantly feature boys.[5]

Exploitation: Spelunking into a Nightmare | 145

Leaks	Most Liked Leaks					
Random Girl	#	Name	Country	Pics	Vids	Siz
All Girls	#1	Maria ▮	Brazil	8	14	40.
By Country	#2	Anna ▮	Germany	45	0	27.
Top Leaks	#3	Alyssa ▮	Philippines	272	239	1.8
Videos	#4	Abbey ▮	United States	52	13	72.
IP-Cams	#5	Goldie ▮	Australia	369	0	16€
Recently added	#6	Aeris ▮	Singapore	31	0	3.2
Recent clips	#7	Akascha ▮	United States	84	0	10:
	#8	Priya ▮	India	244	0	26.

Dark web child sexual abuse material marketplace "Sexy Teen Girls" snapshot (names redacted).

Considerable efforts by big tech companies and governments to curb child sexual abuse material have failed. One study found that, over a five-year period from 2018 to 2023, over 11 percent of all dark web searches over the Tor network explicitly sought out child sex abuse material and one fifth of all onion websites share CSAM.[6] Distributors of child pornography trade links to sexually exploitative images in plain sight on platforms like YouTube, Facebook, Twitter, and Instagram using coded language to evade detection tools.

While awaiting an answer from these search engines, we had a long call with Halima to help assuage her fears and terror over the cyberattack. I told her that not only was the dark web site difficult to find, but its primary function was to infect travelers with malicious software. In other words, anyone trying to purchase and download her pictures would instead find themselves under attack. The chances that anyone who knew her would stumble on the site were almost zero once we removed links to the big search engines. As we spoke, she brightened. We had given her hope to buttress her confidence.

Eventually, the major search engines removed all the links Tom and I meticulously researched to various teen leak sites portraying

Halima's images. But Halima suffers post-traumatic stress because of the personal and explicit nature of the attack. Every few months, she calls me to discuss a fear that her phone has been hacked or that someone is listening through her laptop. While she can be assuaged knowing that friends, family, and future business partners googling her name will not stumble upon the unfortunate pictures in search results, she knows that those images persist somewhere on the dark web. This knowledge keeps her up at night. Finding resolution after a personal cyberattack is a lot like surviving a home invasion. You never really feel safe after.

Occasionally, law enforcement swings and hits a home run, and Germany is on a hot streak. In May 2021, German police arrested four members of a cybercrime group who managed Boystown, the world's biggest child abuse image website, with more than four hundred thousand members worldwide. The German federal officers raided seven addresses across Germany and arrested five men between the ages of forty and sixty-five for distributing indecent images and videos of children. Three of the men arrested were accused of founding and maintaining the forum, while another was one of the forum's most active contributors, with over 3,500 posts.[7] Computer scientists Gareth Owen and Nick Savage wrote a research paper for the Global Commission on Internet Governance in 2015 titled "The Tor Dark Net." It found 900 child sexual abuse sites, like Boystown, on the dark web; they received an average of 168,152 requests per day.[8] As the dark web has grown, so has the prevalence of exploitative websites, despite yeoman's efforts by law enforcement to stamp them out.

In December 2024, German authorities took down Manson Market, a massive dark web marketplace where cybercriminals bought and sold stolen banking credentials, credit card data, and personal information used in online fraud schemes. This matters because much of the phishing, identity theft, and financial fraud hitting everyday consumers starts in places just like this. In the same week, German police also shut down Crimenetwork, the country's largest cybercrime forum, where everything from fake documents to illicit drugs and hacked accounts were up for sale. These takedowns deal a serious blow to organized cybercrime, showing that the digital underworld isn't as untouchable as it thinks.

But Germany isn't just going after financial crime—they're going after monsters. In a major international operation that spanned from 2022 to April 2025, German and Europol authorities also took down Kidflix, a disturbing dark web platform dedicated to child sexual exploitation, with over three thousand users across the globe. Unlike most platforms, Kidflix allowed users to stream child exploitation content, using a twisted token-based system where offenders earned access by uploading material, tagging videos, and verifying titles—then paid in cryptocurrency to unlock higher-quality versions. These dark web marketplaces are digital evil—global, anonymous, and devastating—but every takedown proves that justice can still shine through the shadows.

Not to be totally outdone by Deutschland, in 2021 the FBI's Criminal Investigative Division arrested Eric Eoin Marques, a dual national of the United States and Ireland. Marques was sentenced to twenty-seven years in prison for running a hosting service on the dark web that facilitated over two hundred child exploitation websites. This service housed millions of child exploitation images, many involving sadistic abuse of infants and toddlers.

Another significant U.S. case involved Homeland Security Investigations (HSI) in collaboration with Brazil's Federal Police. In 2022, the joint task force dismantled a criminal network involved in the production and sale of illicit imagery of children through a website that falsely promised modeling careers. This operation identified over one hundred twenty victims and uncovered approximately two hundred thousand images and videos.[9]

These efforts are part of broader international collaborations to combat child exploitation. Missions like Operation Predator by ICE have resulted in numerous arrests and rescues of children in different countries. For instance, in November 2022, HSI special agents arrested multiple individuals in the United States for crimes related to child pornography, rescuing several children from abusive situations.

Tom has conducted his own research into dark web exploitation of all sorts, particularly CSAM. After we got off a Zoom call with Halima, we continued our discussion over a beer at Baby Cat Brewery in the suburbs just north of Washington, D.C. You wouldn't think an ultramarathon runner would touch alcohol of any sort, but our discussion needed fortification.

"What do you think is behind this?" I asked Tom.

We sat up on the roof deck over the brewery. The owners had converted an old car garage into a social hall that maintained the former aesthetic, with grand doors on the facade that rolled up. Within a year of opening in what had been a suburban bar desert, they had to expand to the quieter roof deck that looked out over local train tracks.

"You have kids," he answered.

"Two teenagers and a tweenager."

"How hard is it to keep them off devices?"

I sighed, sensing where he was going. "Not easy at all."

Tom took a sip from his skinny pilsner glass. This was the kind of place that properly glassed the chosen brew. "I have the same problem with my kids. It's like an addiction. But can you blame them?" He shook his head. "They look at stuff from computers, smartphones, tablets . . . and today almost all children under twelve are using the internet. Even kids as young as seven!"

"I can't image giving a seven-year-old a wi-fi connection," I said. "Juliana and I decided on phones at fourteen." I grinned. "There was great moaning and gnashing of the teeth from our oldest two."

Tom winked. "But I bet they were more responsible by the time they got those phones."

"Maybe more mature," I agreed. "And they didn't have a prior internet history. We made certain of that."

"Which is the right call. Kids online get bullied, see obscene and frightening content that they're not ready for. They suffer from digital addiction. Also, all those early social media profiles on platforms like

TikTok, Instagram, YouTube, and Snapchat can be leveraged for future cyberattacks."

"Reconnaissance to learn about your target and coerce them into clicking a link," I suggested.

"That's the FBI investigator talking," Tom said. "Now think like a criminal." He finished his beer and plunked the class down on the table. "Children are particularly interesting to cybercriminals, especially teenagers. They have pristine credit ratings that can be data mined for identity theft. Worse, many blindly trust what they see online. They haven't been hardened against the prevalence of degenerates who trick them into exploitative situations."

I glanced at the empty train tracks and thought of some of the worst cybercrimes visited on our vulnerable youth. "Our children are under threat every time they chat online."

THINK LIKE A SPY

- Children are vulnerable targets for cybercriminals. Studies reveal that children are increasingly targeted by cybercriminals for identity theft, with a significant number falling victim to such crimes. Children under the age of seven, given access to social media, are the easiest targets.

- Many parents are unaware of the need to monitor their children's Social Security numbers and credit reports, leaving them exposed to potential identity theft. Lax supervision of children's social media usage provides cybercriminals with ample opportunities to exploit them. Parents need to be proactive in monitoring and educating their children about online safety.

- Every parent should contact all three major credit bureaus for each of their children. A report typically exists only if someone has stolen an identity in order to open accounts or if the child has been added as an authorized user on an adult's credit card. If such a report exists, parents should work with the credit bureau to freeze their child's credit to prevent additional fraud.

- Social media platforms serve as a primary gateway for cybercriminals to target children. Parents should educate their children about the potential dangers of sharing personal information online and the risks associated with downloading games or applications, which can serve as avenues for cybercrime.

- Educating children about the dangers of social media, identity theft, and online scams is crucial. Parents should engage in ongoing conversations with their children, emphasizing the potential consequences of reckless online behavior. By instilling awareness and caution early on, parents can help protect their children from becoming victims of cybercrime.

- Nearly everything created and transmitted across the internet is stored or copied in one way or another—from embarrassing emails to the most private pictures and images. Criminals seek out this information to defraud, extort, and scam the unwary.

- Spelunking the dark web is like stepping into a den of digital predators. It's a shadowy realm where the most nefarious characters lurk, dealing in everything from cyberattacks to illicit trades, including drugs, weapons, and even human trafficking. Anything can be bought and sold. Human depravity at the touch of a button.

ELEVEN

Exploitation: No Blank Pages

Hey

I can't imagine exactly what went through seventeen-year-old Jordan DeMay's mind when he read that three-letter greeting that popped up in his Instagram messages, but I can guess. Late on a frigid March night in Marquette County, Michigan, Jordan received an alert on his phone. One of his social media accounts had pinged him and demanded his attention. He paused from packing. The next morning, he planned to trade the freezing winds that blew south off Lake Superior for sunshine and spring break in Florida. Had Jordan ignored his phone or placed it on Do Not Disturb to pack uninterrupted, he might have made his plane.

Instead, at about 10:00 p.m., he thumbed his phone and opened the direct message on Instagram from someone he did not know, named Dani Robertts. It said only "Hey."

Dani's social media account displayed images of a beautiful teenage girl with brown hair and an enchanting smile. Her arms were wrapped around a shaggy German shepherd.

Jordan learned that Dani went to high school in Georgia and that they had a friend in common. He continued their discussion while he packed for his trip. Two hours later, Dani's DMs changed from playful to flirtatious. She sent him a nude photo of herself and demanded he reciprocate. Jordan sent his own naked selfie. Soon, things went horribly wrong. The girl Jordan had flirted with for hours transformed into someone sinister. The chat between Dani and Jordan that followed will terrify every parent.

Dani: I have screenshot all ur followers and tags can send this nudes to everyone and also send your nudes to your Family and friends Until it goes viral . . . All you've to do is to cooperate with me and I won't expose you

Dani: Are you gonna cooperate with me

Dani: Just pay me rn [right now]

Dani: And I won't expose you

Jordan: How much

Dani: $1000

Dani: Pay me rn

Jordan transferred three hundred dollars to the attackers that called themselves "Dani" and thought it would end, but the attackers persisted. Three hundred wasn't enough to meet their demands. When Jordan complained that he had no more money to give them, the conversation turned violent.

Dani: Goodbye

Dani: Enjoy your miserable life

Jordan: I'm kms rn [I'm kill myself right now]

Jordan: Bc of you [Because of you]

Dani: Good

Dani: Do that fast

Dani: Or I'll make you do it

Dani: I swear to God

Jordan: I am begging for my own life

"Dani" sent Jordan an image of a collage, with Jordan's nude picture surrounded by pictures of his school, family, and friends. As Jordan stared in horror, Dani began a countdown, threatening to send Jordan's naked picture to his girlfriend.
"Ten . . . nine . . . eight . . . seven . . ."
Jordan lost hope. He retrieved his father's pistol and shot himself. At 7:40 a.m., his father, a former police officer, called in his son's suicide. Jordan was found by police sitting upright in his bed, a pistol in his lifeless right hand. The cell phone in his lap still flashed notifications as "Dani" continued their devastating exploitation.

The police and FBI worked together and subpoenaed the entire Instagram chat history from Meta. Faced with a court order, the social media giant turned over a full, raw, five-hour Instagram message exchange between "Dani Robertts" and Jordan DeMay. Fortunately for police, the time stamps for each chat message included a unique IP address. When the police plugged the IP address into a lookup tool, they received coordinates for an address in Lagos, Nigeria.

Dani Robertts was not Dani Robertts. The original Dani Robertts's Instagram account had been compromised and offered for sale on the dark web. On that fateful night in March 2022, Jordan's conversation was really with Samuel and Samson Ogoshi, two brothers in their early twenties who had purchased the Instagram account and used it for more than a year to target over a hundred victims, including at least eleven minors.

Had you encountered the Ogoshi brothers in person, you'd never guess they harbored a secret cybercriminal alter ego that exploited innocent teenagers and pressured some to take their own lives. They were raised in a middle-class family by a father who had retired from the military and a mother who ran a small business. The brothers played on the neighborhood soccer team and sang in the weekly church choir. One studied sociology at Nasarawa State University; the other trained to become a cobbler. Apparently, they also had the right amount of charisma and sociopathy to excel at cybercrime.

One of the brothers would reach out through their stolen Instagram account to a teenage boy while the other would google the victim's online history. This reconnaissance would provide details about where the victim lived, attended school, and all the information they could learn about friends and family. A bonus occurred whenever they discovered the identity of a girlfriend who they could use as a wedge in the exploitation attack.

According to court records, on more than ten occasions, they induced minor teenage children to send images of themselves masturbating. Each time, they coerced the victim into sending explicit images by first engaging in hours-long conversations, posing as an attractive teenage girl who ultimately sent a naked picture of herself to the victim. As soon as the victim sent their own image, the Ogoshi brothers switched the chat to a high-pressure exploitation scheme that frequently convinced victims to send them money through simple payment applications like Apple Pay and Zelle. I suspect they got away with their crime because victims who paid did not tend to report the embarrassing situation.

Nine months after Jordan's father called 911 in November 2022, the U.S. District Court for the Western District of Michigan indicted the Ogoshi brothers and a third coconspirator for sexual exploitation and other criminal acts. Another nine months passed before the FBI coordinated with Nigerian law enforcement to arrest the brothers at their Lagos home and extradite them to the United States. By April 2024, both brothers pled guilty to conspiracy to sexually exploit a minor, a federal crime under Title 18 of the United States Code, which demands a minimum prison sentence of fifteen years and restitution fines up to $250,000.

In September 2024, the Ogoshi brothers were each sentenced to 210 months in prison and five years of supervised release for conspiracy to sexually exploit minors.[1] I hope they rot in prison. Then–Attorney

General Merrick Garland must have agreed with me, because he issued the following dire warning to future predators:

"These defendants sexually exploited and extorted more than 100 victims, including at least eleven minors, resulting in the tragic death of a 17-year-old high school student. These sentences should serve as a warning that the perpetrators of online sexual exploitation and extortion cannot escape accountability for their heinous crimes by hiding behind their phones and computers. The Justice Department will find them, no matter where they are, and we will bring them to justice in the United States."

When they were arrested, law enforcement found that they'd made online searches after learning that Jordan had taken his life, a curiosity almost as vile as the sin. The searches included topics such as "Michigan suicide," "is suicide a sin," "Instagram blackmail death," and "how can fbi track my ip from another country?"

The FBI produced a sobering report regarding the life-or-death situations caused by sexual extortion (aka "sextortion").[2] At least twenty minors died by suicide due to extortion through sexually explicit photos from October 2021 to March 2023. Seven more suicides linked to sextortion were reported by April 2024. The FBI received over seven thousand reports of online sexual exploitation and extortion of minors that year. While only a small minority chose to end their lives, the psychological damage to teenagers over time is catastrophic.

Teens coerced into sending nude pictures by cybercriminals frequently experience heightened levels of anxiety and depression, driven by the fear that their images will be shared widely, compounded by intense feelings of shame and guilt. This violation may severely impact self-esteem and self-worth, leading to a sense of lost control over their lives and bodies. The experience can erode a victim's ability to trust others, complicating the development of healthy relationships. Many victims withdraw from social interactions out of fear of judgment or further exploitation, resulting in social isolation that exacerbates their feelings of loneliness and depression. The trauma of such manipulation can lead to post-traumatic stress disorder, characterized by flashbacks, severe anxiety, and uncontrollable thoughts about the incident. In severe cases, the psychological impact can escalate to suicidal thoughts and behaviors, as the intense shame and fear make some teens feel trapped with no way out.[3]

The National Center for Missing and Exploited Children (NCMEC) runs a reporting mechanism called the CyberTipline.[4] Both the public and electronic service providers routinely use it to report instances of suspected child sexual exploitation. Sadly, exploitative and abusive material related to children on the internet continues to grow. In 2023, the CyberTipline received more than thirty-six million global reports of circulation of pictures and videos of children being sexually abused. CSAM includes more than just pictures. It can include posts or chats asking a child to view pornographic images or videos; predators requesting a child to perform sexual acts, expose themselves, or share a sexual image of themselves; or discussing or sharing indecent images of children.

According to NCMEC, over the past three years, the number of CSAM reports has increased over 20 percent, and the number of urgent, time-sensitive reports where a child is at risk of harm has grown by more than 140 percent. In 2023 alone, the CyberTipline received over 186,000 reports regarding online enticement to share sexual images—precisely what happened to Jordan—a more than 300 percent increase from 2021.

Reporting CSAM can help remove the material from the internet, or at least reduce its prevalence, particularly because dark web criminals and predators routinely reproduce and share exploitative images. NCMEC's technology seeks to stop this by determining the hash value of the exploitative image or video. A hash value is like a digital fingerprint of a file that allows NCMEC to use matching technology to automatically recognize future versions of the same images and videos. A list of these hash values is then sent to all the major technology companies that enable mass video and image sharing (companies like Facebook and Instagram). These companies are then armed with the ability to search for the unique image fingerprint and remove the exploitative content.

Another important service in the battle against CSAM is called Take It Down.[5] This anonymous, free service helps victims of internet CSAM remove nude, partially nude, or sexually explicit photos and videos taken before they turned eighteen. Take It Down uses NCMEC's hash-value technology to assign a unique digital fingerprint to the sexually explicit content. Services like Snapchat, Facebook, Instagram, and TikTok then use the hash-value list to detect reported images on their sites and remove the content. Take It Down has global reach, is translated into twenty-five languages, and receives more than two million page views a year. But the fight against child exploitation requires continued awareness of the issue, and parents and guardians need to be constantly vigilant to protect children from internet predators.

At a recent keynote, a mother came to the microphone during my Q&A session to follow up on a story I'd told about restricting my teenage daughter from TikTok. She smirked up at me, shook her mane of blond hair, and said, "Your daughter has a TikTok. They all do, it's a fact." I grinned and explained the lengths I had to go to strip dangerous applications from my children's devices. TikTok's owner, ByteDance, as a Chinese-owned company, is subject to laws requiring it to provide data to the Chinese government if requested. While TikTok has denied such access, the law in China requires its companies to provide data for state purposes. Add to that the fact that the TikTok application collects a broad range of user data, including location, device information, browsing activity, keystrokes, and even biometric data like face and voiceprints, making it an incredible espionage tool.

Like all parents, I have waged a continuous war of information control. Delete the app, and the kids will find a way to create a shadow account through a web browser. Block the web page address on the device, and they'll use a VPN to get around security. I finally had to reprogram my home router to block TikTok at the server level. If you try to access the Chinese-owned spyware in our home, an "access denied" message now pops up on the screen. It's only a matter of time before my children find a way to yet again breach security and force me to repeat the cycle. I shouldn't be surprised. Indeed, perhaps I should be proud. I've raised a family of spies.

For those less inclined or without the wherewithal to reprogram routers or battle your children's technological expertise, the best recourse is a softer approach. Talk to your kids about the dangers prevalent online. Impress upon them that what they post online lasts forever and can be used against them years later. Most importantly, let them know they can always come to you, no matter how embarrassed or ashamed they may be. We are both the first and last line of defense for our children, and their final refuge to turn to when hope seems lost and wolves are howling at their door.

This is particularly the case because software updates and patches are not enough to stop our children from spying on us. Our children are masters of observing their parents, learning their routines, and knowing when to cast a sneaky eye over their shoulder to clandestinely memorize a password. If their goal is more time on devices, and parents control the keys to that time, our children will plot elaborate plans to gain access. When my daughter Emma was eight years old, we caught her streaming a TV show that she did not have permission to watch during a time when Apple Screen Time should have bricked all tablets. After a round of interrogation, we learned that Emma had shoulder-surfed my wife to clandestinely memorize her six-digit device passcode. Emma unlocked the phone and added her fingerprint without Juliana noticing. She would then ask for more Screen Time from her tablet and run to the phone, open it with her fingerprint, and accept the Screen Time request before anyone noticed.

But someone did notice. Emma's older siblings, Hannah and Lukas, caught her watching during Screen Time downtime and got her to cough up how she'd done it. The three formed a conspiracy centered around my wife's phone. First, they went into Screen Time and quietly changed the downtime settings to something more appropriate for binge-watching. Then they went into the password settings and learned the master password for Netflix. They used this to go into my account and elevate each of their permissions to inappropriate maturity ratings. Emma told me that letting her siblings in on her scheme was her Christmas present to them that year. A most celebratory Christmas it was . . . until I found out.

Parents must nurture this cleverness but must also educate our children about the pitfalls and traps for the unwary online. Cyber exploitation often includes bullying and harassment, typically to shock the victim and coerce them to pay. But sadly, sometimes the bullying is the point of the exploitation. In their 2023 study, Javelin found that 70 percent of children active on YouTube have been cyberbullied and that figure has tripled since 2019.[6] Worse, only 11 percent of cyberbullying victims turn to their parents for help. Children on popular platforms like YouTube, Snapchat, TikTok, and Facebook face heightened risks of cyberbullying due to direct chat or message features favored by criminals. This accessibility makes it easier for children to isolate themselves and conceal their online activities from adults. Many resort to blocking parental access or creating alternative "shadow" accounts, making it harder for parents to discover the problem.

As if cyberbullying through chats wasn't bad enough, incredible advances in image creation by generative AI tools has taken a terrifying problem and turned it into a crisis. A student named Audrey would learn this the hard way . . .

* * *

Audrey attended a private grade school in California. Her eighth-grade year would soon end, and she could see over the horizon of final exams to summer break and then beginning her freshman year as a high school student. She played lacrosse and would spend the summer in a camp to prepare her to make the high school team. She'd spend another week on the coast with her family and every other moment of an endless summer with her "crew," a group of girls she'd known since grade school. Her life felt perfect.

Until she walked past a table of boys at lunch crowded over their phones. Curious about the "spilled tea," Audrey caught a peek before one of the boys could turn his phone away.

Somehow, impossibly, the image looked like one of her close friends. Except this friend was naked. Audrey pushed between two of the boys and grabbed the phone, ignoring his protests. With athletic poise granted by years dodging defenders on the lacrosse field, she spun away from his attempts to pull the phone from her and examined the photo. And then swiped to the next. And the next . . .

Audrey tried not to make things worse by sickening up all over the cafeteria floor. The last image showed her, naked across a bed with her legs in an impossible position . . .

She screamed and hurled the phone across the room.

This story is one among many, happening at increasing rates due to the ease and accessibility of generative AI. At a high school in Washington State, boys used a "nudify" app to remove the clothes of girls who attended the school's homecoming dance. In New Jersey, tenth-grade boys shared sexually explicit images of female classmates they created using generative AI. A California school district expelled five eighth graders who face swapped sixteen of their classmates (i.e., real faces superimposed on AI simulated nude bodies) and shared the images through messaging applications.

Generative AI has allowed perverts, predators, and perpetrators to expand the market of sexually explicit images available online. Dozens of generative AI applications are available online that can undress a body, predominantly female, in just seconds. These applications rely on algorithms trained on vast datasets of images. In the case of so-called nudify applications, the AI might be trained on ten thousand images of naked females to nudify a single image in a swimsuit.

This flavor of AI is called a generative adversarial network (GAN)—a class of machine-learning frameworks designed to generate new, synthetic data that resembles a given training dataset. Typically, GANs are used to enhance or clarify images by taking one image and re-creating it with greater detail. You can use a GAN to restore and add detail to an old photograph of your great-grandfather found in an attic, or to transform a quick sketch scrawled on the back of a napkin into a photorealistic image of a cat. But as with all generative

AI accomplishments, there are downsides. Face swap was one such tool clearly made accessible to the boys in Audrey's eighth-grade class. These kinds of applications take two images or an image and a video and swap one face for another. If you have scrolled through any social media memes recently, you'll find countless videos of politicians and celebrities with their heads swapped into famous movie clips. My favorite are clips where the heads of Presidents Obama, Trump, and Biden have been swapped for three teenagers telling lame jokes to one another. Obviously, these sorts of memes are nonconsensual, but are at least parodistic and lighthearted.

The social media analytics firm Graphika has spent the last few years looking into the more disturbing phenomenon of exploitative websites.[7] For example, in September 2024, twenty-four million people visited nudify websites that use generative AI to undress images of people. Advertisements for nudify services pop up on social media platforms like Instagram and TikTok, driving revenue and drawing in everyone from the curious to the malicious. Since the beginning of 2023, the volume of referral links for nudify applications has increased by more than 2,000 percent on platforms like Reddit and X. Graphika identified fifty-two nonconsensual intimate imagery groups on Telegram with at least one million users in 2024.

Screenshot of Undressapp AI, a nudify website on the surface web.

Imagine a situation where, instead of looking over a classmate's shoulder, Audrey had received images or videos of herself in compromising sexually explicit situations from an online attacker. The exploitative images could be used to extort money, accede to demands, and even lead to self-harm. Anyone can create such images or videos online in moments for a small fee.

The downside in the growth of generative AI is how easily it facilitates the harmful production and distribution of child sexual abuse and exploitation materials. As AI evolves, new pathways to exploitation open up, with better-quality deepfakes and deepnudes, and even on-demand live streaming of child sexual abuse and exploitation material.

Education leads to agency. Guidance, support, and a firm hand on technology by parents is necessary to ensure our children understand the threat and are armed against exploitation by online predators, cybercriminals, and even jealous peers. My concerns reach beyond the immediate exploitation teenagers and young adults suffer through online assaults, however. The problems AI pose to our youth go beyond exploitation image modification and generation.

As of this writing, my children Hannah and Lukas are in high school. Like many other innovative schools, Hannah's college preparatory school uses Apple's iPad as the primary learning tool. Her textbooks are digital, and assignments are created and submitted on the single screen. Communication with classmates and teachers is instantaneous and often occurs during class. The adept way Hannah maneuvers an Apple Pencil would put the best magicians to shame. My youngest daughter Emma's grade school uses Chromebooks in much the same manner.

On a recent flight home from a speaking event in California, I was trapped near the back of the plane, waiting for an available restroom. As I waited, I couldn't help looking at the young woman in seat 35D's laptop screen. The page was open to a multiple-choice exam. It didn't take a former FBI investigator to see that she was a college student. The online exam had been prepared by her university and the on-screen logo matched the one on her baggy sweatshirt.

Remaining inconspicuous, I scanned her laptop screen (I was bored!). The question related to a sociology class. Having studied criminology and psychology at Auburn University, I thought I could figure out the correct answer. Before I could read past answer choice C, the student swapped tabs to ChatGPT. She had already prompted the AI to respond as a sociology student with the best answer to a multiple-choice question—all of which she pasted into the generative AI. In seconds, her ChatGPT responded that B was the best answer and why.

Without reading the explanation, she switched back to the test and picked B. Before I made it to the restroom, the student and AI co-conspirator had answered every question and finished the test. The software immediately returned her test grade. She got a 100.

In my (solidly Gen-X) day, each of my children and the college student in 35D would receive an assignment from their teacher to write an essay and would pull a blank sheet of looseleaf from their backpack. Imagination would spark, a No. 2 pencil would scratch, and an idea would shape itself on the page. Today, our children, young adults, and younger generations of employed professionals address creating far differently. Most open ChatGPT and ask the generative AI to write an essay for them on the assigned topic. What comes next is not creating, it is editing.

Generative AI cleverly regurgitates but does not create. Instead, AI mimics and extrapolates from existing data, making it inherently derivative. AI is limited by the scope of its training data, able to produce high-quality content within these confines, but it struggles to venture beyond them. Humans are not bound by these limitations. We dream and create using a complex interplay of mental faculties that not even the best neuroscientists and psychologists truly understand. Humanity's progress from discovering fire and inventing the wheel to creating generative AI itself has steamed forward through time on railways of novel ideas, reaching beyond immediate knowledge and experience. Human creativity evolves, leading to continuous innovation, while generative AI depends on the quality and diversity of its training data, advancing through technological improvements.

In other words, AI cannot learn and grow without human ingenuity feeding the data it relies on.

But what happens when humans rely on AI and stop creating? As we allow technology to exploit ourselves away from light-bulb moments, we move closer to an idiocracy. We are, in a sense, exploiting ourselves. Artificial intelligence is an incredible resource to assist, investigate, and enhance ideas of our own making, but what happens when imagination is stifled by AI? What happens when there are no longer creatives to dream and inspire? What happens when there are no blank pages?

THINK LIKE A SPY

- Sexual extortion, also known as "sextortion," is a form of blackmail in which individuals are coerced into providing sexually explicit images or videos, often through online means. Bloomberg's report highlights the devastating consequences of sextortion, including suicide among minors who become victims of this heinous crime.

- At least twenty minors took their own lives in 2022 and 2023 as a result of sextortion. By April 2024, seven more suicides linked to sextortion were reported. These incidents emphasize the urgent need for awareness and prevention efforts to safeguard vulnerable teenagers from falling prey to such exploitation.

- The rise in online sexual exploitation and sextortion cases among minors highlights the dangers posed by unmonitored social media usage, unrestricted internet access, and the misuse of generative AI. Parents must actively engage in their children's online activities, providing guidance, supervision, and education to ensure their safety in the digital landscape.

- Child sexual abuse material (CSAM) includes more than just pictures. It can be posts or chats asking a child to view pornographic images or videos; requests by predators for a child to perform sexual acts, expose themselves, or share a sexual image of themselves; or talking about or sharing indecent images of children.

- The CyberTipline serves as a critical reporting platform for suspected instances of child sexual exploitation and CSAM. In 2023, the CyberTipline received over thirty-six million reports worldwide concerning the circulation of sexually abusive pictures and videos of children, highlighting its essential role in addressing and preventing such heinous crimes. Here is the link: https://www.missingkids.org/gethelpnow/cybertipline.

- Numerous generative AI applications are accessible online, enabling rapid image manipulation such as undressing bodies or swapping faces. These applications employ algorithms trained on extensive datasets to re-create images with enhanced detail and can be misused to create explicit content without consent.

- Among the prevalent generative AI tools is face swapping, which seamlessly exchanges faces in images and videos and "nudifies" them, which will remove the clothing from any subject in an image.*

---

* For more information see my Top Ten Tips to Avoid Online Sextortion Scams and What to Do if Victimized in The Spy Hunter Tool Kit on page 273.

TWELVE

Destruction: Inside the Fishbowl

Back inside the NGO's offices, I met with our small coterie of cyberthreat hunters in a cozy, second-floor conference room. Aptly named the Fishbowl, one glass wall looked out over a lonely hallway that curved toward a small kitchenette and coffee station. Each of the employees in the room were well into their second cup by the time I arrived. Exhausted faces turned to me, their eyes weary and grim. Like me, they had all reached their limit with the LockBit ransomware attack.

There was Ben, who sat behind a laptop that cast his face in a sickly blue glow. A cable snaked from a port to where it disappeared into the center of the table. He punched a few keys, and a PowerPoint presentation livened up a flat-screen monitor dominating one wall. Beside him, Jill stared sourly into the middle distance. Our agenda included two crucial points: assessing the extent of the data breach and determining if we needed to notify potential victims about their compromised information. I imagined that the thought of a cybercriminal using Jill's account to infiltrate our network was still raw.

David nodded from Ben's other side as I approached. His intelligent eyes told me that he had a secret he wanted to tell. I hoped the news was good.

I took a seat across from them next to Mary. The NGO had fortunately hired the fiery Southerner as a data privacy officer only months before the attack. Great timing for the NGO, and unfortunate for Mary. Mary would ultimately decide whether our amateur code-breaking hour would end with a data breach disclosure that rocked the NGO world and destroyed the company's reputation. Every person at the table hoped to avoid that situation.

"We've gotten a lot of forensic analysis behind us since last we met," Ben began. He clicked his mouse and a graph appeared on the screen. "This is a representation of our outbound network bandwidth." He looked at me. "Eric's right. It's . . . slow."

"That's an understatement," David chuckled. "Connecting to SharePoint from home is a lesson in patience." As the person in charge of the NGO's Data Protection Unit, David also had critical decisions to make in the next few hours.

"There's a reason for that," Jill interjected. "Microsoft throttles the bandwidth from our servers outbound to the internet unless we call and ask them to open the spigot."

"A security measure," Ben said. "And good for us. We ran the test Eric asked for and there is no possible way LockBit stole three terabytes of information."

Jill pointed at the graph. "The dwell time was a matter of hours. To extract even a terabyte would take days."

"That's good news." Mary brightened. "But not good enough. We know they stole something; we just don't know what. If we can't identify what they stole, we unfortunately must assume they stole the worst data."

I knew what she meant. A week after, we knew a lot about the who, what, when, and how of the attack, but we still didn't have enough information to prove a negative. We couldn't yet show that the attacker *did not* steal what we most feared. And we had plenty to be concerned about. Ben, Jill, David, and the cybersecurity consultants they hired had spent nights and days reconstructing LockBit's faded footprints through our server by carefully reviewing transaction journals collected by the operating system. This was like chasing echoes when we needed to tail a suspect close enough to see his shoes. The problem was that those footprints clearly led through the Executive and Human

Resources drives on the Headquarters server. We didn't know what, if anything, had been stolen from that sensitive data.

"Let's go over what we know," I suggested, "and then decide how that helps avoid ruining Mary's year."

Ben replaced the graph with a timeline. "The point of attack happened last weekend through the service desk web server," he said. "That server is connected to the internet so employees can use it to reset passwords and submit help desk tickets to IT. The server didn't have multifactor authentication turned on."

Before everyone started kicking themselves, David picked up the thread. "The attacker exploited a Microsoft Windows vulnerability through an unpatched issue with Service Desk. This let LockBit mine for the username and password of the last person to log into the server."

"That was me." Jill took a laborious breath. "I knew about the patch but couldn't get it installed correctly on Friday."

I jumped in to save her from further self-recriminations. "The attackers, LockBit, were lurking around the periphery of our systems and exploited the tiny window of opportunity—just two days—to exploit the flaws in Service Desk and Windows."

"They used the stolen credentials," Ben continued, "to create their own account called GlobalNGOsysadmin." The stolen credentials were Jill's.

"The GlobalNGO account," Jill said, "was then used to install a remote access tool called Any Desk that allowed LockBit to control our server, change permissions, access drives, create folders, and so much more." She made a disgusted face. "Sorry. It's cold."

"Like the trail from there," David quipped. "We know from the journals that LockBit's data mining stayed on the Headquarters server. He spread ransomware to destroy the company as far and wide as possible, but during his limited time before triggering the ransomware attack, he performed data exfiltration on just the one HQ server."

"Which is good news," Jill said, opting for the positive. "Once we identified when the attacker had first compromised the service desk server, we restored all infected systems, laptops, endpoints, etc., from a clean backup prior to the infiltration—otherwise we would have returned to a state where the attacker had a foothold, and he could renew his attack."

"He's lurking outside right now," Ben said. "Probing and prodding and trying to find a way in."

A few of us glanced toward the glass wall of the Fishbowl as though we'd see a hacker peering in from the outside. The attack had us all on edge.

"He's pissed we haven't paid," David said, shrugging.

"We've been stalling," I said. "LockBit provided us a full file tree of what he stole as a sign of life. Everything from the HR and Exec drives. H and E, right down to the file name."

"Now the bad news," Mary said. We leaned closer to her. "I looked at the documents in those drives. The big three of required disclosure for data breaches of personally identifiable information are on there. Health, financial, and beneficiary information."

"Hold on," Ben said. "We minimized the impact! We shut down all our systems, closed our VPN connections between offices, and asked all our employees to stop working." He sighed. "No one worked on a company laptop for a week! Everyone had to use Slack and work on their personal phones."

"That might have saved us from a disaster, but stolen information means required disclosures to the employees, partners, vendors—oh God, I hope no beneficiaries—whose information LockBit might have sitting on a dark web server somewhere," Mary said, raising two fingers. "Disclosures mean consequences." She added a third finger. "Consequences are both financial and reputational."

"LockBit refused to send us actual files," I said. "Just the file tree and plenty of demands that we pay."

"He has some," David said. "We are eighty percent sure. Hard to know one hundred percent because he covered his tracks by destroying network logs. That makes it hard to see precisely what he exfiltrated."

David added that, based on transaction journal entries, they knew he created four folders and extracted information into two of them. They could see what he copied into each folder except for the largest one. He compressed the folders and sent them to himself, but because he deleted the network logs, they couldn't determine where the data was sent. However, the firewall logs were encrypted, which he couldn't access, and these logs helped them figure out the size of the data that left their network.

David signaled to Ben, who clicked his mouse. The screen changed to a list of four items.

Files1.zip—12 MB
Files2.zip—3 MB
Examples.zip—10.7 MB
Examples2.zip—14.1 MB

"A review of the journals gave us the contents of Examples.zip and Examples2.zip and the size of all files," David said.

"That's a win," I pronounced.

"Halfway there," he noted. "But you were right, the total amount exfiltrated is less than forty megabytes. That's hardly three terabytes. LockBit was bluffing all along."

But we still had a serious problem. We had no clue what files LockBit had compressed into the Files1 and Files2 folders. Just fifteen megabytes of information, the size of a few digital images or downloaded songs, would make or break the NGO. And our time had run short.

I tapped my pen on the table, driving home my next point. "LockBit says if we don't pay, they are releasing all our information on their dark web message board."

If we couldn't determine what LockBit had sent itself in two files totaling fifteen megabytes, they would succeed.

I had an idea. One that I was willing to bet against a proposed $5 million ransom.

"Here's what I want you to do," I began.

* * *

Not long ago, destructive cyberattacks were the secret weapons of choice in the arsenals of cyberespionage and terrorism. The ancient espionage art of destruction involves the deliberate use of sabotage, subversion, or covert action to disrupt, damage, or neutralize enemy targets, assets, or capabilities. Destruction is typically carried out clandestinely, and any future war in the West will be waged in a cyber battleground that targets critical infrastructure.

Nation-state threat actors orchestrated one of the most famous and destructive attacks in history, driven not by political will but by revenge: Sony Pictures Entertainment's nightmare before Christmas in December 2014. The Monday before Thanksgiving in the United States, Sony employees arrived to find grinning red skull images on locked computer screens. Later investigation would show that North Korea had attacked Sony in retribution for a planned release of the movie *The Interview*, starring James Franco and Seth Rogen, in which the actors played reporters sent to North Korea to assassinate dictator Kim Jong Un. From November 24 until late December, Sony scrambled to continue operations in the wake of the disastrous attack. The company disconnected its network from the internet, shut down normal communications channels, replaced smartphones with old BlackBerries dragged from storage, and swapped computers for paper and face-to-face meetings. The attackers stole hundreds of gigabytes of data and published it on the internet, seeking to bring down Sony's entire company network for good. Sony hadn't prepared for the unprecedented act of aggression from a foreign country and was forced to respond while simultaneously examining its cybersecurity, determining how the breach occurred, and hardening defenses against continuing attacks by a pissed-off North Korean tyrant.

One would think that the lessons learned by Sony in 2014 would have impressed upon the world the need to prepare for crisis situations *before the crisis*. Sadly, time and again, novel chaos events have proven that lack of preparedness often causes more damage than the crisis. In May 2021—still in the midst of the COVID-19 pandemic, while societies argued whether the science supported lockdowns and enclosing faces in masks and how much we should trust in natural immunity from the virus as opposed to vaccines—a destructive ransomware attack shut down the transmission of gasoline from the West Coast to the East Coast of the United States.

The East Coast accounts for nearly one third of the United States' gasoline consumption. In early May, the southeastern and Gulf Coasts of the United States, from Maryland to Mississippi, suffered a severe gas shortage and a sudden increase in gas prices wherever gas was available. My own sleepy neighborhood in suburban Maryland, just north of the Washington, D.C., Beltway, experienced lines of cars waiting for an available gas pump. Everyday people, already stretched to the limits of resilience by the pandemic, feared a sudden fuel-shortage crisis that should not have impacted an affluent suburban neighborhood whose residents primarily spent their days at home during lockdown.

By May 11, governors in Florida, Georgia, South Carolina, North Carolina, and Virginia all declared states of emergency after drivers had run out of fuel. A day later, the Consumer Product Safety Commission issued a series of tweets and warnings—among them were "Use only containers approved for fuel" and "Do not fill plastic bags with gasoline." Apparently, during the gas-buying frenzies, numerous images of people at gas stations filling odd containers cropped up on social media. Hoarders filled their tanks and their spare gasoline cans, then went on to fill bottles and empty milk and detergent jugs, and worst of all, trash bags.

I understand how fear can drive a person to hoard gasoline in various plastic containers. During the pandemic, societies saw hoarding of toilet paper, paper towels, masks, surgical gloves, hand sanitizer, and cleaning products, to name a few. What I can't understand is what would drive a person to attempt to transport gasoline in a trash bag. Ignore the fact that getting it home without spilling some in the car would require a balancing act and plenty of luck. But what do you do with it when you get home? Dump it in the bathtub? None of this seems safe. That's how you get tweets like this from the Consumer Product Safety Commission:

> **US Consumer Product Safety Commission** ✓
> @USCPSC
>
> We know this sounds simple, but when people get desperate they stop thinking clearly. They take risks that can have deadly consequences. If you know someone who is thinking about bringing a container not meant for fuel to get gas, please let them know it's dangerous.
>
> 10:29 AM · May 12, 2021
>
> 💬 99   🔁 1K   ♡ 5.8K   🔖 20   ↑

US Consumer Product Safety Commission warning snapshot.

What caused the shortage that led to such chaos? Four days earlier, just before 5:00 a.m., a control room employee at Colonial Pipeline checked in to work to find a ransom demand on his computer screen. The company followed a standard response procedure and immediately began shutting down pipeline operations. Joe Blount, president and CEO of the company, would later state, "By the time that I was notified, we'd already gone about the task of shutting down fifty-five hundred miles of pipeline. The employees are trained to do so when they perceive a risk; as you can imagine, we didn't know what we had at that point in time. We knew we had a threat; we knew that threat had to be contained, and therefore we shut the pipeline down in order to do that."[1] By 6:10 a.m., roughly an hour after discovering the ransomware attack, Colonial Pipeline had shut down all operations. According to Blount, Colonial could not immediately confirm whether the cyberattack had placed the IT or Operational Technology (OT) systems at risk or whether a physical risk threatened the pipeline, so they decided to terminate it all as a precaution.

Colonial Pipeline is one of the largest gasoline and jet fuel pipelines in the United States and therefore part of the nation's critical infrastructure. The company manages approximately three million barrels of petrol a day across fifty-five hundred miles of pipeline from the West to East Coasts. When a ransomware attack forced Colonial to turn off the gas, the national economy swirled into chaos. Typical of situations where security is examined in a pressure situation, what Colonial *didn't know* concerned the company, the White House, and the FBI more than the immediate cyberattack. The government had to wonder whether the ransomware attack was a precursor to a physical attack on the pipeline by a nation-state seeking to compromise U.S. critical infrastructure. Had the United States suffered an act of war?

In a world where "there are no hackers, there are only spies," cybercriminals can look a lot like foreign intelligence units. Colonial would soon discover that DarkSide, a somewhat legendary Russian cybercrime syndicate, had meticulously breached their systems starting in late April. The earliest compromise was through a virtual private networking account that allowed a former employee to access the system remotely. The attackers had stumbled upon the password for the VPN log-in on the dark web. Apparently, the Colonial employee had used a complex password for the account, but had also used that same password for at least one other website that had suffered a breach.[2] The breached usernames and credentials had found their way to the dark web for sale, and enterprising DarkSide cybercriminals had scooped them up. The log-in was no longer active after the employee had departed, but the account hadn't been deleted. This was a critical mistake, especially because the VPN account lacked a second layer of multifactor authentication for protection. Passwords have become powerless. People tend to use the same password across every account they own and most of those passwords end up for sale on the dark web. This makes it easy for attackers to bid a few dollars on a collection of usernames and passwords and mine that information for a nugget of gold—like the password for an unsecured remote access account to a critical company responsible for U.S. energy infrastructure.

The cybercriminals also launched phishing emails that targeted contractors and employees. As DarkSide compromised additional accounts, they installed the Tor Browser on victim machines to ensure that they could access and control those accounts without detection. DarkSide additionally created a second command-and-control channel using a Red Team software called Cobalt Strike, an offensive security software that allows security teams to launch attack simulations (so-called Red Team attacks) to test security. By carefully embedding Cobalt Strike stagers, DarkSide could connect to unique remote servers and continuously communicate with and control computers on Colonial's IT system. The pandemic played into and assisted the success of this attack. DarkSide focused on virtual desktop accounts created by Colonial so that employees and consultants could work from remote locations. As they mined usernames, passwords, and other data from hundreds of virtual computers, they quietly deleted their presence from the logs. The attackers displayed a high level of sophistication that placed DarkSide right at the top of the FBI's Most Wanted list for cybercriminals. One method they used to defeat cybersecurity was to avoid systems in Colonial's network infrastructure that deployed endpoint detection and response sensors.

On May 6, the attackers stole 100 gigabytes of data and encrypted a significant portion of Colonial's IT system data. A day later, DarkSide demanded that Colonial pay millions of U.S. dollars in return for a key to decrypt their data (the ransom). They also threatened to release the gigs of data they stole to the public if Colonial did not pay promptly.

The FBI and CISA quickly realized that the Russian cybercrime syndicate DarkSide had most likely orchestrated the attack. DarkSide had spent the pandemic perfecting their own version of a double extortion ransomware attack that included stealing and locking data. This one-two punch solved a problem enterprising criminals had with innovative cybersecurity data backup tools. Victims used to defeat ransomware attacks by ignoring ransom demands while the company carefully restored infected systems from trusted backups, thereby turning back the clock to a safe place before the attack ever happened. In response, DarkSide evolved their attack to extort their victims by not only locking data with ransomware, but stealing it, and then threatening to release critical information like company emails or intellectual property into the public if the victim refused to pay.*

DarkSide had also created a dark web syndicate of what they called "affiliates" who served as lower-tier ransomware attackers in a ransomware-as-a-service (RaaS) model. The associates would use DarkSide's dark web infrastructure of proprietary ransomware development, Bitcoin collection capabilities, technical support, and knowledge bases. In return, the affiliate attacker would pay DarkSide a share of the proceeds as a service fee. DarkSide's criminal operations were highly organized, blending business acumen with cybercrime. They developed a profitable RaaS model, created a dark web data leak site, and established a communications team with a press center. In October 2020, DarkSide even donated $20,000 to charity. But by attacking Colonial Pipeline, a critical part of U.S. energy infrastructure, DarkSide may have bitten off more than it could chew.

Colonial reported the attack to the FBI once it had shut down its operations. Pressure mounted on Colonial Pipeline, the Biden White House, and ultimately Putin's government as U.S. gas stations emptied and gas prices rose. Late-night hosts joked about gasoline in trash bags. By the end of the day, Colonial Pipeline paid seventy-five Bitcoin—then equivalent of $4.4 million dollars—to DarkSide in ransom and hired cybersecurity firm Mandiant to investigate and respond to the attack. "It was the hardest decision I've made," Joe Blount later told a congressional hearing about his decision to pay.

All hands jumped in to address the crisis. On May 8, Colonial publicly announced the ransomware attack. The FBI, CISA, and the NSA collaborated to identify the servers DarkSide had used to steal 100 gigabytes of Colonial's data and took them offline.

The White House went public on Sunday, May 9. President Joseph Biden declared a state of emergency and increased the ability of trucks to transport fuel by road. While he didn't point his finger directly at

---

* For more information on how to stop ransomware attacks, read my Ten Tips on How to Help Prevent Ransomware Attacks in The Spy Hunter Tool Kit on page 275.

Putin, President Biden announced that the attacks were of Russian origin. On May 10, the FBI issued a press release confirming that DarkSide was responsible for the attack on Colonial. The FBI didn't say it, and Biden didn't go there, but I will. I suspect that DarkSide operated with the knowledge and sanction of the Russian government. The U.S. security and intelligence apparatus has long known that Russian intelligence turns a blind eye to criminal cyberattacks against Western countries and will often use the criminal brain trust as surge forces for nation-state attacks. DarkSide ransomware automatically checks device language settings like Cyrillic keyboards to avoid victims in Russia, and it actively recruits Russian-speaking affiliates and partners.[3] In other words, DarkSide's own technology ensures that neither they, nor their affiliates, attack any of the Commonwealth of Independent States friendly to Russia.

By 5:00 p.m. on May 12, Colonial Pipeline restarted most of their services and resumed basic operations. They'd waited five days from the initial ransomware demand to ensure that DarkSide had not compromised other critical systems and that Colonial had scrubbed the scourge of ransomware from its data. Nevertheless, it took many more days for the depleted fuel supply chain to deliver gasoline to thousands of stations across the United States. Despite press releases from Colonial assuring renewed operations and attempts from state governors to calm citizens, drivers panicked and hoarded gasoline.

One silver lining shook the ransomware crime world—at least for a minute. On June 7, the FBI announced that it had compromised DarkSide's Bitcoin cryptocurrency wallet and moved DarkSide's digital currency into a wallet the FBI controlled.[4] In other words, the FBI stole Colonial's ransom payment back from the thieves. DarkSide had moved the cryptocurrency through at least six digital wallets. The FBI gave chase and eventually repatriated about 63.7 Bitcoin, or $2.3 million of Colonial's money.

As for DarkSide? They went dark. The crime syndicate's destructive attack against U.S. critical infrastructure had crossed a line that brought unwanted political pressure on the Kremlin. On May 14, DarkSide sent a statement to the *New York Times* complaining that it had lost access to its public-facing systems, including a blog and payment server, and that its website would go offline within forty-eight hours. DarkSide closed its affiliate program of criminal service providers with a final message: "Stay safe and good luck."

DarkSide's high-profile attack on Colonial Pipeline might have ground their operations to a halt, but only after an extremely successful crime spree. In its first seven months as a criminal syndicate (beginning August 2020), DarkSide netted around $60 million, $46 million of that amount in the first quarter of 2021 alone.[5] Within a year, DarkSide rebranded into the now-famous ALPHV cybercrime syndicate. Having established deep roots in critical infrastructure attacks after Colonial Pipeline, recall that ALPHV would go on to target MGM hotels in the Vegas strip ransomware attack. After the FBI sought to shut them down for the second time, DarkSide/ALPHV sprouted up again to launch their coup de grâce, the attack on Change Healthcare, which decimated countless aspects of the health-care industry in the United States and affected more than 100 million patients.[6] In the pantheon of destructive critical infrastructure attacks, Colonial Pipeline is second only to Change Healthcare as the most prominent attack on critical infrastructure by a dark web cybercrime syndicate.

If you are starting to worry about getting a prescription filled at a pharmacy, flipping a switch and seeing the lights come on, or pulling up to a pump and seeing a closed sign, you are in good company. These are the things that keep me up at night. Destructive attacks on critical infrastructure are growing, and companies, regulators, and the public have not learned the lessons of the past to protect against the attacks of the future.

State-sponsored actors from countries like China, Russia, North Korea, and Iran have consistently targeted the critical infrastructure of Western countries for years. In May 2023, Chinese state-sponsored spies breached communications networks at a U.S. outpost in Guam and targeted Kenyan government ministries to gather intelligence on debt owed to Beijing.[7] In 2023, Chinese spies known as Volt Typhoon infiltrated the Littleton Electric Light and Water Departments in Massachusetts, maintaining access for over three hundred days. They breached both IT and operational technology systems, attempted to exfiltrate sensitive infrastructure data, and potentially set the stage to disrupt power and water services. Russian and Iranian hackers have also been linked to significant attacks on water systems in Texas and Pennsylvania, demonstrating their capability and intent to disrupt critical infrastructure. Where spies play the long game to prepare for future wars, cybercriminals, our new bank robbers, seek to smash and grab and escape in their dark web cryptocurrency getaway cars. Attacking critical infrastructure is incredibly dangerous because it draws the attention of global law enforcement, but it is exceptionally lucrative. And wherever you find a big payday, you'll find a cybercriminal. Especially the ones who call themselves Big Game Hunters.

* * *

Imagine sitting down at your office computer on a mundane, inconsequential Wednesday morning. It's May and the warm spring weather has you glancing out the window, already imagining a weekend of friends, family, and outdoor BBQs. Your municipal job as an emergency dispatcher for the City of Dallas's 911 system is an important one. Your responsibilities save lives, prevent crime, and literally stop fires from spreading.

As you try to boot your computer to log in to the city's dispatch system, the day leaps from inconsequential to a crisis. The system crashes to a black screen, and you attempt to shut down and restart. When your monitor finally flickers to life, you see the strange image of a white chess piece on a dark background that you recognize as the king. The word "Royal" floats beneath the image. Below that are two lines of text:

Please read carefully the "readme" file you got from us.

If you still have a problem, use our contact form.

Royal

Please read carefully the "readme" file you got from us.
If you still have a problem, use our contact form.

Go to contact form

Royal Ransomware lock screen screenshot.

You wiggle your mouse, and the cursor moves. All you can do, however, is hover over a clickable button beneath the two lines of text that say "Go to contact form." Remembering your security training, you don't click the link. Instead, you focus on the two lines of text. "What readme file?" you ask yourself. A glance around the dispatch center reveals that your colleagues have the same problem. Some are futilely mashing the keyboard or holding the power button to cold boot systems. Others are frantically on the phone with tech support. Phones continue to ring. People needing help. Without the computer-assisted dispatch system, the team starts to write down reports of emergency calls from Dallas citizens on paper.

None of the technology in the office works, until suddenly as though possessed, printers click and whirl as they come online and spit out sheets of paper. The eerie moment stills the room to silence, and you can't help thinking about the last Stephen King novel you read.

Holding your breath, you pull the single sheet of paper from the printer beside you and scan the bizarre message written across it.

Hello!

If you are reading this, it means that your system were hit by Royal Ransomware.

Please contact us via:

You frown at the next line, which is a web address, but nothing you recognize. It begins with the word "royal" and then a long string of random characters and letters in such a jumble it makes your eyes cross. At the very end, instead of the expected .com of web addresses, the long string of characters terminates with .onion.

"IT is saying to keep all these ransom notes." One of your colleagues waves his note in the air and shouts to the room.

Ransom, you think, and read on.

In the meantime, let us explain this case. It may seem complicated, but it is not!

Most likely what happened was that you decided to save some money on your security infrastructure.

Alas, as a result, your critical data was not only encrypted, but also copied from your systems on a secure server.

From there it can be published online. Then anyone on the internet from darknet criminals, ACLU journalists, Chinese government (different names for the same thing), and even your employees will be able to see your internal documentation: personal data, HR reviews, internal lawsuit complaints, financial reports, accounting, intellectual property, and more!

```
Hello!
      If you are reading this, it means that your system were hit by Royal ransomware.
      Please contact us via :
      http://royal2xthig3ou5hd7zsliqagy6yygk2cdelaxtni2fyad6dpmpxedid.onion/12345678900987654432123456789809

   In the meantime, let us explain this case.It may seem complicated, but it is not!
   Most likely what happened was that you decided to save some money on your security infrastructure.
   Alas, as a result your critical data was not only encrypted but also copied from your systems on a secure server.
   From there it can be published online.Then anyone on the internet from darknet criminals, ACLU journalists, Chinese government(different names for the same thing),
   and even your employees will be able to see your internal documentation: personal data, HR reviews, internal lawsuitsand complains, financial reports, accounting,
   intellectual property, and more!

      Fortunately we got you covered!

   Royal offers you a unique deal.For a modest royalty(got it; got it ? ) for our pentesting services we will not only provide you with an amazing risk mitigation
   service,covering you from reputational, legal, financial, regulatory, and insurance risks, but will also provide you with a security review for your systems.
   To put it simply, your files will be decrypted, your data restoredand kept confidential, and your systems will remain secure.

      Try Royal today and enter the new era of data security!
      We are looking to hearing from you soon!
```

Royal Ransomware "readme" ransomware note screenshot.

The note goes on, but you are distracted by frantic 911 calls coming in that you now must find a way to dispatch without the computer system they trained you to use. You begin calling police officers on their cell phones and field radios as though a time loop had sent you back to the 1980s. A supervisor comes by to collect the note and you put it out of your mind. The city is in crisis, and you are sitting at ground zero.

Cities shoulder a myriad of responsibilities: maintaining essential services such as electricity provision, water supply, and emergency medical services. Modern cities are driven by technology. Essentially, each municipal department is a distinct tech company, susceptible to attacks that can grind vital services to a halt. This makes cities particularly vulnerable to cyber spies and criminals.

Dallas learned this the hard way. Throughout the city on that Wednesday morning, countless city employees received similar notes and were confounded by locked computer screens. Police communications and IT systems crashed, and the Dallas County Police Department's website went offline. Anyone who tried to browse to https://dallaspolice.net received a "Secure Connection Failed" message. Dallas Fire-Rescue also had their operations impacted. Difficulties in contacting the police and fire services sent waves of concern through Dallas urbanites. The municipal court system canceled all jury trials and jury duty. The online payment system and meter-reading software for Dallas water utilities stopped working. Even the Dallas Public Library's reservation system went offline, and everyone who had borrowed books was told to keep them until the system came back online.

The City of Dallas is the ninth-largest city in the United States, with a population of around 1.3 million people. Like most cities, over forty different departments, multiple offices, and several boards support and operate Dallas. Across these many departments and offices, nearly nine hundred computer applications support approximately one hundred technology and business services. The attackers had a large menu of services, functions, and networks to choose from.

At 2:00 a.m. on Wednesday, May 2, 2023, a Big Game Hunter cybercrime syndicate named Royal Ransomware launched their attack. Just like LockBit and ALPHV, the Royal Ransomware group has somehow evaded law enforcement. Like their criminal brethren, Royal extorts victims by stealing data and threatening to publish it on their dark web message boards if the victim refuses to pay.

Royal first cut their digital teeth targeting hospitals. So much so that the U.S. Department of Health and Human Services (HHS) issued an advisory to warn hospitals to beware attacks from the ransomware group. A true royal pain to the health-care industry, Royal Ransomware infiltrated hospitals and extorted between $250,000 and $2 million depending on the size of the organization. This was all a precursor for their grandest attack to date.

It would take the City of Dallas more than five weeks to cleanse Royal from their servers and networks before it could bring all their services back online. In the aftermath of the attack, Royal exfiltrated 1.169 terabytes of data, including potentially stealing the personal information of 26,212 Texas residents and 30,253 individuals as they infiltrated finance, emergency services, human resources, and even waste management servers. It's "potentially," because in cybercrime cases, threat hunters can forensically identify what attackers accessed, but often cannot precisely predict which accessed information the criminals stole. That is, until the information appears on the dark web—and by then the house has burned to the ground.

How did Royal execute the attack against one of the most formidable U.S. cities? The Big Game Hunter cybercrime syndicate modeled the best espionage infiltration attacks. Dallas might have learned about the attack on May 3, when Royal executed malicious software they had seeded throughout the city's many networks, but the attack began nearly a month earlier. From April 7 until go time on May 3, Royal silently slipped into the City of Dallas like cloaked assassins under cover of night. They began with careful reconnaissance against the city, learning every potential avenue and doorway they could exploit to find a foothold. They found one by compromising a single service account, most likely through spear phishing or simply purchasing the username and password for the account on the dark web. The credentials for the stolen account gave Royal access to a single server. Imagine the first assassin dressing in the stolen clothes of a vegetable vendor who is allowed through the walls to sell her wares. Once inside the circle of trust, she uses this infiltration to open doors late at night when the guards are less vigilant, allowing her companions to slip in unnoticed.

In the modern era, the first point of access leads to careful analysis of network connections from the first compromised server to the next, and so on. Like a spy who has infiltrated a city and walks the streets, disguised and unnoticed, the Royal cybercriminals navigated Dallas's digital infrastructure using legitimate remote management applications. These applications (called beacons) allowed Royal to communicate back and forth with Dallas servers from the outside without triggering cybersecurity. Most importantly, it allowed the quiet exfiltration of just over a terabyte of data that the criminals could later hold hostage against the city.[8]

When printers across the city began spitting out ransom notes, the City of Dallas's cybersecurity operations center had already begun ringing an alarm. The city shut down impacted servers and isolated Royal to prevent the ransomware from spreading. Within twenty-four hours, Dallas felt confident they'd kicked Royal's assassins out of the castle, but the damage left in their wake was extraordinary. Dallas could not restore the impacted servers they took offline until teams of external cybersecurity spy hunters and their own IT staff worked round the clock to scrub away every trace of Royal. Like an infection that is not completely cleaned and leaves a mote of bacteria behind, the illness can continue to spread. For over a week, the Dallas Police 911 and 311 responses, customer service applications, municipal courts, water utilities, animal services department, the secretary's office, and development services could not use their computer applications. All this work comes at a cost. The Dallas City Council approved a budget of $8.5 million to hunt Royal, kick them out, recover from the attack, and restore servers with more resilient protections. Like many other cities and organizations that have their data exfiltrated by crafty spies and criminals, Dallas purchased expensive identify theft and fraud protection services and breach notification services to hand out to all people and business partners who potentially had their data stolen.

To add insult to injury, or perhaps a display of a morbid sense of humor, Royal baited Dallas in their final few paragraphs of the ransom note:

Fortunately we got you covered!

Royal offers you a unique deal. For a modest royalty (got it; got it?) for our pentesting services we will not only provide you with an amazing risk mitigation service, covering you from reputational, legal, financial, regulatory, and insurance risks, but will also provide you with a security review for your systems.

To put it simply, your files will be decrypted, your data restored and kept confidential, and your systems will remain secure.

Try Royal today and enter the new era of data security!

We are looking to hearing from you soon!

Of course, at the same time Royal offered their cybersecurity services, they turned the knife to get their ransom. In a post on Royal's Happy Blog website, the criminal syndicate threatened to share "tons of personal information of employees (phones, addresses, credit cards,

SSNs, passports), detailed court cases, prisoners, medical information, clients' information and thousands and thousands of governmental documents."

After the high-profile attack against Dallas in May, the FBI deployed cyber agents across the dark web to hunt Royal down. Unfortunately, they did not manage to burn out all the weeds. In November, the FBI and CISA issued a joint cybersecurity advisory that reported that since September 2022, Royal had attacked over 350 global victims and demanded more than $275 million USD in ransoms.[9] Then, to continue evading law enforcement, the Russian ransomware gang continued their digital rampage with a new moniker. On August 7, 2024, the FBI and CISA issued a follow-up joint advisory announcing the rebrand of Royal to BlackSuit.[10] According to the advisory, BlackSuit operates by first exfiltrating data and threatening extortion, then encrypting systems if ransom demands aren't met, often gaining initial access through phishing emails. After infiltrating networks, they disable antivirus software, steal large amounts of data, deploy ransomware, and use a leak site to publish stolen information from nonpaying victims. The ransom demands typically range from $1 million to $10 million in Bitcoin. The Royal of old stuffed into a shiny new black suit.

```
Good whatever time of day it is!
Your safety service did a really poor job of protecting your files against our
professionals.
Extortioner named BlackSuit has attacked your system.
As a result all your essential files were encrypted and saved at a secure
serverfor further useand publishing on the Web into the public realm.
Now we have all your files like: financial reports, intellectual property,
accounting, law actionsand complaints, personal filesand so onand so
forth.
We are able to solve this problem in one touch.
We (BlackSuit) are ready to give you an opportunity to get all the things back
if you agree to makea deal with us.
You have a chance to get rid of all possible financial, legal, insurance and
many others risks and problems for a
You can have a safety review of your systems.
All your files will be decrypted, your data will be reset, your systems will
stay in safe.
Contact us through TOR browser using the link:
```

BlackSuit ransomware note snapshot. Source: Tripwire.com

You may have noticed that cybercriminals are nothing if not vindictive. Just as ALPHV resurfaced after its FBI takedown to wreak havoc on the U.S. medical supply chain following the MGM Las Vegas attack, Royal, rebranded as BlackSuit, had its own "Empire Strikes Back" moment—this time targeting the automotive industry.

The June 2024 ransomware attack on CDK Global by BlackSuit was a seismic event, disrupting nearly fifteen thousand car dealerships across North America. CDK Global is a critical software vendor providing dealer management systems for sales, financing, and repairs. BlackSuit's ransomware brought dealership operations to a grinding halt, forcing many to revert to manual processes. The financial damage was staggering, with car dealerships collectively facing over $1 billion in losses, while customers endured delays and frustration.

The chaos rippled far beyond the dealerships. Automakers like BMW, Nissan, and Honda experienced widespread operational disruptions, and sensitive customer and business data accessed by BlackSuit raised serious security concerns. To make matters worse, phishing scams proliferated during the outage, targeting both dealerships and their customers. BlackSuit's ransom demand skyrocketed from an initial $10 million to over $50 million. Though CDK Global began restoring systems within weeks, the attack exposed the fragility of critical supply-chain software and demonstrated the catastrophic ripple effects ransomware can have across entire industries.

Whether Royal, BlackSuit, or some other name, the constant threat demonstrates the need for spy hunters who understand the myriad ways criminals compromise our data. Otherwise, we'll wake up one morning wishing we had prepared for a forced vacation to medieval times.

THINK LIKE A SPY

- Destructive attacks on critical infrastructure are growing and companies, regulators, and the public have not learned the lessons of the past to protect against the attacks of the future.

- One would think that the lessons learned by Sony in 2014 would have impressed upon the world that we must prepare for crisis situations *before the crisis*. Sadly, time and again, novel chaos events have proven that lack of preparedness often causes more damage than the crisis.

- Attacking critical infrastructure creates chaos beyond the damage caused by the cyberattack. When citizens believe their necessities and comforts are jeopardized, they will react irrationally and unpredictably. Like filling up trash bags with gasoline.

- In a cyberattack it is often what you don't know that causes the most chaos. Proving a negative, that critical systems or data were *not* compromised, is very difficult during the attack.

- Passwords alone are Achilles' heels. People often use a single password across multiple accounts. A single breach on just one account creates a single point of failure for all accounts. When people and organizations fail to turn on multifactor authentication, the password becomes the easiest failure point in security.

- Breached accounts eventually end up on the dark web, where usernames and passwords are sold in dark web marketplaces. Cybercriminals routinely bid a few dollars on a collection of usernames and passwords and then mine that information for a nugget of gold—like the log-in credentials for a company responsible for critical infrastructure.

- Cybercriminals target critical infrastructure with ransomware attacks because they know the pressure to restore systems quickly from regulators, the public, and consumers will be categorically high. This corresponds to an increased pressure on the compromised organization to pay. Cybercriminals who attack critical infrastructure call themselves Big Game Hunters.

- Modern cities are driven by technology. Essentially, each municipal department is a distinct tech company, susceptible to attacks that can grind vital services to a halt. This makes cities particularly vulnerable to cyber spies and criminals.

THIRTEEN

Destruction: Up at Night

One June evening in 2024, the sky unleashed a downpour over our tiny suburban town. Summer had encroached on spring and a riot of pollen dusted every surface like a smothering cloud of sneezes waiting to erupt. After the first rumble of thunder, Juliana and I raced to our front porch with the kids to watch the torrent fall. The lightning strikes made us jump.

A sharp crack, then light filled the sky. We squinted against a fork of lightning that struck right up our street. Juliana pointed to the top of a tree engulfed in flame. Beside it, the blackened power line coiled on the ground like a dead snake. "That's why you don't go running around outside during a lightning storm," she said to our children, claiming the teachable moment. "You never know when lightning will . . ."

The porch light flickered and died. Along the street, houses darkened as though the universe had flicked a master switch. In the time it took us to share a glance, our small bulb returned to life. I fished my phone out of my pocket and checked the Tesla application. Our home had switched to the Powerwall installed in our basement.

"Let's tell them we lost power," Juliana whispered. "We can play board games with candlelight."

With another tap, I brought up our home security system and cut the lights to our porch. We'd save our children from the toxic allure of screens for at least one evening.

The lightning storm that followed made the local news in a town that hadn't made the news since Colonial Pipeline's disaster led to arguments at the gas pump. Half the neighborhood lost power for hours while Pepco repaired the damage. Despite the white lie Juliana and I told our children, we'd only lost it for seconds.

I spent most of the miserable lockdowns of 2020 conducting research for this book. And as most of the world moved sluggishly toward a more hopeful 2021, I decided to purchase a solar generating system because I've long seen the grim writing on the wall. I did this despite the massive supply-chain problems that plagued the world, driving a high cost and low inventory of everything from lumber and nails to components, batteries, and silicon chips.

Contractors from Lumina Solar Inc. swarmed across my roof and installed twenty-five solar panels. A Tesla Powerwall—essentially a wall-sized battery—ensured that sunlight absorbed by the panels would not just power my home but provide a reserve in the event the grid failed. While deep in the pressure situation of the pandemic, I planned for the next crisis: a critical infrastructure attack launched as an act of war.

The May 2021 ransomware attack against Colonial Pipeline would later justify my overabundance of caution and large out-of-pocket costs. Attacks on global critical infrastructure are steadily increasing. Many have already plagued us. There are more to come.

The World Economic Forum Annual Meeting was held on January 18, 2023, in Davos, Switzerland. During that meeting, a great number of brilliant cybersecurity leaders made a prediction that continues to chill me. Over 93 percent of those cyber leaders and 83 percent of business leaders at the event started a doomsday prediction clock: by February 2025, a "far-reaching, catastrophic cyber event is likely."[1] This so-called catastrophic global mutating event (CGME) will most likely take the form of a large-scale, destructive attack on critical infrastructure. While February has come and gone, the near constant probe attacks, disruptions, and infiltration by state-sponsored espionage units and cybercriminals alike has me deeply concerned about a catastrophic loss of power before the end of 2026. Covering my roof with solar cells is an investment for a near future where my family may have plenty of occasions for candlelight board games.

When I mention critical infrastructure to audiences I speak to worldwide, most think of necessities like power transmission, water from the tap, and gas at the pump. The frightening reality is that threat actors have an enormous menu of critical infrastructure categories to choose from. The sixteen most critical (in alphabetical order) are: (1) chemical, (2) commercial facilities, (3) communications, (4) critical manufacturing, (5) dams, (6) defense industrial base, (7) emergency services, (8) energy, (9) financial services, (10) food and agriculture, (11) government facilities, (12) health care and public health, (13) information technology, (14) nuclear reactors, materials, and waste, (15) transportation systems, and (16) water and wastewater systems. With so many sectors to defend, and each one distinctly critical to preventing chaos and ensuring human welfare, threat actors are currently seeking to exploit, dismantle, and destroy these critical industries.

In June 2021, the IC3 began tracking ransomware attacks against all sixteen critical infrastructure sectors.[2] Ransomware attacks victimized the health-care, financial, IT, manufacturing, government, commercial, food, energy, and communications sectors more than any others that year. By the time their 2023 report rolled out, the IC3 reported that fourteen out of the sixteen critical infrastructure sectors fell victim to at least one ransomware attack.[3]

Disrupting the flow of energy has long enticed spies and criminals to invest in cyberattacks. In 2015, the Main Directorate of the General Staff of the Armed Forces of the Russian Federation (still commonly known as the Russian military intelligence group, or GRU) shut down Ukraine's power grid in the dead of winter. The Russian cyber warfare group APT44, code-named Sandworm, stole power from 250,000 Ukrainians. Then they did it again in 2016. Sandworm is most notoriously known for the 2017 NotPetya ransomware attack that hit computer systems in Ukraine and then spread destruction to computers across the globe. This ransomware, which had no decryption key, cost worldwide organizations more than $10 billion[4] and rendered nearly 100,000 computer systems inoperable across Ukraine, Russia, Europe, North America, and reaching as far as Australia.[5]

Sandworm has sought to disrupt the U.S. energy grid for years. They inserted malware on the networks of U.S. electric utilities in 2014 before their catastrophic attack on Ukraine. In May 2020, the NSA released an advisory that Sandworm had launched a sophisticated email vulnerability exploit campaign against U.S.-based organizations.[6] The specific email server vulnerability would allow an attacker to send specially crafted email to execute commands that allowed Sandworm to install programs, modify data, and create new accounts. According to the FBI, Sandworm had sought to compromise "a wide range of US-based organizations and educational institutions," including the energy sector.[7]

It is no surprise to any current or former intelligence operator that foreign services like Sandworm have successfully infiltrated U.S. industrial control systems. Why haven't the spies triggered a catastrophic shutdown? Because these probe attacks are preparing for the conflicts and wars of the future.

Energy remains the holy grail of infrastructure cyberattacks for foreign intelligence units and cybercriminals. Foreign state actors know cyber war theaters ignore borders. Kinetic military attacks require trained military forces, logistics, mobilization, travel, and extensive material resources. Just look at the trouble Russia has faced in Ukraine. Cyber warfare attacks only require planning, espionage reconnaissance, and a keyboard. Disrupting a nation's energy resources immediately throws the enemy into chaos, but the other fifteen critical infrastructure sectors are also fair game.

The October 7 terrorist attack against Israel by Iran's proxy Hamas transformed a decades-long theoretical conflict of saber rattling, skirmishes, and air strikes into a gladiatorial war. But prior to that horrendous kinetic attack, the true battle between the countries began in cyberspace. In 2010, a 500-kilobyte computer worm infiltrated over fifteen of Iran's nuclear facilities and destroyed centrifuges critical to enriching uranium for the country's nuclear weapons program.

Many speculate that the United States and Israel jointly developed and deployed the uniquely unprecedented cyberattack. In the decade that followed, Israel and Iran have fought a covert cyber war. Most recently, in April 2020, Iran allegedly struck Israeli water systems within the civilian critical infrastructure. Over a two-day period, the attack sought to compromise the control systems of numerous water and sewage facilities across the country. Fortunately, Israel's Water Authority and National Cyber Directorate stopped the attack before the water supply could be interrupted. At a CyberTech conference in Tel Aviv, Prime Minister Benjamin Netanyahu addressed the attack and stated that "Iran is attacking Israel on a daily basis. We monitor it and prevent it every day."

The same critical infrastructure mischief happened a year later in the state of Florida. Two days before the 2021 Super Bowl in Tampa Bay, an employee at Oldsmar's water-treatment facility saw his mouse moving purposefully across his screen. He ignored it, thinking that perhaps the facility's IT staff had used TeamViewer software to remotely administer his computer.

Later that afternoon, his mouse moved again. This time the employee took notice and watched as the phantom creature changed the levels of lye from 100 parts per million to 11,100 parts per million. Lye, or sodium hydroxide, is a chemical used to manage the town's potable water PH levels. I've spent time in the past two years helping my daughter with seventh- and eighth-grade science, and I can attest that even a middle schooler understands that such a high concentration of sodium hydroxide in water is dangerous to touch. Sodium hydroxide is the main ingredient in the viscous drain cleaner we use to clear those obnoxious hairballs. Imagine the catastrophic damage for Floridians who drank the water or bathed their children in it.

The threat to drinking water and the surge of stories across media raised the Oldsmar story to national attention on par with the Colonial Pipeline attack. Congressional inquiries followed, the FBI and Secret Service investigated, and the director of the Cybersecurity and Infrastructure Security Agency used the Oldsmar event to elevate a $1 billion grant program for states and localities. Testifying before the House Appropriations Committee about CISA's Fiscal Year 2023 budget, CISA Director Jen Easterly raised the specter of the attack and the importance of the grants. "I would draw your attention in particular to water," she said. "Water entities that, frankly, are very target rich—as we saw with Oldsmar in February 2021—but resource poor, and so being able to provide grant money to help them raise their cybersecurity baseline, I think, is really important."

A joint advisory from CISA, the EPA, and the Multi-State Information Security and Analysis Center found that Oldsmar used the outdated Windows 7 operating system, which Microsoft had stopped supporting. The water-treatment plant had numerous problems above and beyond a cyberattacker.

The investigation never found a culprit and, in a head-scratching cliffhanger, reversed course in later statements about the attack. *Sort of.* The FBI later stated that there was no conclusive evidence of an external cyber intrusion. In a statement to CyberScoop, the FBI reported that "through the course of the investigation the FBI was not able to confirm that this incident was initiated by a targeted cyber intrusion of Oldsmar." In FBI-speak, this means that there is something going on that the FBI does not want to reveal. Former Oldsmar city manager Al Braithwaite suggested that the incident might have been caused by an overzealous employee rather than an outside cyberattacker. Neither are willing to comment further, which makes me wonder whether the attack has national security implications or some other *for-your-eyes-only* consideration.

A similar attack took place in San Francisco a week before Oldsmar and should have put all water-treatment plants on notice. The attacker used a stolen username and password from a TeamViewer account to access the Bay Area water-treatment system, then deleted a program that the plant used to treat drinking water. Fortunately, plant operators discovered the sabotage within a day, changed passwords to kick the attacker out, and essentially got very lucky. If the water-treatment plant had used multifactor authentication, the stolen username and password would have been useless. Had the treatment center conducted good cyber hygiene and removed access for the departed employee whose credentials were stolen, I wouldn't be writing this paragraph.

Of course, an axiom I've learned about cybersecurity regulation is that things must continue to get worse before real action is taken to make them better. Since Oldsmar, the FBI has reported a slew of attempted ransomware attacks against water and wastewater systems (WWS) facilities. In March 2021, an unknown ransomware variant hit a Nevada-based facility, impacting its SCADA (Supervisory Control and Data Acquisition) and backup systems. In July 2021, ZuCaNo ransomware affected a Maine-based facility's wastewater SCADA computer, forcing operators to run the system manually until restoration. In August 2021, a California-based facility was compromised by Ghost variant ransomware, which had infiltrated the system for a month before being detected on three SCADA servers.[8] In November 2023, an Iranian group named Cyber Av3ngers hacked into a water authority northwest of Pittsburgh and took partial control of an infrastructure system that regulates water pressure. Previously, the group claimed responsibility for global attacks, including against those numerous water-treatment stations in Israel.[9]

The threats to critical infrastructure have become so dire that, in January 2022, the FBI, the CISA, and the NSA issued a joint warning against Russian cyber spies targeting the United States. Anytime those three agencies wholeheartedly agree on anything, we should take notice. According to the warning, Russian intelligence has attacked a wide range of U.S. organizations using everything from spear phishing and brute-forcing accounts to exploiting known security vulnerabilities to probe our critical infrastructure. The spies have lurked undetected in compromised networks—including cloud environments—by using legitimate credentials, most likely procured from the dark web.

Calling all bounty hunters! If you can find one of the six Russian intelligence officers behind Sandworm, you can make millions. The

The Department of State Rewards for Justice Program bounty imagined in the style of a Wild West wanted poster.

Rewards for Justice Program was established by the Department of State through the 1984 Act to Combat Terrorism. Its stated mission is to "offer rewards for information that protects American lives and furthers US national security objectives."[10] The current reward for information leading to the arrest of Sandworm is $10 million.

While Russia's Sandworm garners much of the spotlight for its brazen probe attacks on critical infrastructure, China's approach to cyberwarfare is no less chilling. According to the Department of Defense's 2023 Cyber Strategy Summary,[11] Beijing's cyber efforts are not merely preparatory—they're designed to dominate. China has embedded malicious code within critical U.S. networks, targeting everything from power grids to water supplies that support both civilian life and military operations. In January 2024, FBI director Christopher Wray testified before the U.S. Congress that Chinese cyberthreat actors have positioned themselves within U.S. critical infrastructure to "wreak havoc and cause real-world harm to American citizens and communities."[12] The FBI has been aware of China's plan for some time. Wray continued: "If or when China decides the time has come to strike, they're not focused solely on political or military targets. We can see from where they position themselves, across civilian infrastructure, that low blows aren't just a possibility in the event of a conflict. Low blows against civilians are part of China's plan."

* * *

If Russia and China weren't enough, the rise of generative AI has opened the floodgates to innovative new attacks that translate from the digital to the kinetic. In an interview with CNBC, Stuart Madnick, an MIT professor of Engineering Systems and cofounder of Cybersecurity at MIT Sloan, expressed concerns that cyber-generated physical attacks may be the next target of cybercrime.[13]

Madnick and his team have simulated attacks in their lab and proved that cyberattacks can lead to kinetic explosions. They hacked into computer systems to cause motors driving pumps to overheat, compromised temperature gauges, jammed pressure valves, and circumvented circuits to cause catastrophic equipment failures. Any of these actions by a malicious threat actor would physically take systems offline, causing far more disruption than a pure cyberattack like ransomware or DDoS.

Artificial intelligence used by cyber spies and criminals adds another frightening dimension to Madnick's concerns, and to defend against them, the best cybersecurity companies have enlisted their own AI squad. As in Disney's 1982 film *Tron*, where computer programmer Kevin Flynn is transported into a digital world where programs battle each other for control of cyberspace, today's new breed of cybersecurity professionals leverage AI to fortify defense mechanisms. Cybersecurity AI can detect, analyze, and neutralize threats in real time—all faster than a human threat hunter. By analyzing vast amounts of data and identifying patterns indicative of cyberattacks,

AI-powered defenses already play a pivotal role in safeguarding all our data. But if you like, we can pretend the AI are battling it out across an infinite arena straddling motorcycles made of light.

* * *

There is a final, furious struggle that worries me just as much as the cyberthreat to our critical infrastructure: quantum computing. For years, cybersecurity professionals have feared a quantum crime and espionage spree that could upend global societies and put all our data at risk. The strongest protection against wholesale theft and use of our most critical data is encryption. Numerous breaches, from small to mega, have stolen enormous quantities of data. Encryption continues to protect most of this stolen data and makes it useless to anyone without the secret decryption key. Quantum computing turns this protection on its head.

Encryption relies on prime numbers—those special numbers that are only divisible by themselves and one, like 2, 3, and 5. These prime numbers are used as private keys in encryption, forming the basis of the calculations that protect data. The bigger the prime number, the harder it is to break the encryption. For example, the number 15 can be broken down into 3 and 5 (3 x 5 = 15), which is simple. A grade schooler can process this in her head. But when you use much larger numbers, the math becomes incredibly complex. In fact, it once took scientists two years and hundreds of computers working together to factor a number with 232 digits.

In 1994, Peter Shor, a professor of Applied Mathematics at MIT, developed a quantum algorithm that efficiently calculates the prime factors of large numbers by using a computer with many quantum bits, or qubits. Qubits work faster than their two-state, 1/0 bit elders and theoretically could factor large numbers quickly. Fortunately, scale prevents Shor's algorithm from tearing encryption to pieces. So far, no researchers have managed to use sufficient qubits to reach quantum supremacy—defined as the point where quantum computers overtake classical ones. To achieve this, quantum engineers would require a computer with millions of qubits. Since the race to quantum supremacy began in the 1990s, researchers around the world have built stronger quantum computers. China has also invested heavily in the technology. Whoever wins on the quantum speed track will have an incredible espionage advantage.

Cyber spies have stolen encrypted data for decades in what are called "store now decrypt later" (SNDL) attacks. With the knowledge that quantum computers are no longer theoretical, but a matter of time, spy agencies have scooped up massive amounts of encrypted data from all industries. At risk are critical data from the world's banking, military, energy, biochemical, business innovation, and countless other verticals, all locked behind encryption that may soon fall to a quantum skeleton key. The dark web has taught us that information stolen by spies eventually becomes the property of criminal and terrorist groups. Moreover, if criminal syndicates get their hands on access to quantum computing, cyberattacks may become impossible to prevent.

Fortunately, the U.S. National Institute of Standards and Technology (NIST) did not wait for the quantum pressure situation to materialize before examining security. In July 2022, NIST published a list of the first-round winners in a six-year competition to determine the best algorithms to protect data from quantum decryption. Three of the four winners already worked for IBM's quantum division. IBM hired the fourth. Not to be left behind, Google jumped into the quantum game with a $50 million investment to research universities in the United States and Japan. IBM's investment soared to $100 million in 2023, demonstrating that the race to quantum is a serious undertaking.[14]

Quantinuum Ltd., a global company with headquarters in Colorado and the UK, partnered with JPMorganChase to set the new quantum supremacy record, outperforming Google's best machine by a factor of one hundred and using thirty thousand times less power.[15] This advancement underscores the rapid progress in quantum computing, focusing on building more reliable qubits. Such innovations are crucial for reaching practical quantum supremacy in the West, potentially earlier than anticipated.

Don't count China out. By 2023, the CCP upped their government investment in quantum computing to $15.3 billion. For comparison, the investments in Germany ($5.2), the United Kingdom ($4.3) and the United States ($3.8) together do not meet that level.[16] Europe is leading the development of the European Quantum Communication Infrastructure, aiming to create a secure communications network that spans the twenty-seven European Union member states and overseas territories using fiber-optic networks and satellites. The EU is nipping at the heels of China, which has already implemented a similar network between major cities, covering over four thousand kilometers. Quantum communication leverages quantum mechanics to encrypt and transmit information in a way that is nearly impossible to intercept or decode. This unparalleled level of security has made quantum communication a holy grail that every global power fervently pursues with a knight's zeal.

Russia and China might be ahead of all others. According to reports from the *South China Morning Post*, scientists from Russia and China have successfully created a quantum communication link from a ground station near Moscow to another near Urumqi in China's western Xinjiang region.[17] Using secure keys transmitted by a quantum satellite deployed by China, the allied countries transmitted two images secured by unbreakable quantum keys over 3,800 kilometers. This achievement highlights the feasibility of a highly secure quantum communication network among nations aligned with Russia and China. It also creates a future intelligence disaster for Western countries who will not be able to intercept and decode signals intelligence (SIGINT) from these rival nations.

Quantum computing is like an unstoppable golden bullet at the end of a winding maze. The first world power to perfect scalable quantum computing and communications will skyrocket in its advantage against all other nations. Here's hoping that companies like Google and IBM thread the labyrinth before a foreign threat actor or cybercriminal perfects the technology and the SNDL ticking time bomb explodes. We can only hope that mathematical geniuses on the side of the angels solve the problem before the bad guys receive the most powerful tool imaginable.

THINK LIKE A SPY

- Critical infrastructure spans many sectors that are required to live our lives safely, peacefully and with prosperity. The sixteen most critical are: (1) chemical, (2) commercial facilities, (3) communications, (4) critical manufacturing, (5) dams, (6) defense industrial base, (7) emergency services, (8) energy, (9) financial services, (10) food and agriculture, (11) government facilities, (12) health care and public health, (13) information technology, (14) nuclear reactors, materials, and waste, (15) transportation systems, and (16) water and wastewater systems.

- The Russian cyber warfare group APT44, code-named Sandworm, is a foreign threat actor responsible for critical infrastructure attacks, the NotPetya ransomware worm, and numerous vulnerability exploit campaigns against the power grids servicing Western countries.

- The U.S. Department of State Rewards for Justice program has posted a $10 million bounty for information leading to the arrest of Sandworm operatives.

- Energy remains the holy grail of infrastructure cyberattacks for foreign intelligence units and cybercriminals. Criminals who can disrupt power know they can place victims in a desperate position to pay ransoms.

- Water-treatment facilities in the United States are particularly vulnerable to cyberattack because they are seen as lucrative targets with poor cybersecurity.

- Threat actors have deployed AI to patiently probe and identify flaws in targeted operating systems, deploy countersurveillance that detects and avoids cybersecurity, and draft malicious code to launch novel attacks.

- The advent of quantum computing presents a crisis for security and a boon for espionage. Cyber spies have stolen encrypted data for decades in what are called "store now decrypt later" (SNDL) attacks. Quantum computers will have the capacity to decrypt this stolen data.

PART II

ACT LIKE A SPY HUNTER

PAID

Prepare: Preparation requires proactive measures to anticipate, detect, and neutralize threats. This includes understanding adversarial tactics, fortifying security defenses, training personnel in recognizing and responding to attacks, and continuously monitoring for potential breaches. Effective preparation occurs prior to a pressure situation caused by a breach of security.

Assess: Assessment is the ongoing process of evaluating the effectiveness of security measures and identifying potential vulnerabilities. It involves analyzing current threat landscapes, reviewing and testing existing protocols, and gathering intelligence on emerging tactics used by threat actors. Continuous assessment ensures that security strategies are updated and adapted to address new risks and changing circumstances.

Investigate: Investigation is the systematic process of identifying, tracking, and dismantling threat-actor activities. It involves conducting surveillance, collecting and analyzing evidence, and assessing potential breaches. The goal is to uncover the methods used by threat actors, rapidly neutralize attacks, and prevent the compromise of sensitive information. Effective investigation ensures that all actions are documented, legal standards are upheld, and security breaches are thoroughly addressed.

Decide: Decision requires timely and effective choices to execute security plans, especially under pressure. It requires evaluating gathered intelligence, assessing current threats, and determining the best course of action swiftly. Successful decision-making ensures that actions are taken promptly to protect sensitive information, prevent breaches, and adapt to dynamic security challenges, emphasizing a proactive stance to avoid failure.

FOURTEEN

Intro to PAID

During my time as an FBI Ghost, I hunted numerous spies—from Russian intelligence officers to rogue U.S. citizens and everything in between. Most spies are highly trained, continually cover their tracks, and deploy countersurveillance to try to spot the hunter. A single mistake can lead to devastating consequences. For that reason, careful tactics of *preparation, assessment, investigation,* and *decision* (PAID) are the prescriptive keys to successfully catching a spy. I've developed the PAID method through years of cybersecurity thought leadership and as a national security strategist, but looking back, I first formulated these tactics while running surveillance operations for the FBI.

Late one chilly afternoon, my team of Ghosts was tasked to trail a known Russian intelligence officer (IO) from his embassy in Washington, D.C., to a densely wooded national park in northern Virginia. Sources had indicated a potential meet between the IO and an unknown subject (UNSUB). The FBI was keen to identify the unknown subject and determine whether the contact was an American mole. Our surveillance began with *preparation*. The target would drive from Washington, D.C., to Virginia, but would then proceed on foot to the potential meet. I was chosen to jump out into the park after the IO. My teammate was code named Covergirl. Ghosts do not choose their code names; they are chosen for us by our squad mates. I got Werewolf because of an incident at the FBI Academy when I howled at a full moon. Covergirl could probably have modeled if she hadn't become an FBI Ghost. We decided that we would trail the IO hand in hand, playing the role of a couple out for a Saturday hike.

Thus prepared, we *assessed* the who and what of the target. Huddled in the squad room, we scrutinized recent photos and committed to memory height, weight, face, and even discussed asymmetrical characteristics like gait and walking speed. We pored over maps to determine the most likely trail through the park to the best meeting points. A critical precept of any successful spy hunt is never to go into any situation blind.

The *investigation* resulted in me and Covergirl following the IO along a windswept trail through a forest of mostly leafless trees. Occasionally, an evergreen would block sightlines with canopies of pine needles, but for the most part, our only cover was to sell the fiction that we were a couple. The meet took place in a crumbling amphitheater at the center of the park—precisely where our analysis had predicted they would find each other. People moved through the area—enough to provide me cover, but we needed to *decide* quickly how to proceed. Most operations fail because of lack of decisive action. The best spy hunters know to prepare, analyze, conduct the investigation, and then act quickly to win the day.

We carried forward our romantic fiction. Covergirl posed on the old steps while I pretended to take pictures of her. In reality, I captured the target and UNSUB on film as they came together, shook hands, and spoke quietly. When they turned toward us, Covergirl impulsively kissed me—acting without hesitation to sell her undercover role. Her decisive action led the IO to turn back to his UNSUB with a shrug, already disregarding us. The pictures we later developed allowed us to identify the UNSUB. The rest is classified.

In a shell game, the dealer tricks the unwary by promising a cash reward if they can guess under which cup a ball is hidden. In truth, the ball is palmed, it never makes it under the cup, and the dealer deceives his mark. Savvy people know the trick and walk away without playing. To think like spy hunters, we must see the shell game in every interaction online—even the ones we instinctively trust. In cybersecurity, trust must be earned.

FBI trainees spend a lot of time in the classroom learning practical disciplines required to become law enforcement officers, but most of the training takes place in the field, either through practical exercises or ghosting actual targets (mostly ones that won't shoot you over a mistake). In that way, investigative training is like Miyagi-Do Karate from the eponymous movie *The Karate Kid*. You learn by doing and—suddenly, almost magically—you understand.

Believe it or not, just as Daniel-San learned a precise chop block from waxing Mr. Miyagi's car and an up-block from sanding his fence, DI^{2}CED has taught you to recognize threats and understand when you must switch your mind from archaeologist to spy hunter. Part 1 of this book taught you to block the cyberattack before it hits your face. Part 2 focuses on *how* to strike back.

The PAID methodology is a loop. You must prepare before the attack by intrinsically understanding what data you must protect, where that information resides, and who has access to it. Knowing this will allow you to build an incident response plan that layers protection around your most critical data. Because no plan survives first contact with the enemy, you must constantly assess your security, particularly when circumstances change. This assessment allows you to apply the counterintelligence skills you learned from DI^{2}CED to situations that may be scams or cyberattacks. Once you identify a potential attack or breach, investigation kicks in to rapidly hunt the threat and neutralize it before the cybercriminal escapes with your data. Finally, the courage and aptitude to make rapid decisions, often under pressure, round out the four-step methodology. Once you've survived a cyberattack (and hopefully thrived), you must revise and strengthen your plan with lessons learned from sparring with a cybercriminal.

As you dive into the next four chapters, remember that the PAID methodology applies to everything from global enterprises with thousands of networked systems and endpoints to a single person with a laptop. The only difference is scale. PAID is a road map for security officers and information technology security professionals. It's also a powerful tool you must use to examine your security before the pressure situation of a cyberattack throws your life into crisis.

Dark web cybercriminals must win to survive. They only get paid when they successfully breach a company or infiltrate and exploit your most important information. To stop them, we must not only know all the ways they attack, but we must fight back and make our data work for us, not against us. Counterintelligence agents call this operational control.

The FBI taught me to understand the techniques, tactics, and behaviors of the adversary and to hunt those threats wherever they tried to hide. Now it's time to teach you how to attack.

FIFTEEN

Prepare

When Ben called me early on a Saturday morning, I was comforted by the fact that the NGO had a plan to execute. Our checklist included calling the insurance company and data privacy attorneys, hiring a cybersecurity company (and having them on retainer) to investigate and remediate the breach, and ultimately telling every employee to close their laptops and walk away. Ben and I updated the board of directors and executive team at regular intervals. We switched our internal communication from Microsoft Teams to closed groups in Slack, Signal, and WhatsApp. Ben organized a fleet of global IT professionals from his personal cell phone.

My cybersecurity work with the NGO began shortly after a European regulation concerning data protection created a massive headache for every global organization that did business in the European Union. That regulation, called the General Data Protection Regulation or GDPR, might have saved the NGO from LockBit's ransomware attack. In May 2018, the GDPR sought to harmonize data privacy laws across Europe. It also required any company, wherever domiciled, to invest in reasonable cybersecurity policies and technology and establish systems for data control. The EU wanted to make certain that anyone with access to their citizens' data took steps to protect it.

I worked with the NGO and its attorneys to make the global organization GDPR-compliant. Fortunately, employees like Ben and David understood that the cost of a cyberattack far outweighed the investment in cybersecurity. They used the regulatory requirements of the GDPR (the NGO had programs in EU member countries) to wrangle budget from the tight-fisted board. A plan started to come together.

The NGO's investment in a cybersecurity policy was a key component of our response.

The best cybersecurity policies are tailored to the specific complexities, work, and size of an organization and outlines steps to safeguard against and respond to cyberthreats. An insurance company will require minimum IT and cybersecurity standards before coverage. For many organizations, meeting these standards serves as a vital framework for building internal policies that control access to critical systems, respond with incident plans, manage IT inventory, enforce strong password management, and execute other aspects of data protection. An effective policy not only reduces the potential for catastrophic cyberattacks, but it also helps when auditors and regulators come knocking; properly documented policies can lower an organization's rates in cyber insurance coverage.

The NGO's plan saved the organization, short and simple. Without it, Ben and Jill would not have identified the ransomware early on, before the attack spread beyond containment. Without that plan, the NGO would not have had a checklist of who to call and when. Two weeks could have resulted in two months of compromised and broken systems, exorbitant ransom payments, and loss of confidence from donors and partners who are the lifeblood of charitable work. Instead, we shut down for two weeks, continued to communicate through alternative channels, restored critical systems from verified backups, installed cybersecurity that chased LockBit from the NGO's systems, and ultimately told the attacker to take a long walk off a short pier.

Context Is Key

When Colonial Pipeline learned of their ransomware attack just before 5:00 a.m. on that Friday morning, they ceased all operations.

In the initial hour, when they identified DarkSide's ransomware, Colonial could not determine whether the attack had compromised IT systems or had spread to operational systems that might pose a physical threat to the pipeline. Colonial followed their plan and, out of an abundance of caution, shut everything down. Similarly, when LockBit compromised the NGO with ransomware and Ben called me that Saturday morning, we also shut everything down. Like Colonial, the NGO did not have the cybersecurity architecture to immediately determine which of the global IT systems and networks LockBit had compromised.

Cybercriminals know that lack of context is standard across many industries. Every protection plan against cyberattacks begins from the ground up. The best cybersecurity is intrinsic. Intrinsic security integrates security measures and principles into the design, development, and operation of data systems and networks. Most organizations make the mistake of adding security as an afterthought. This is like painting over a wall that might suffer from mold or rot. You've covered up the problem but never rooted out the weakness. Security must be built into every infrastructure layer, from hardware to software and processes to training.

In earlier chapters, we've discussed endpoint detection and response and likened it to a muscled bouncer at the door of the exclusive club where one's critical data holds court. The best cybersecurity today extends this protection to all the hallways and corners of that club. It contextually understands every connection between rooms and lounges, catwalks, and even that small window in the bathroom. It constantly monitors who has entered the club, who they're talking to, and who they try to leave with. When someone not on your exclusive list is found chatting up someone who shouldn't be anywhere on the premises, an alert is raised, and that person is ejected.

This heightened level of security is called extended detection and response (XDR). XDR uses machine learning and AI telemetry, provided in real time from subscriptions to cloud-based servers, to watch for anomalies in your data across numerous security layers including endpoints, firewalls, networks, email, servers, and user accounts.

Subscribing to threat intelligence services is crucial for staying informed about the latest cybersecurity threats.

Context and intrinsic security provide the following benefits to companies that build security into their infrastructure (we'll get back to the individual soon):

1. **PROACTIVE DEFENSE:** Cybersecurity continually addresses security at every level, reducing flaws and vulnerabilities that limit the attack surface for attackers. This zero trust principle trusts no entity (inside or outside) that seeks to access data networks by default. Instead, *every* access request must be verified, even for those within the circle of trust. You never know when you might have a spy in your midst.

2. **EARLY DETECTION:** Continuous monitoring and automated responses detect threats before they can cause significant damage.

3. **CONTEXTUAL INFORMATION:** Machine learning and cybersecurity AI provide a deeper understanding of potential threats, allowing for more accurate identification of attacks and faster responses.

4. **EFFICIENT RESPONSE:** Security teams can respond rapidly to threats, mitigating potential damage.

5. **ADAPTIVE SECURITY:** Systems with intrinsic security and contextual awareness can adapt to evolving and unknown threats, ensuring robust protection.

For organizations, building context into cybersecurity requires time and investment, but the payoff is worth the cost. Cybercriminals continue to increase their sophistication, reach, and scale of attacks. Failures by law enforcement to arrest criminals have made them more aggressive, and criminals who do not fear consequences are dangerous. It is therefore up to every organization to protect itself from cyberattacks. This applies to individuals as well. The only difference is scale.

Context gives threat hunters the edge they need by answering three essential questions: what, where, and who. It starts with understanding *what* matters most. Think of your critical data as the crown jewels. *What* information, if lost or compromised, would cause the most damage? Identifying it is the first step, because you can't protect what you don't recognize as valuable. *Where* is your most critical information stored? Picture this like mapping out a vault system. A thorough audit helps you locate your sensitive data, segment it, and lock it away in the inner sanctum—accessible only to a select, trusted few. The more isolated and protected it is, the harder it is for attackers to crack the safe. Finally, every great detective knows that the key to solving a case is figuring out *who* has access and who might be a risk. Segment your data so that the most sensitive information is accessible only to a small group of trusted individuals, with the highest level of security layered around it. In the FBI, we called this information *compartmentalization*. Only those with a "need to know" are granted access to the most top-secret information. This process is where the James Bond term "for your eyes only" comes from. In the world of cybersecurity, we call this process "access control" and the principle is called "least privilege."

The same road map applies to individuals who own a single laptop, a tablet, and a phone. Where is your most important data stored? Is it on the laptop hard drive or on cloud servers like Microsoft OneDrive, Apple iCloud, Google Docs, or Dropbox? Who has access to that data? Do you share your password with your family and friends? Or have you compartmentalized the data to just you and perhaps your partner or spouse? Like any secret ever whispered, the more people who know a thing, the easier it is lost.

The effort needed for everyone from a freelance graphic designer with a single laptop to a global multinational organization to establish intrinsic security depends on scale. A single person can organize data on a laptop with folders protected by a reliable cybersecurity application. I recommend vendors who use cloud-based updates, scan emails for threats, provide ransomware protection for critical files, and offer secure backups in case of a breach. An organization will require far more complex processes, procedures, and controls, with IT staff and external cybersecurity consultants. Ultimately, intrinsic security understands data the way a chemist understands molecular structures, or a mechanic understands an engine down to every nut and bolt. Knowing how things fit together allows a spy hunter to identify when information is compromised, changed, or accessed without authorization. Cybersecurity cannot passively wait for an attack to land; it must constantly hunt the threats that are hunting all of us. But you must also personally hunt threats. DI²CED showed us that cybercrime runs on an engine of deception. Preparation is a people problem.

The Password Is Not Enough

Use strong passwords that you do not repeat across accounts. But don't passively trust them. We've already discussed how most of our usernames and passwords are already for sale on the dark web. Attackers know that most people use the same password for everything, from our business and bank accounts to the rewards program at our local ice cream store. In mega breaches, all the usernames and passwords for account holders are dumped into dark web bargain bins. Bottom-feeder cybercriminals buy these in bulk and then try usernames and passwords on every potential log-in after spending a little time learning about their targets through social media reconnaissance. Worse, as computational power grows, AI has become masterful at guessing or cracking even the most complex passwords.

In July 2024, just as I was finishing a draft of this book, a data dump called RockYou2024 exposed nearly ten billion passwords—9,948,575,739 to be exact—making it one of the largest password compilation leaks in history. This dump included passwords gathered from previous leaks and breaches, significantly increasing the risk of cyberattacks for millions of users worldwide. Most of your passwords are likely in there. If you've ever wondered why suddenly there are new playlists on your Spotify account or new additions to your Netflix My List queue, someone may have compromised your account by scooping up your overused password from the dark web, cracking it with a fast computer, or simply guessing it by learning about you from social media.

Password manager solutions like Bitwarden and 1Password (*Wired* rated them among the best) can help ease the burden of ensuring unique, complex passwords for every account. While they take time to learn and manage, they are worth their weight in gold against cyberattacks. My best friend, Mike, also uses his password manager as contingency planning in the event the worst happens. His wife, Viv, has access to the master password for his password manager account (memorized, not written down), and they share access to the global application that opens the password door. If aliens suddenly abduct Mike and take him away to a distant galaxy, never to return, Viv won't have to guess passwords to critical accounts and websites while she mourns her kidnapped soul mate.

The best way to ensure that no one guesses or compromises your password is not to rely solely on the password. Enable two-factor authentication (2FA) or multifactor authentication (MFA) for everything from that ice cream shop rewards program to your 401(k) retirement account; 2FA or MFA adds a second layer of security to your account. After entering the password, you will be prompted to enter a secure code that comes to you through a second trusted source. These might include a text to your personal cell phone, an authenticator application on your phone, a code sent to a separate email account, or even a physical USB key that you insert into your laptop. I prefer the authenticator application. Each code is generated as a one-use code and changes every thirty seconds, and I can configure the app to work the way I wish. If you are curious, the compromised VPN accounts on the Ukrainian control systems from chapter 3 relied on just a username and password for security. Relying on a password alone is like protecting a doorway with plastic wrap. With a little effort, the attacker can walk right through.

I predict we will soon escape the flawed sense of security passwords impress upon us. Many organizations have already dumped passwords entirely for cloud-based single sign-on (SSO) applications that allow one tap on an application sitting on your phone to connect to secure data networks. Another technology already changing how we access data is biometric authentication. Many of us already encounter this when we peer at our phones to unlock them. These security solutions might verify through a face scan, fingerprint, or even full palm scanning like something out of *Mission: Impossible*.

Tech companies are also evolving away from the password to protect individuals and consumers like me and you. In September 2021, operating system powerhouse Microsoft announced an option to eject the password. Microsoft Outlook, OneDrive, Family Safety, and Xbox users can abandon passwords for the Microsoft Authenticator app, a security key, or a verification code. If you have a camera on your computer, you can log in using Windows Hello, which conducts a biometric face scan. All these authentication techniques are superior to a simple typed password entry.

In April 2025, Microsoft upped the ante on their password elimination goal by rolling out a new sign-in and account-creation process that centers around passkeys. A passkey is a secure, password-free log-in method that uses cryptographic authentication, typically tied to your device or biometric data—like unlocking your phone with your face or fingerprint—making it far harder for hackers to steal or reuse. Microsoft's move comes in response to a surge in password-related attacks—which reached seven thousand per second in the first quarter of 2025—as traditional passwords increasingly fail against AI-driven phishing and sophisticated hacks.

Apple innovated to passkeys in 2022, one step ahead of Microsoft and after Apple pioneered Face ID in 2017. When Face ID debuted, reports trickled in of children who opened their parents' phones by fooling the software. You might recall the story of a six-year-old in Arkansas who opened her mother's phone by pressing her sleeping finger against the home button. While her mother dreamed, little Ashlyn bought $250 of virtual Pokémon. When my wife and I upgraded years after Apple further secured the technology, we let each of our children try to unlock our phones, just to be certain (they couldn't). According to Apple, the probability that a random person could use Face ID to unlock another person's iPhone or iPad is less than 1 in 1,000,000. With each update, they make this less plausible.

LockBit took advantage of the NGO's overreliance on passwords when they attacked. LockBit exploited a vulnerability in a third-party help desk server to steal Jill's username and password. If the help desk server had 2FA enabled, the attacker might never have been able to demand a ransom. Similarly, if Colonial Pipeline had enabled 2FA for the vendor account that DarkSide used to gain access, people on the East Coast wouldn't have filled trash bags with gasoline. Turning on 2FA or using passkeys for your accounts is the most important step you can take to protect your data from attackers.

Email Is Security's Achilles' Heel

Your junk mail is a no-man's-land of scams, phishing emails, clickbait, and other garbage that lies in wait on the desperate hope you click. Unfortunately, junk mail filters are imperfect, and a trickle of coercive emails sneak into our inboxes. The more deadly concern is spear phishing emails that evade the best filters. Without careful diligence and good cybersecurity software tools, the unwary might click on a link or open an attachment that opens the door to an attacker. If data is the currency of our lives, email is the attacker's lockpick.

Some time ago, I began to segment my email boxes based on an importance hierarchy. The decision to do this began out of necessity. I have seven separate email accounts (I literally had to count), each with its distinct purpose. Each of my businesses (three) has a separate email account that I check through one unified application. The account reserved for public speaking shares an application with my iCloud account—which is only used for Apple-related information. I use a Gmail account to correspond with friends and family; my Hotmail account, the oldest I maintain, is used for every sort of registration and subscription. I am diligent not to use my name or refer to myself in any way on this account, and I use a single application just for this account. While this might sound paranoid, my multiple email boxes are a system of information compartmentalization. My three business accounts are only used for business. I can check the iCloud account when I need to monitor my children's use of Screen Time and authorize applications on their Apple devices. A single account organizes all requests for me to speak and converse with my agents. My Gmail account keeps me up to date with friends and family. Finally, my Hotmail account takes a bullet for the rest because I use Hotmail for subscriptions, and registrations, spam, phishing emails, and every sort of scam plagues that inbox. I never click on a link or open an attachment in my heroic Hotmail account.

Remember that thinking like a spy hunter requires you to practice email archaeology. Verify the spelling of web addresses and email addresses that may seek to imitate friends, family, work colleagues, or legitimate companies. Sometimes attackers will spoof emails by changing letters that might escape everything but forensic scrutiny. One of the most common is to replace a small *l* with a capital *I* (e.g., O'Nei*ll* instead of O'Nei*ll*). It is better to be pleasantly surprised to find a safe email than to be caught unaware.

Have a Backup Plan

After LockBit compromised the NGO's HQ server and hundreds of laptops with ransomware, our incident response plan contemplated restoring operations from secure backups. The NGO's servers backed up daily to an encrypted cloud service that LockBit couldn't access. Restoring from a recent backup seemed straightforward, but without knowing the exact timing of the attack, we risked restoring infected data. Thus Ben, David, Jill, and I, along with a team of outside cybersecurity experts, had to determine when the attack started to restore from a clean, preattack backup.

There are countless backup systems and vendors available to aid in this. The most effective includes ransomware protection and secures backups to offsite facilities that encrypt your data and prevent the attacker from altering your backup. Many organizations and individuals that relied only on backups built into their operating systems paid exorbitant ransoms when the only way to restore their data was to purchase it from their attacker. I use a combination of cloud-based backups for all my critical files, as well as a weekly backup of my entire laptop drive to physical hard drives. I keep one physical backup at my house, and another safely hidden at a friend's. That way, if my house ever catches fire again (God forbid), I'll know my data remains safe and secure.

Don't Overshare on Social Media

Juan and his family have weekly Zoom conferences. His sister lives in Denver with her new husband and family. His younger brother just began university in Mexico City, and their parents and extended family live in Chile. Juan works a stressful job as an accountant in Los Angeles and looks forward to the weekly meetups that they started during the COVID lockdowns. Seeing the faces of his growing family brought him the joy needed to muddle through each week.

During a Zoom call, his sister Isabella pasted a link in the chat with the comment "check out these pics." Everyone in the family clicked the link except Juan's abuela, who didn't know how to open the chat function. Everyone but Abuela had their identity compromised. A cybercriminal group had surveilled Isabella's public Facebook account and had noticed the post on her wall sending the Zoom link to her family group. The comment had not come from Isabella, but from impostors using the screen name "Isabel1a"—replacing an *l* with a numeral one (1). Juan's family could have protected themselves by preparing for this common Zoom-bomb attack by password-protecting the Zoom conference and ensuring that their social media accounts were set to private.

MGM Resorts International succumbed to a $100 million ransomware attack because an impostor fooled a help desk professional into resetting an employee's username, password, and 2FA to an account the attackers controlled. Scattered Spider learned all the details they needed for the con by surveilling social media. When the attacker posing as Jonathan scammed Mary into sending him tens of thousands of dollars in romance fraud, he first learned all about her through Facebook. When Jennifer DeStefano received a frantic phone call from her fifteen-year-old daughter, Brie, screaming that she had been kidnapped, the attackers that deepfaked Brie mined their information from social media.

Social media is a goldmine of information for attackers. Limit what you post and who you share your information with. Make your social media accounts private and never share critical personal information such as your address, vacation plans, or your children's ages publicly.* Once you've locked down your social media account, ensure that 2FA is turned on for every one of them. Usernames and passwords for social media are sold on the dark web for pennies.

The Cybersecurity and Infrastructure Security Agency publishes a wealth of how-to information about cybersecurity in their *Secure Our World* blog. One of my favorites is CISA's post titled: "Protect Our World with MFA."** CISA's three easy steps to turn on MFA apply generally to most applications, and every person should follow them:

1. Go to "settings" in your application. It may be called Account Settings, Settings & Privacy, or similar.

2. Look for and turn on MFA. It may be called two-factor authentication, two-step authentication, or similar.

3. Confirm MFA is turned on. Select which MFA method to use from the options provided by each account or app. Examples CISA gives are:

---

* For more information on how to set your privacy settings in social media applications, see my Ten Tips to Prevent Your Social Media Applications from Disclosing Private Information, available in The Spy Hunter Tool Kit on page 276.

◊   Receiving a numeric code by text or email

◊   Using an authenticator app: These phone apps generate a new code every thirty seconds. Use this code to complete logging in.

◊   Using biometrics: This uses our facial recognition or fingerprints to confirm our identities.

As a public figure, I frequently post to accounts on X, Instagram, LinkedIn, and YouTube and to my weekly newsletter on Beehiiv. I treat each of these public accounts as tools that enhance my brand and get the word out to readers like you that we need to make the world safe from cyberattacks. I am cautious about what I post and when I post it. For example, I often post information and pictures from my speaking events, but typically after the event is done and when I'm already home. Criminals will reconnoiter social media to determine the best time to launch attacks, usually when the target is out of pocket and unable to identify or respond to the attack. If I were a cybercriminal, I'd attack a public speaker just after he posted "I'm taking off on my flight to Vegas to speak at BlackHat," knowing that he'd likely be off the internet for a few hours in the air. Similarly, if I wanted to rob your home, I'd do so after you posted a picture of your beautiful family smiling at the airport on your way to a two-week beach trip. Assume that anything you post online can be used against you. If you must post about your plans, do so when you are home after the vacation and only to private groups in your social network. Take care when posting private moments into the public arena.

Don't Trust Your Lying Eyes (or Ears)

When a scammer posing as Ferrari's CEO, Benedetto Vigna, tried to con a top Ferrari executive using a sophisticated AI deepfake voice clone, the exec didn't panic—he went full detective. The scammer reportedly asked, "Hey, did you hear about the big acquisition we're planning? I could need your help." Trusting his cop instinct, the executive played along just long enough to spring a trap: a personal question only the real CEO would know. The question? What book had the CEO recently recommended to the exec—an obscure title the impostor couldn't fake. The scammer flubbed it and hung up, foiling what turned out to be a plot to push Ferrari into a phony financial deal. Thanks to one sharp executive and a simple two-factor authentication question, Ferrari dodged both a multimillion-euro loss and a major PR disaster.

Have a plan for deepfakes. To recap, deepfakes include AI-generated synthetic media that manipulate images, videos, or audio to create hyperrealistic but deceptive content. When the financial officer in Hong Kong logged on to his virtual conference system and saw his CFO there, he immediately trusted his eyes. When Jennifer DeStefano heard Brie crying over the phone, she recognized her daughter's voice. We are trained to believe our senses, but deepfakes turn trust upside down. In a new era where deepfakes will hound us at every cyber turn, we must establish systems to verify what we see and hear. The financial officer could have immediately called the CFO's office to verify the transactions before sending wires totaling $25 million. Jennifer could have asked her daughter for a code word. The Ferrari exec challenged the fake CEO with a book title.

When I worked counterterrorism with the FBI, we established code phrases known only to our closest family members and locked them in a sealed envelope with our squad. If kidnapped, we would need to verify the code phrase before the FBI would believe the terrorist on the other end of the phone. We called this a "sign of life."

I have a sign of life with my family, a code phrase that we have all memorized and can ask if I ever receive a call from one of my children claiming to be kidnapped. I've also established a phrase with my business partners in the event one of them makes an odd request on a Teams or Zoom meeting. In a future where 90 percent of the internet will be synthetically generated and we cannot readily trust what we see and hear, thinking like a spy and acting like a counterintelligence agent can save you from a cyberattack.

Protect Your Children from Exploitation

Recall the story of Jordan DeMay chatting with a girl named Dani Robertts on Instagram, and how he couldn't have known that the cute girl was a puppet Instagram account controlled by criminal brothers in Nigeria. Jordan couldn't have imagined that he'd ultimately take his own life after the criminals extorted, bullied, and shamed him.

Halima confronted a similar extortion, when criminals stole intimate photos from her phone and published them on the dark web. She immediately involved her cousin, who called me. Tom and I were able to spelunk into the dark web and, in explaining how difficult the pictures were to access, relieved Halima of her panic.

Both stories are similar in that Jordan and Halima each felt deep shame over nude pictures that the attackers threatened to expose. I'm eternally grateful that Halima contacted me. Tom and I walked her through a process that helped her feel protected and safe at a time when her world had unraveled. I wish that Jordan and so many others like him who are preyed upon by exploitative cybercriminals also had someone to reach out to.

Parents and guardians should talk to their children about social media account scams and attacks like the one that cost Jordan DeMay his life, devastated Halima's, and horrified Audrey when she looked at faked nude pictures of herself over an eighth-grade classmate's shoulder. In our household, Juliana and I practice "phone at fourteen" and allow limited social media at twelve. Children do not need to be on social media until they are mature enough to understand that 99 percent of what we see on social media is misstated, untrue, parody, or downright harmful. Juliana and I resisted social media until our children turned twelve and we routinely discuss the pitfalls and dangers with them. Cyberbullying is a crisis, and unfortunately, most children do not reach out to their parents for help. Reinforce with children and teenagers that look up to you that if they are in a situation like the one confronting Jordan, Halima, or Audrey, they should come to you immediately—and that there will be no judgment, only love. Read chapter 11 with your children and discuss it together. Let them know that you are there for them and will help them through.

Finally, monitor your children's use of AI. Make certain that your children know how to create and dream on their own without using AI to do most of the work. Give them a blank page. They will thank you for it one day.

ACT LIKE A SPY HUNTER

- Develop a cybersecurity plan before the pressure situation places you or your organization into a crisis.

- One resource that organizations can rely on to improve preparedness before and resilience from active cyberattacks is the National Institute of Standards and Technology (NIST) Cybersecurity Framework. NIST's approach is organized into five key functions: identify, protect, detect, respond, and recover. This comprehensive approach to deploying cybersecurity can be scaled to organizations of any size and complexity through handy guides and documentation, all free on NIST.gov.[2]

- Invest in cybersecurity insurance that is tailored to your organization to mitigate financial losses when a cyberattack occurs.

- Ask what, where, and who for all your sensitive data:

    ◊ Know **what** your most critical data is (define it).

    ◊ Know **where** your most critical data is (compartmentalize it). Begin with an audit of your data. Segment your data so that the most sensitive information is accessible only to a small group of trusted individuals, with the highest level of security layered around it.

◊ Know **who** has access to your critical data (privilege it). Limit administrative privileges to only a few trusted users who genuinely need access and have a "need to know." This is called the *principle of least privilege*.

- Layer security around that data (protect it). Invest in cybersecurity tools that include robust firewalls, Next-Generation Anti-Virus (NGAV) software, virtual private networks (VPNs), data loss prevention (DLP), and critically important, but often overlooked, two-factor/multifactor authentication (2FA/MFA) systems.

- Understand your data with intrinsic security and context. Intrinsic security integrates security measures and principles into the design, development, and operation of data systems and networks. The best cybersecurity is called extended detection and response (XDR) and leverages the principle of zero trust. XDR uses machine learning and AI telemetry, provided in real time from cloud-based servers, to watch for anomalies in your data across numerous security layers including endpoints, firewalls, networks, email, servers, and user accounts.

- Have a backup plan. Routinely back up your data to secure locations like cloud-based third-party solutions or a physical drive you store in a safe place.

- Do not rely on passwords alone to protect your data. Two-factor authentication methods like passkeys, biometrics, text and email codes, and authentication applications and devices are the most critical parts of a plan to protect your important accounts and applications from cyberattacks.

- Establish a plan to identify and discard phishing emails. Invest in cybersecurity that scans emails and attachments and quarantines malicious messages.

- Segment your email boxes into different applications with a hierarchy of trust. Do not use critical email accounts for personal communications or online registrations.

- Think like an email archaeologist. Scrutinize emails from a zero-trust mentality.

- Have a plan for deepfakes. Establish a "sign of life" code phrase with your family and friends to prevent deepfake fraud and extortion. As an example, my family uses the first line from a favorite poem. Use a code word that will be easily remembered and instantly recognizable to your family.

- Be smart with the use of social media. Lock down all your social media accounts to private. Share posts only with close friends. If possible, post pictures and plans for vacations *after* you come home. Criminals who know that you will be gone and where you are going can use this information to develop impersonation attacks or physically rob your home while you are away.

- Protect your children from exploitation. Talk to them about social media account scams and establish routine checks of their accounts to ensure they are not hiding exploitation or bullying from you. Encourage your teenagers to read chapter 11.

SIXTEEN

Assess

Early at the FBI Academy, my squad was called to an "emergency" surveillance that involved tracking a "rabbit" (our term for the primary target) to a potential meet. The meticulously organized practical exercise involved highly skilled FBI operatives who took pride in ensuring that newcomers failed. Alternatively, we rookies were desperate to show the veterans up.

The game of spy vs. spy began with vehicular surveillance. I drew the short straw and trudged to the surveillance van, a blocky white monstrosity that stood out like a sore thumb from a mile away. This meant I'd wait at the periphery of the surveillance, apart from the exciting maneuvers to change the *eye* on the target and keep him in *pocket* until he *landed* (i.e., parked) somewhere.

When our rabbit finally stopped his Machiavellian surveillance detection run and parked in the first row of a supermarket parking lot, dusk had settled around us. I didn't have to worry about my quarry spotting the van—which we called Moby Dick—as it trundled into the small parking lot. When our rabbit parked his Ford Explorer and paused to watch rearview and side mirrors to see who followed, *I was already there*. Forced to stay on the outside of the surveillance, I had decided to stay ahead of the rabbit wherever possible and practice positioning my behemoth at choke points where I predicted he might land.

My assessment paid off.

When the rabbit exited his car, hiked up his pants, and spared a not-so-subtle glance around before walking toward the supermarket, I was ready. A video camera on a tripod recorded his slow walk toward the brick facade. Through the same broadside window, I furiously clicked through rolls of film on my FBI-issued Nikon N90s telephoto camera. The tinted window made lighting my target difficult, but it also protected me from his occasional glances toward the parking lot behind him.

Snap. I captured his face in profile.

Snap. I caught him approaching an ancient pay telephone hanging off the brick wall. A lamp above his head spotlit him and allowed me to push my camera to maximum zoom.

"He's making a telephone call," a member of my team said through the field radio.

Another one said, "That's an operational act, right?"

"Looks that way," the first responded with a little less confidence.

I ignored them and focused on my photography training: Extend the zoom. Open the aperture and reduce the shutter speed to bring more light to the sensor. Focus on the target and, above all else, hold the hands steady! Deep breath in, release half of it, hold and . . .

Snap. Rabbit continued his phone call. Was it just a phone call?

Snap. Rabbit glanced down. No way we followed him for eight hours to catch him making a phone call we couldn't listen to.

Snap. What's that with his right hand?

Zoom. *Snap. Snap. Snap.* Can't tell but he was hanging up the phone.

I keyed my radio. "Werewolf to team, target is moving. Repeat, target is on the move . . ."

My skepticism paid off. The phone call was a cover to hide his ulterior purpose, a *dead drop* of information taped under the pay phone. My naked eyes hadn't seen it, nor did the running video camera, but my careful photography had won the day.

The next morning, when our squad of trainees collected for our classroom debrief, we learned the hard truth of skepticism. "Trust not what you see," the instructor lectured. "Spies bury the evidence you need behind sleight of hand, mundane actions, and your false sense of confidence." He glared at us. "Question. Everything."

Then he held up a single photo that showed a close-up of the rabbit's hand, palming a business card stuck against a piece of duct tape. I had zoomed in enough to just make out the name on the business card. Points for Gryffindor.

FBI undercover operatives are always checking their security. In counterintelligence, it's essential to regularly assess how well security measures are working and to spot any weaknesses. Ongoing assessment ensures that the security plan you carefully designed remains effective over time.

This is where many organizations and individuals fail. A cybersecurity plan cannot be set and forget. In the same way that one must routinely patch and update their software to prevent vulnerabilities and flaws from leading to cyberattacks, you must constantly assess changes in your security environment and rework your plan.

Organizational Assessment Strategies

In a society built on connections through data, we are only as strong as the neighbor with whom we share information. Every outside network that connects to our data presents a weakness that an attacker can exploit. Adding new systems, technology, software, or cloud services may expose your data networks to outside attacks. Regular assessment ensures that these new technologies are securely configured and integrated into the intrinsic security framework. No man is a digital island unto himself.

Days before LockBit attacked the NGO, Jill struggled to patch a known vulnerability in the help desk server managed by a third-party company. In spirit, her assessment of the NGO's cybersecurity was on point, but in practice, the delay in patching opened the door to a Russian cybercrime syndicate.

Organizational restructuring like mergers and acquisitions or changes in critical internal personnel can introduce new networks, IT systems, and potential vulnerabilities. Recall that UnitedHealth Group acquired Change Healthcare in October 2022 for $8 billion, only a short time before ALPHV attacked Change Healthcare and launched the most damaging critical infrastructure ransomware attack in history. In response, UnitedHealth sought to update and improve Change Healthcare's antiquated systems, including ensuring that multifactor authentication protected access to core data. On May 1, 2024, UnitedHealth's CEO Andrew Witty testified before the House Energy and Commerce Committee Subcommittee on Oversight and Investigations.[1] In his testimony, Witty stated:

> We're continuing to investigate as to exactly why MFA was not on that particular service. It clearly was not. I can tell you I'm as frustrated as you are about having discovered that as we've gone back and figured out how this situation occurred.
>
> Change Healthcare was a relatively older company with older technologies, which we had been working to upgrade since the acquisition. For some reason, which we continue to investigate, this particular server did not have MFA on it.

Colonial Pipeline had prepared for a cyberattack and invested in excellent cybersecurity, but fatally missed a critical step in assessment. A former employee's VPN account remained undeleted after their departure. DarkSide infiltrated Colonial's system using the VPN account by obtaining the password from the dark web. The absence of multifactor authentication further exacerbated the vulnerability. When employees leave, or vendors and consultants are no longer contracted, remove their accounts and access. When outside parties are granted access to your data, monitor that access and ensure that their standards for cybersecurity are as robust as yours.

Assessments should be conducted whenever new staff are hired or existing employees gain more access. Major changes—like layoffs, new hires, or allowing remote work—require a fresh look at security. The zero-trust approach means verifying everything. Think of it as using careful checks to build trust. These checks are especially important in today's hybrid work environment, where remote work has distanced employees from their companies. Remote work expands the potential for security breaches, making it necessary to review access controls and endpoint security.

A venture capital client brought what looked like a routine diligence investigation to me and my partner at The Georgetown Group. They had acquired a company in the fashion industry that had grown meteorically from startup to Fifth Avenue player in only a few years. The VC group wanted the company in their portfolio, but they first requested an assessment of the C-suite. Most of the value in the company came from the visionaries at the top, and my client wanted to ensure a bad apple didn't spoil the bunch.

We dialed up our competitive intelligence apparatus and investigated the company's three founders. The CEO and COO checked out, with a few speeding tickets between them and a list of eye-rolling social media posts we advised taking down. Our report on the CFO was less sanguine. We identified serious gambling debt that he'd hoped to recover through the purchase of the company. Countless trips to Vegas and Atlantic City on the company dime resulted in a deeper hole that sought to swallow him. Had the VC client brought him over as part of the deal, his debt and addiction could have presented a vulnerability to the company's bottom line, reputation, and growth potential. A small amount of critical assessment at a key decision point by the venture capital group might have saved it from years of buried financial problems.

Whenever new laws or industry regulations change the compliance landscape, assess and revise your security policies and practices. Failure to comply with regulations and required standards can lead to penalties, increased risk, and arguments with your insurer about coverage after an attack. When the European Union issued the European General Data Protection Regulation, it forced the NGO to assess its cybersecurity to comply with the regulation. A good thing too! Had the GDPR not forced their hand, the board of directors may not have allocated sufficient budget to prepare the NGO for LockBit's ransomware attack.

The digital island principle also applies on the personal level. Next time you're on your cell phone, ask yourself these questions: How many pictures do I have stored on my phone? Are there private pictures of friends and family that I do not want shared? Are there ones of myself in embarrassing situations that I wouldn't want seen by my employer or grandmother? If the answer to these questions is a resounding yes, check the privacy settings on all your social media applications to see if your social media accounts have access to your full photo library. By granting access to a third party, you've potentially compromised all your photos. When we grant any third party access to our data, we are trusting data to an organization we do not control. Halima learned this the hard way when attackers compromised her phone through a Snapchat attack and stole her entire photo reel. If Halima had blocked her social media applications full access to the Photos application on her iPhone, the private photos Halima had shared with her boyfriend would not be for sale on a Russian server with the label "sexy teen pictures."

Don't Expose Your Data

Don't leave your sensitive data lying around for others to stumble across. If you, say, leave the VRBO you rented for a getaway weekend, log out of Netflix and other accounts you may have logged in to to watch your favorite shows in another person's home. And take care when using unknown wi-fi hotspots, especially free hotel wi-fi, as you might accidentally log in to an "evil twin" network. Always deploy personal VPNs to hide your identity when accessing public wi-fi at Starbucks or places like your local library, airports, or even on airplanes. Personal VPNs like those offered by ExpressVPN or NordVPN are simple applications that you install on your phone or laptop and activate whenever you require an extra layer of security. When choosing a VPN, ensure that the company does not log your activity. Verify the VPN provider's privacy policy for a clear "no-logs" commitment, ensure that it is independently audited and avoids storing data on hard drives, and prioritize VPN providers based in jurisdictions with strong privacy laws.

If you receive a prompt to log in using your personal email or social media accounts, that's a clue you may have inadvertently connected to an evil twin. If a cybercriminal living next door to a Starbucks set up his own wi-fi router and set the service set identifier (SSID) to "Starbucks Guest Wi-Fi," the store's patrons might unknowingly log onto the criminal's evil twin wi-fi router, thus handing over their information. I recall a case in which an Australian man was arrested for setting up evil twin wi-fi networks at airports and on flights to steal sensitive data from unsuspecting passengers. He mimicked legitimate networks, prompting users to log in with personal credentials, which he then harvested to access their accounts. To avoid falling victim to these attacks, manually forget public networks from your device after using them. This prevents your device from automatically reconnecting to rogue networks impersonating legitimate ones in the future.

If you're using public devices, like hotel room televisions or shared computers, always log out of private accounts like email or Amazon after use. Leaving your account logged in creates an open invitation for the next user to access your personal information, change your settings, or even misuse your account. Think of it like leaving your front door wide open—better safe than sorry.

Constantly Assess and Revise Security

During his remarks at the National Defense Executive Reserve Conference in November 1957, President Dwight D. Eisenhower remarked, "Plans are worthless, but planning is everything."[2] The thirty-fourth president went on to explain that emergencies are unexpected and will not always happen the way you planned. Eisenhower was prescient, but perhaps former heavyweight boxing champion Mike Tyson stated it better: "Everyone has a plan until they get punched in the mouth." Tyson had made that remark to a reporter who asked whether he was concerned that his fight plan would not account for his opponent, Evander Holyfield. Tyson lost that fight despite Vegas betting odds of 15:2 in his favor. Maybe Tyson should have reassessed his plan.

In cybersecurity, a key method to reassess security is to conduct vulnerability assessments and penetration testing. Organizations routinely hire threat hunters like my dark web spelunker pal, Tom, to play the role of cybercriminals and seek to breach their security. This can expose hidden flaws and vulnerabilities that allow you to shore up weaknesses in your plan. Organizations that survive cyberattacks typically come out the other side more secure.

Patch and Update Systems

Everyone from the largest Fortune 500 company to a retired grandparent or a teenager with their first phone can immediately assess and improve security by patching systems. Large organizations may rely on services that scan and triage the most critical vulnerabilities and list them in a patch hierarchy. You and I can personally spend a few minutes every week updating applications on our phones, tablets, and computers and ensuring that our operating systems and cybersecurity software are up to snuff. Wherever possible, I set my systems to automatically update, including my internet of things (IOT) devices like thermostats and home security cameras and the wi-fi routers in my home. Some may be skeptical of this approach, particularly after, in July 2024, cybersecurity company CrowdStrike issued a flawed update that crashed 8.5 million computers running the Windows operating system and cost Fortune 500 companies alone more than $5 billion in direct losses.[3] But, in general, it is always better to patch quickly. The NGO learned this lesson the hard way, and Change Healthcare even harder. Keep critical systems updated and reduce the attack surface for cybercriminals.

Prevent Malicious Applications

Paul founded Tres Ríos, a vacation rental company that helps exhausted workers find their perfect vacation. As the CEO and sole proprietor, he ran the entire company from his brand-new, top-of-the-line laptop he had purchased from the first year's profits. One morning, Paul's clients began to call and email him frantically. Apparently, he'd spent the weekend emailing them links to "The Most Amazing Rental Opportunity." Everyone who clicked on the link was asked to place a refundable deposit on a future half-price rental using their credit card. Within moments, fraudulent charges abounded. My team investigated and learned that every Friday and Saturday night, Paul's son Raul snuck out of bed and played Fortnite on his dad's high-performing laptop. Raul had installed the free game and had also installed a special browser that a friend told him would generate free in-game currency so Raul could buy new flashy outfits for his character. The malicious browser connected to the cybercriminals who had created it and seeded it within game forums popular with teenagers. Paul could have protected himself by installing robust cybersecurity on his laptop that prevented application installation without a password. That way, any time his son tried to install something, Paul would receive a notification and could look into his son's late-night gaming habits.

In your corner of the world, make sure to implement an application control process to prevent downloading and installing applications that are unverified and potentially malicious. Look for unauthorized applications and connections to your data. Robert Hanssen was famously caught installing a keylogger on an FBI computer system. When he was caught, he argued that he needed the password to install a new printer. For some reason, the FBI bought this sad excuse. Had they questioned his actions more critically and assessed the sudden breach of security accurately, they might've stopped the most damaging spy in its history years before I was sent undercover to catch him.

Don't experiment with your sensitive data. Always install your applications from application stores like Apple and Google Play that verify and monitor for malware. Be cautious, however because criminals have occasionally infiltrated even these stores. Only install applications that you need and trust. A threat researcher like Tom will use a clean laptop to test applications before trusting them. With two teenagers and an aspiring middle-grade hacker in my family, I've restricted the installation of any application on any of our computers and handheld devices without my approval. This allows me to assess whether I'm willing to allow a new application into our secure environment.

If It Appears Too Good to Be True, Don't Trust It!

When Jonathan reached out to Mary on Facebook, the first blush of romance, her loneliness, and confirmation bias made her want to believe in her connection with a handsome stranger. Had she read this book, Mary would have known to reserve her heart until she discovered she could trust Jonathan. Assessing the situation would have led Mary to conduct diligence before she sent Jonathan a single dollar.

I can't blame Mary, because I nearly succumbed to a similar situation. I wasn't seduced by a person, but by the promise of professional recognition—and the confirmation bias that made me believe I'd cross visiting Cape Town off my bucket list. I should have paused my excitement for a moment to assess the situation. Numerous clues would have led me to diligence and investigation before I shelled out $10,000 for a first-class ticket. When the Hillsong pastor first reached out to me, I should have scrutinized the email closely and questioned why an established organization had reached out to me with a Gmail address. I also should have noted that the letter they sent offering to fly me to South Africa to speak had an incorrect signature. I should have thought like a spy hunter and questioned whether I could trust the email in my inbox.

Similarly, had Edward read this book before he received a seemingly innocuous text simply saying "Hello?" he would have deleted it immediately and never spoken to Karthi. The cybercriminal would never have stolen Edward's pension and ruined his afternoon tea. The silver lining for Edward is that the crisis made him pack up and join his daughter in America, penniless in fortune, but happy in family. I like to imagine that Edward would have made it to his daughter's home in America regardless of the cyberattack. I'm an optimist about such things.

Life is filled with offers and scams that promise something for nothing. A great rule of thumb for cybersecurity as well as personal security is to verify first and trust later. When you suddenly think you've won the lottery, or a prince from another country chose *you* to inherit his fortune, step back, take a breath, and assess the situation. Ask yourself, "Is this too good to be true?" If the answer is "yes," you now know what to do.

Your plan provides the framework and tools to lay the foundation for cybersecurity. Routine assessment enhances and revises the plan as circumstances change, but also places you in the right state of mind to spot cybercriminals before their attack succeeds. Now that you know how to think like a Spy Hunter, it's time to teach you to act like one. A careful plan and knowing assessment will help you spot the scam, but the real work of a spy hunter relies on investigation.

ACT LIKE A SPY HUNTER

- None of us live on a digital island. In a connected society, our security depends on our information-sharing neighbors. Every new system or technology can be a potential vulnerability, requiring regular assessments to ensure secure integration.

- Organizational changes like mergers, acquisitions, or personnel shifts can introduce new vulnerabilities. Regularly reassess security during such transitions to identify and mitigate risks.

- Remove access for departing employees, vendors, and consultants promptly. Monitor third-party access to ensure their cybersecurity standards match yours.

- Significant staff changes or new hires necessitate security assessments, especially with remote work increasing the attack surface. Adopt a zero-trust approach to verify all access diligently.

- Update security policies and practices to comply with new regulations and industry standards. Noncompliance can lead to penalties and increased risk.

- Conduct regular vulnerability assessments and penetration testing to uncover hidden flaws. Employ threat hunters to simulate attacks and strengthen defenses. Schedule regular security audits conducted by external experts. Always document the security audit process and results.

- Personal digital security is crucial; ensure privacy settings on social media do not compromise sensitive data. Trusting third parties with your data requires vigilance over their security practices.

- Avoid logging into evil twin wi-fi hotspots by skipping free wi-fi networks that require email or social media credentials to log in, always use a VPN to encrypt your data and secure your connection, disable file sharing to prevent unauthorized access to your device, and manually forget public networks after use to avoid automatic reconnections.

- Patch systems regularly to keep them updated and reduce the attack surface. This applies to everyone, from large enterprises to individual users.

- Implement application control processes to prevent unverified and potentially malicious downloads. Use trusted app stores like Apple and Google Play for installations.

- Assess whether an attacker has compromised your username and password. Discover whether they appear in known data breaches using resources like HaveIBeenPwned.

- Be skeptical of offers that seem too good to be true. Verify first and trust later to avoid scams. This mindset will enhance both your cyber and personal security.

SEVENTEEN

Investigate

Now that your curiosity is piqued, it's time to step into the area and act the part of a spy hunter. This is where investigation becomes crucial. The counterintelligence art of investigation involves systematically identifying, tracking, and dismantling threat-actor activities through surveillance, evidence collection, and breach assessment.

Your work as an investigator begins once you assess that there is a problem. Then you must switch to actively verifying whether your instincts are correct. When online, imagine yourself standing in the center of a minefield where flashy signs everywhere are coercing and influencing your steps. If the World Economic Forum's top researchers are correct, recall that before, the majority (90 percent) of the internet will be synthetically generated by artificial intelligence in just a few years. It will take an investigator to sift the truth from all the lies. Verify everything. In cybersecurity, a little suspicion goes a long way.

Act Like a Spy Hunter

When Hillsong reached out to me to perform a keynote in Cape Town, my assessment came almost too late, but fortunately, my suspicions triggered just in time. I should have assessed right away that the offer was too good to be true and moved directly into investigation. My training as an investigator should have then carried me past the surge of excitement that led to confirmation bias. I didn't need my previous FBI training to ultimately investigate: Google Hillsong, go to the contact page on their website, and call the church directly. For the cost of a long-distance phone call, I could've immediately uncovered the scam. There were plenty of clues that I blindly ignored. The email failed to use the correct domain for the official communication. Hillsong owns the Hillsong.com domain. An official email would end in hillsong.com. The emails I received came from a Gmail address. A small thing to investigate that could have saved me hours of wasted time.

Poor Edward might have taken a step back from his burgeoning friendship with Karthi to call Bergstromm & Billings. An hour of investigation would have discovered that the company did not exist. Perhaps Edward might have insisted that Karthi join him for one of his afternoon teas before investing his pension with Karthi's finance company. Countless excuses would have delayed a meeting that the cybercriminal had no intention of attending. Had Edward insisted on a face-to-face before investing his money, Karthi could never have pig butchered him.

When the finance employee for a Hong Kong multinational corporation received an email from the chief financial officer inviting him to a video conference, the employee had no reason to deny his boss's request. But when the CFO began emailing the employee to send more than a dozen wires to various bank accounts, the employee should have investigated. One call to the London branch would have exposed the elaborate deepfake confidence scheme. That simple act of diligence would have saved his company $25 million in stolen funds.

Similarly, when Guillaume proposed that Camille install a new payment application, she should have followed her first instinct—the one that tickles our belly when we identify that something is off or wrong—and called her supervisor. I call this the cop instinct. Law-enforcement officers develop these spider senses through hours of working crime scenes. You have already developed this defense against cyberattacks by studying part 1 of this book. Cybersecurity turns the old saying *It's better to ask forgiveness later than ask permission* upside down. It's better to ask permission now than experience the unforgivable later.

Beware Impostors

Business email compromise, the most basic impostor attack, is a $55 billion-per-year crime.[1] Victims have reported BEC scams to the FBI IC3 from all 50 states and 177 countries, with over 140 countries receiving fraudulent wire transfers. This massive increase in crime is partially due to difficulties in transforming the global workforce into a hybrid-first environment and living through the most incredible expansion and adoption of internet communication technology in Earth's history. Thinking like an investigator is the only way to stop the avalanche of stolen funds from storming into dark web war chests. Scrutinize emails for every flaw. Establish second and third levels of verification, especially for every financial transaction. Train employees at every level. Set in stone that executives will never request odd transactions outside the normal company policies. Reach out directly to friends who contact you through email or social media to send wires or invest in strange business schemes.

Establish other communication channels with everyone important to you. My family knows that if I ever ask them to send money, I will use a particular "sign of life" code phrase. Businesses should require a phone call or even a video conference plus a digital signature for every requested transaction over a certain amount. Think like a spy. These signs of life have protected undercover agents for centuries.

Finally, monitor what you and your family share on social media and public websites. Cybercriminals will research and take advantage of vacation details for executives, promotions, recruiting, and especially organizational charts. They will launch attacks against families when the person they seek to impostor is traveling and unable to answer a phone call. They want to learn not only who to target, but when. If I wanted to attack your company, I would use resources like LinkedIn and the company website to learn the names of the CEO, CFO, and everyone in the finance department. I would then seek to compromise the executives' accounts and send emails to all finance employees demanding wire transfers when the executive is on vacation or traveling and cannot readily respond to verify the email. I'd even impersonate the CEO with a deepfake phone call or video conference with the employee to enhance the deceit.

I developed this personal checklist, with some great advice from the FBI's IC3, to avoid impostor scams that plague my email inboxes:

- Cease all contact immediately with someone you suspect might be an impostor. Scammers often use emotional manipulation to extract more information or money.

- Document the incident. Keep records of all communications, including emails, text messages, or any other interactions. Take screenshots if necessary.

- Never send a wire payment to someone you do not know. Most wire payments cannot be reversed and cybercriminals will immediately move money into dark web cryptocurrency where it cannot be repatriated.

- Report the scam:

    ◊ To the website or platform where the scam occurred (e.g., social media, e-commerce sites).

    ◊ To your bank or credit card company. If financial information was shared or money was sent, contact these institutions immediately to stop payments and potentially reverse transactions.

    ◊ To your local police department, especially if money has been lost.

◊ To the Federal Trade Commission (FTC) at reportfraud.ftc.gov. For identity theft concerns, visit identitytheft.gov.

◊ To the FBI's Internet Crime Complaint Center (IC3) at ic3.gov, if the scam involved cybercrime.

- Require business transactions to use registered company email accounts. Be suspicious of emails that come from free, web-based accounts like Gmail, Yahoo, or Outlook.

- Turn on two-factor authentication and additional verification techniques EVERYWHERE. The best email impostor attacks rely on first compromising an account. Passwords alone will not protect you from cyberattacks. Without something stronger, email accounts are easy to compromise.

- Monitor social media and public websites for shared details about vacations, promotions, or organizational charts. Cybercriminals exploit this information to launch targeted attacks, especially during travel or executive absences.

- Be wary of requests that are "highly confidential" or require immediate action. Impostors pair their deceit with pressure situations to convince the target to act quickly before they have a moment to think about what they've been asked to do.

- Eye any sudden changes in business practices with suspicion. If your policies require two digital signatures using encrypted processes (for example, Adobe Sign) before processing a wire transfer, a sudden request from the CEO in a Teams chat to wire $1 million to Nigeria should turn that cop instinct tickling your stomach into a one-hundred-foot drop on a roller coaster.

- If you date online, do so with an eye toward investigation. Investigate and verify before trusting your heart with an online romance. Conduct diligence research on your potential paramour's social media accounts. Accounts with minimal information or lacking history may clue you in to a scam. Conduct a reverse image search to determine whether pictures of your crush are stolen from other sites or are deepfakes.

    ◊ Right click and "copy" an image from a social media account or one the person sent you in an email or chat.

    ◊ Point your browser to https://images.google.com and paste the image.

    ◊ Google will identify any websites that host the image online.

    ◊ If you see the image among similar pictures on a different social media account or from stock photo websites, you have successfully investigated and identified a scam.

- To spot deepfakes, I fight fire with fire—AI versus AI. My go-to tool for detecting synthetically generated images is Winston AI, a Montreal-based company founded in 2022 that builds AI-powered content detection tools for businesses.

    ◊ Point your browser to https://app.gowinston.ai/image-detection and sign up for a free account. Save the picture you want analyzed in a folder on your computer.

◊ Drop the picture in Winston AI's chat function and ask the AI to investigate the picture and determine whether the image was created by AI.

◊ As a test, I dropped the picture ChatGPT 4.0 generated of Jonathan from chapter 8 into Winston AI's deepfake detector.

◊ Winston AI's synthetic image detector returned a result stating that Jonathan's image was 80 percent AI and 20 percent human.

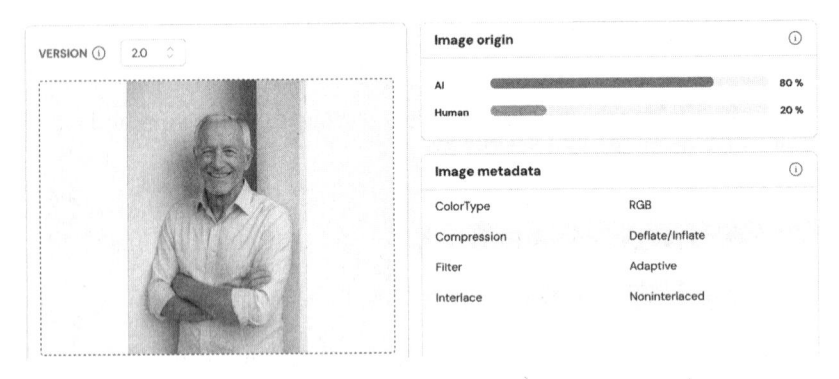

Winston AI's synthetic image detector result snapshot.

◊ Be cautious with AI detection tools. Hyperrealistic synthetic media—images, video, voice—is advancing so fast it's outrunning many deepfake detectors. Case in point: I asked ChatGPT's own deepfake detector if its AI-generated image of "Jonathan" was fake. It confidently told me Jonathan was a real human. Nice try, ChatGPT!

◊ Finally, always ask to meet potential impostors in person. A criminal will never arrive at a set meeting and risk arrest. Instead, they will offer countless excuses for why they abruptly missed the meeting.

The Parent Spy Hunter

A question for all parents reading this: If an unfamiliar car driven by an unidentified person arrived at your home and your teenage son or daughter dashed outside to jump in, would you stop them? Of course you would (assuming you're a good parent). Yet, letting your children use social media unsupervised is essentially allowing them into countless cars with strangers. Just as you'd scrutinize someone appearing at your doorstep, you need to carefully examine the risks in online interactions. It may be tedious, but it's necessary work.

Even better, teach your child to think critically and spot potential dangers online. Build trust with them so they feel comfortable discussing any concerning online situations with you. Parents who are present with their children may get exasperated eye rolls, but inaction may lead to bullying, exploitation, and even self-harm and suicide.

Here is a checklist to investigate potential criminal online interactions with your children on social media:

- Monitor your child's online activity. Just as you enforce curfews or decide whether your teen can attend a party or social event, make judgment calls on what they can do online and who they can communicate with. Use parental control software to track internet usage. I use Apple's Screen Time with my family. To reduce the time we all spend online, every Sunday we determine who has the biggest screen time. The loser cleans the downstairs bathroom.

- Educate yourself and your children. Learn about the social media platforms your children prefer and understand their features. Stay informed about current online threats and tactics used by predators. Assume that your children will find workarounds for all your social media controls. Inform them of all the risks so that they know to make healthy decisions for themselves online. Establish trust so that your children will report any suspicious interactions with you.

- Regularly check your children's browser history and social media accounts. My wife and I require that our kids provide us with their cell-phone passcodes, and we will continue this until they are eighteen. We use enforcement policies to prevent the deletion of browser history and conduct spot checks on our kids' phones. I can't tell you how many times we have had the "as long as you live under this roof, and we are paying for your phone" conversation.

- Know who your children are communicating with. Just as you know the names of your son's or daughter's closest friends, check their connections on social media. Investigate to look for adults you do not know communicating directly with them or suspicious profiles among their contacts. Look for inappropriate language, requests for personal information, or attempts to meet in person. These might all be signs that an adult is grooming your child.

- Investigate red flags. Children who are victims of online exploitation, abuse, or grooming may seek to hide the information from you. Keep an eye out for secretive behavior around devices. Scrutinize their bank accounts for unexplained increases in funds. Look for sudden gifts like jewelry, games, or items your child cannot afford. Finally, watch for sudden changes in mood or behavior related to online activity.

- Preserve forensic evidence. Save screenshots of concerning online interactions or chats. Keep records of dates, times, and usernames of those you think may be online predators or criminals. Such records can assist law enforcement.

Monitoring is important but cannot solve all potential dangers. Building trust with your child so they feel comfortable discussing online experiences with you is most important of all. Balance investigation with respect for your child's privacy as appropriate for their age. An informed child is their own best investigator when it comes to online threats.

Know When to Seek Help

When LockBit attacked the NGO, Ben and I rapidly assessed the situation and decided we needed assistance from a top cybersecurity incident response team. In other words, we knew we didn't have the capabilities or the resources to handle it ourselves. We consulted our cyber insurance provider and hired the team they suggested. Without support from outside consultants with expertise in investigating and remediating cybercrime, Ben, Jill, and I would not have had the capacity to discover the critical *how*, *when*, and *where* of LockBit's attack before the criminals spread throughout the network. We couldn't have shrunk the attack surface around them faster than they could compromise our network without outside help.

Large, sophisticated companies like Colonial Pipeline, Kaseya, and SolarWinds invested in incident response consultants to stop attacks from spreading, identify the attackers, and prevent future such attacks from compromising their data. The City of Dallas, with all its resources and budget, brought in outside help to contain the attack by Royal Ransomware. Individuals must do the same, albeit on a smaller scale. When Halima lost her photos to a criminal extortion gang, she came to me and Tom for help. So did Angelo when criminals stole his identity to open bank accounts to move stolen funds to drop accounts on the dark web. Knowing when to investigate does not require a degree in cybersecurity. It only demands attention to detail, a quick eye to spot a criminal attack before it causes untold damage, and the willingness to seek immediate help.

ACT LIKE A SPY HUNTER

- Use DI^{2}CED to recognize threats and understand when you must switch your mind from threat hunter to investigator. Think like a spy. Act like a spy hunter.

- When online, develop a trust-nothing mindset. Verify everything. A little suspicion goes a long way to keeping your data safe.

- Assess every situation that appears too good to be true. If you have any concerns, begin an investigation. Cybersecurity turns the old saying "it's better to ask forgiveness than permission" upside down. It's better to ask permission first than experience the unforgivable later.

- Investigate potential impostor attacks. Thoroughly examine emails for any errors or suspicious elements. Implement multiple layers of verification, particularly for financial transactions. Provide comprehensive training to all employees across the organization. Firmly establish that executives will not request unusual transactions that deviate from standard company procedures. Use a sign-of-life code phrase with friends and family members to verify their identities online.

- Monitor what is shared on social media and public websites. Criminals will use your social media as reconnaissance to learn about you and your family and time their attacks.

- Identify romance fraud by researching the social media account of your new online friend. Conduct a reverse image search to determine whether pictures they send are stolen from other sites or are purchased from stock photos.

- Use AI to fight AI deepfakes. Ask robust AI from reputable companies to scan images and identify whether a photo sent to you was created by generative AI.

- Supervise your child's use of social media to protect them from online bullying, exploitation, and extortion attacks. Build trust with your children so they feel comfortable bringing concerning online situations to you.

- Investigate red flags in your children's online activity. Watch for secretive activity related to devices and accounts, scrutinize bank accounts for unexplained funds, look for sudden gifts your child cannot afford, and watch for sudden changes in mood or behavior related to online activity.

- Preserve forensic evidence like screenshots of online interactions and chats.

- When your investigation uncovers an attack, seek help.

EIGHTEEN

Decide

Before I walked into room 9930 at FBI Headquarters to start my undercover investigation of Robert Hanssen, I made the critical decision to accept the case, despite knowing that it would disrupt my life, strain my marriage, and place me in a hellscape of potential danger. Each day of mental sparring with the spy demanded split-second decisions. How to respond, how to act, what to show on my face—any mistake on my part might have led to disaster. If Hanssen confirmed his suspicions that the FBI had placed him under investigation—that room 9930 was an elaborate mousetrap—he might have turned and run, possibly after shooting me.

The biggest decision I made during the case stepped outside the plan the FBI had drawn for me. Hanssen never left his briefcase behind. Whenever he left the office, even for a moment, he brought it with him. Until one afternoon when Hanssen left to visit former colleagues at the Department of State. I glanced into his office and saw the briefcase beside his desk.

My marching orders were clear: Do not search his office, ever. As my dad used to say, "Full stop. Period. End of discussion." I stared at the bag and made a decision that changed everything about the most critical investigation the FBI had ever run. I ghosted into the room, kneeled down, and searched the bag.

The decision paid off. I found a data card, a current passport, financial statements, and a cell phone I'd never seen before. In moments I called in a forensic search team. With Hanssen oblivious, the team copied the data and photographed the rest. I'd later read letters printed from the data card that Hanssen had written to the Russians years before as his alter ego Ramon Garcia. It was the first moment in an investigation full of struggles when we knew, definitively, that Robert Hanssen, FBI Supervisory Special Agent, was the Russian spy we had hunted for decades. My decision to change the plan led to the first major break in the case. One that led to an elated team of agents rapidly assessing and revising the focus of the investigation going forward.

Counterintelligence decisions are always inflection points. They require the rapid assessment of situations, preferably with a period of investigation, but come in small windows that pass quickly. Wait on a counterintelligence decision and the moment passes, the spy escapes, the terrorist sets his bomb, secrets and lives are lost. Careful planning sets the course toward decisions with the best outcomes, but plans change in the moment. Decisions of any merit require courage backed by knowledge.

Colonial Pipeline exuded this when they shut down operations and ceased the transmission of petrol from the West Coast to the East Coast of the United States. Early in the morning, when a ransomware note was discovered on a control room screen, the control room supervisor executed a plan the company had put into place. The supervisor executed stop work authority and shut down operations. Imagine making one decision that would impact millions of people. In that moment, it was the right one. An attack on a fuel pipeline could harm employees, communities surrounding the pipeline, or the environment, each of which could lead to disastrous outcomes. Without knowing the extent of the attack or whether a foreign country was behind it, Colonial made the command decision to shut everything down to give them time to assess, investigate, and decide on a new plan.

To Pay or Not to Pay, That Is the Question

Colonial Pipeline had a second difficult decision to make—whether to pay the $4.5 million ransom to DarkSide and restore operations quickly or continue to remediate the problem and absorb the operational costs for each day the company shut down. To make matters worse, the reputational harm from an angry public standing in line at the gas pump continued to grow, adding pressure to the decision.

Joe Blount, CEO of Colonial Pipeline, described the decision as one that weighed many factors, but ultimately relied on what best served the interests of the United States.[1]

> You don't want to pay the ransom. You don't want to encourage [hackers], you don't want to pay these contemptible criminals. But our job and our duty is to the American public. So when you know that you have one hundred million gallons of gasoline and diesel fuels and jet fuels that are going to go across the Southeastern and Eastern Seaboard of the United States, it's a very critical decision to make. And if owning that de-encryption tool gets you there quicker, then it's the decision that had to be made. And I did make that decision that day. It was the right decision to make for the country.

In contrast, the FBI has adamantly argued that a victim should not pay a ransom. Paying a ransom funds cybercrime syndicates that rely on ransomware income to grow operations, pay affiliates, and manage infrastructure. It also incentivizes and encourages individuals to choose a life of cybercrime. Because criminal syndicates like DarkSide, LockBit, and Royal Ransomware are business enterprises that want future victims to pay, cybercrime syndicates are incentivized to provide decryption keys after receiving the ransom. If you strongly suspected that a ransomware attacker would not hand over decryption keys after you paid the extortion amount, would you ever pay?

Less sophisticated and organized criminal gangs are not so structured or professional. Affiliates may piggyback on the name of a large syndicate, but then disappear with the ransom payment without providing a decryption key. Some criminal gangs and solo attackers might collect payments and disappear out of spite. There is no honor among thieves.

When I counsel victims faced with the decision to pay, I mention the FBI's stance on the matter but don't draw a hard line. The decision to pay is always a personal one and relies on numerous factors, including the sophistication of the attack, whether data was stolen, whether a secure backup exists, the possible reputational harm, and the ease of restoring from backup.

Colonial Pipeline weighed these factors and decided that paying the $4.5 million was better for U.S. citizens in crisis than weeks of restoration, remediation, and cybersecurity threat response. The company had to accomplish that work regardless of the transaction for a decryption key, but operations still ran while the hard work happened behind the scenes.

On the other hand, CNA Financial Corp. chose to pay a $40 million ransom to Phoenix after the cybercrime syndicate compromised fifteen thousand systems with ransomware and encrypted large swaths of company data. They decided this despite spending two weeks restoring customer service and internal email between employees and deploying endpoint detection and multifactor authentication throughout CNA's endpoints to chase the attackers out of their systems. When CNA decided to pay Phoenix, just weeks after Colonial Pipeline made the same decision, the $40 million payment was one of the largest in history.

When REvil infiltrated JBS Foods with a disruptive ransomware attack, JBS paid an $11 million ransom despite having a secure backup. The FBI argued against paying the ransom, but obligations to customers and employees, the cost of rebuilding systems from backup, and the daily loss of business, which exceeded the ransom payment for a single day, informed JBS Food's difficult decision to pay.[2]

Conversely, the NGO had limited options. As a government contractor, the Treasury Department Office of Foreign Assets Control regulations prohibited the NGO from paying LockBit, an entity on the Specially Designated Nationals (SDN) List, commonly known as the terrorism watch list. Paying a ransom would have required a waiver from Treasury. As a government contracts attorney and former government official, I knew restoring from backups and enduring a two-week shutdown would probably take less time than procuring a government waiver.

A major factor in the decision to pay hinges on whether criminals stole data. The NGO was particularly concerned that LockBit had exfiltrated sensitive information. Cybercriminals know that if they can place a victim in a pressure situation, they are more likely to pay. The investigation I conducted with the NGO sought to determine what LockBit had stolen in order to decide who the NGO needed to inform. The most sensitive data that many companies protect is related to employees, customers, and beneficiaries. Loss of such data can cause vast reputational harm, extraordinary costs in identity theft monitoring, and possible regulatory actions and fines. Fortunately for the NGO, Ben, David, Jill, and I identified precisely what LockBit had stolen and avoided a large disclosure.

Finally, the decision whether to pay can cause devastating emotional harm to an individual. I decided not to pay the criminal posing as a Hillsong pastor mere moments before I might have sent the wire. Despite this, the fact that I fell for the scam continues to embarrass and infuriate me. I debated for some time whether to tell my personal cyberattack story, both in writing and onstage. Ultimately, I am happy that I chose to tell the tale. Cybercrime affects all of us, from every business and organization to consumers and spy hunters alike. Learning from each other and developing effective plans of action that lead to better decisions is a critical step in making the world safe from cyberattacks.

Choose Not to Be a Victim

The decision not to become a victim requires analysis and action. Thinking like a spy allows us to spot the attack before it compromises us. Having a security plan, cautiously assessing interactions online, and investigating concerning situations leads to informed decisions. This is where your DI^{2}CED knowledge comes into play.

A healthy amount of suspicion will save you from a spy . . . or a cyberattack. Question what you see. A phone call might hide an ulterior motive. An amazing investment offer from a person you've *never met in person* could initiate a complex confidence scam. The love of your life could be an AI deepfake. When faced with an offer you can't refuse or that is too good to be true, decide to walk away.

ACT LIKE A SPY HUNTER

- When faced with a security breach, training and planning must inform rapid decisions.

- A decision based on the execution of your plan is optimal, but circumstances change. Plans and decision-making must be flexible.

- Paying cybercriminals funds criminal operations and incentivizes and encourages individuals to choose a life of cybercrime. If possible, do not pay the ransom.

- The decision to pay is always a personal one and relies on numerous factors, including the sophistication of the attack, whether data was stolen, whether a secure backup exists, the possible reputational harm, and the ease of restoring from backup.

- A major factor in the decision to pay also relies on whether criminals stole data. The most sensitive data that many companies protect is related to employees, customers, clients, and beneficiaries. Cybercriminals know that if they can place a victim in a pressure situation, they are more likely to pay.

- The decision whether to pay an attacker can cause devastating emotional harm to individuals targeted by cybercriminals.

- You are empowered to protect yourself from cyberattacks. Use DI^{2}CED and PAID to inform your decisions. When faced with an offer you can't refuse or that is too good to be true, know that you can decide to walk away.

- For weekly intel, subscribe to my free newsletter at https://ericoneill.net/newsletter/.

NINETEEN

Congratulations, Spy Hunter

Ben and Jill met me in Kaffa Coffee on the south end of Silver Spring, Maryland. The quiet building, tucked away on a side street intersecting the busier Georgia Avenue, opened into a spacious room surrounding a coffee bar. Couches and lounge chairs sprawled along glass windows. On the opposite side of the bar, wooden tables and chairs waited in precise rows, most commanded by laptop jockeys sipping from the free wi-fi as earnestly as they drank the amazing coffee.

Years working undercover in the FBI had long ago made me a coffee junkie. A second career in law and then as a writer has not helped the habit. Instead, I've leaned into the addiction the way so many others have: I'm now a connoisseur. It's a more genteel term for someone who drinks *way* too much caffeine.

Kaffa was an easy choice. The patrons skewed toward respectable and quiet. The food was as good as the coffee, and for the most part, people minded their own business. It was the sort of place where a spy might meet her agent, heads together as they exchanged secrets or plotted the downfall of a government. The dark wood interior and mood lighting that filled corners with shadow added to the mystique. It was the perfect place to finish a personal criminal espionage journey that had consumed my life for months.

Ben and Jill watched me approach their quiet table in the back. Ben's bright eyes and the hint of a smile foreshadowed good news. For once, Jill's scowl had fallen away to something milder. As I sat across from them, I wondered when she would loosen her death grip on her unwitting role in the attack. The Serenity Prayer came to mind: "God grant me the serenity to accept the things I cannot change, courage to change the things I can, and wisdom to know the difference."

Ben leaned forward. "We ran the exfiltration analysis you suggested. We found the command line LockBit used to create a list of folders and build a file tree."

By "we," I knew Ben meant Jill. As the network engineer, Jill would have investigated the faint footprints of the attacker through the winding hallways of the NGO's data.

"Your instincts were right," Jill said. "We know LockBit created a file tree of the H and E drives."

We paused as the waiter approached and I ordered coffee. Black.

"Mr. LockBit gave us the full file tree of both drives as a sign of life after he and I spoke on the phone."

Jill nodded. "Right. But when we reviewed the files in Examples and Examples2—which we knew from the transaction journals—we found plenty of information to worry about but didn't find the file tree."

"So how did LockBit extract the file tree information?"

Jill finally softened her expression. "We pretended to be LockBit. We remotely connected to the HQ server and ran a PowerShell command to generate a separate file listing of the H and E drives. This time we included the file names in each folder. The output of each command was captured in two separate text files. We zipped the two text files to see the compressed size of each. Below is the result of this initial test."

She pushed a manila folder toward me on the table. I opened it and saw a single sheet of paper.

- dirlist_Edrive.zip = 11,557,824 bytes (11.5 MB)–contains a listing of folders and files on the E:\ drive.

- dirlist_Hdrive.zip = 2,550,863 bytes (2.5 MB)–contains a listing of folders and files on the H:\ drive.

"Remember the zipped file folders called Files1.zip and Files2.zip?" Ben asked. "They were really close in size. Twelve megabytes for Files one, and three for Files two."

The waiter deposited a giant mug of coffee in front of me that might have felt comfortable on the set of the old TV show *Friends*. I sipped gratefully while my mind processed the new information. "Close but no cigar?" I asked.

"Well . . ." Ben winked. "We reasoned that one of the text files in Files one or Files two *must* be the file tree. However, as you can see, the file trees Jill created and compressed are half a megabyte smaller than what LockBit sent you." He raised a finger before I could interject. "Hold on. We can do math too. The file structure that the threat actor copied into a compressed file and sent himself from within our network was more data than the file tree they sent you as a sign of life."

Jill continued. "We reran the process and reconstructed the complete file tree down to the folder and individual file name level for each of the E and H drives." Jill grinned. "The results were extraordinary." She tapped the page in front of me. "We found the missing point five megabytes. Tools that compress files use different compression algorithms, and we don't know the method or tool the threat actor used to compress the two files. Accordingly, we are confident that the contents of Files one and Files two are the complete file structures for the E and the H drives."

"Just the file structure," Ben added with a wide grin. "No confidential data. Zero. Nada."

A smile found my face. Ben had just told me Mr. LockBit had stolen nothing but a list of file and folder names for two of the NGO's many network drives. Our immediate concern was well founded. The drives in question were the Executive and Human Resources drives, both filled with sensitive information. But LockBit hadn't stolen any of that data! Instead, they had copied the names of the files and folders that housed that data, and then bluffed. Classic criminal misdirection. Our hard work had called that bluff.

"You can relax," I said.

"We all can. We'll make minimal disclosures to a handful of people that had information stolen from the Examples folders. But they are all internal employees. The executives decided to give them counseling support and identity theft monitoring."

"And Mr. LockBit?" I asked.

Ben waved a hand through the air. "He's old news."

* * *

Mr. Lockbit didn't call me again, but he had become increasingly upset on his dark web message board. I fired up my Tor Browser for one last conversation.

LockBit: We have given you plenty of time to pay. Time is up. Pay now or we release all your information.

Me: I don't think we are going to pay.

LockBit: We told you not to talk to your insurance. They never want you to pay but the damage will be too much for you to handle.

Me: We know you are a liar. We kicked you out. Reconstructed what you did, and you have nothing. Game over.

Before he could answer, I closed my browser, severing my connection to the dark web and the cybercriminal who had tried to bluff a spy hunter and lost.

* * *

Our data is precious. It preserves our fondest memories through collections of pictures and videos, old poems, and fledgling ideas tucked away for the future. It organizes our lives through shared calendars, legions of email and text communications, and applications of all sorts and sizes. Data helps us manage our time, schedule our lives, and remember important meetings or your daughter's violin concert. It improves our quality of life by ensuring that critical infrastructure transmits, flows, and continues uninterrupted. It air-conditions our homes in the summer, heats them in the winter, sends water when we turn the tap, and illuminates lights when we flick the switch. Data enables and preserves the business we conduct. It secures our intellectual property, communicates over vast distances, connects us financially, and turns the world into a conference room. Data is the currency of our lives. Cybersecurity must empower trust in that data.

Making the world safe from cyberattacks begins with you. With all of us. We humans have established a community of data. As with all communities, large and small, some seek to exploit their fellows for personal gain. These cybercriminals thrive on deceit. Defeating their efforts requires us to know their tactics, recognize their scams, and counter them before they deceive, impersonate, infiltrate, falsely gain our confidence, exploit, and destroy what we hold dear.

Thinking like a spy is the first step in restoring trust in our data. Acting like a spy hunter by preparing before the attack, routinely assessing your security, investigating threats, and deciding to act is the methodology that will empower data to work for us. By understanding the DI^{2}CED methodology and deploying PAID, we will stem the river of cryptocurrency pouring into the pockets of cybercriminals. We can make the world safe from cyberespionage and blind malicious foreign intelligence agencies. We can turn dark web moguls into paupers, collapse their dark web caverns, and make the pirates walk their own plank.

Congratulations, spy hunter. Welcome to the cyber war.

THE SPY HUNTER
TOOL KIT

Top Ten Tips to Stop Unwanted Robocalls and Avoid Phone Scams

1. Ignore unknown numbers: Don't answer calls from unfamiliar numbers. If you do, hang up immediately.

2. Be wary of local numbers: Caller ID can be spoofed. A "local" number doesn't guarantee a local caller.

3. Don't engage with prompts: Hang up if asked to press buttons to stop calls. This often identifies active numbers.

4. Avoid saying "yes": Scammers may record your agreement for fraudulent purposes.

5. Guard personal information: Never share sensitive data like account numbers or passwords over the phone.

6. Verify callers independently: If someone claims to represent an organization, hang up and call back using contact information from their website or other official sources.

7. Resist pressure tactics: Urgency is a red flag. Take time to verify legitimate requests independently.

8. Secure your voicemail: Set a password to prevent unauthorized access to your messages.

9. Use blocking tools: Utilize call-blocking services from your provider or download blocking apps.

10. Register with Do Not Call: Add your number to the National Do Not Call Registry to reduce telemarketing calls. Go to https://www.donotcall.gov/.

For more information, the FCC produces a wealth of resources at https://www.fcc.gov/consumers/guides/stop-unwanted-robocalls-and-texts.

Top Ten Tips to Avoid Romance Fraud Scams

1. Never send money or share financial information with someone you haven't met in person.

2. Be extremely cautious about sharing personal details, especially sensitive information or photos.

3. Move slowly in online relationships and be wary of those who declare love quickly.

4. Use reverse image searches and online searches to verify the person's identity and details.

5. Stay on official dating platforms; avoid moving to personal email or messaging apps too soon.

6. Be skeptical of sob stories or urgent requests for help, especially those involving money.

7. Consult trusted friends or family about your online relationship for an outside perspective.

8. Educate yourself about common romance scam tactics and stay informed about new trends.

9. Set social media profiles to private and be mindful of what you share publicly.

10. Report suspicious profiles or behavior to the dating platform and relevant authorities. File a report at ReportFraud.ftc.gov.

Remember, if something feels off or too good to be true, trust your instincts. It might be a scam.

Deepfake Spotter Checklist

Use this checklist to help identify deepfakes used in clever impersonation attacks. Keep in mind that these scams often rely on creating a sense of urgency, leaving little time for you to think critically. If you start to feel pressured, take that as your cue to pause, slow down, and investigate thoroughly.

Visual Irregularities

- Check for unnatural blinking or awkward eye movements.

- Look for mismatched shadows or inconsistent lighting.

- Inspect skin texture for a lack of pores or fine details.

- Examine facial edges (e.g., around ears and jawline) for blurring or poor blending.

- Assess teeth and mouth movements for unnatural alignment or overly uniform teeth.

Audio Anomalies

- Watch for lip movements that don't sync with the audio.

- Listen for robotic or overly smooth speech patterns.

- Check for inconsistent or missing background noise.

Behavioral and Contextual Clues

- Look for exaggerated or odd facial expressions.

- Observe for stiff or misaligned body movements.

- Question whether the actions or statements seem out of character or context.

Tools and Software

- Pause the video and zoom in to spot abnormalities in facial features.

- Use AI detection tools like Microsoft Video Authenticator.

- Analyze metadata for editing history or missing details.

Physiological Signs

- Inspect eye reflections for unnatural lighting.

- Look for symmetrical movements that should naturally vary.

General Verification

- Look up the source of the video or image for reliability.

- Trust your intuition—if something feels off, investigate further.

Top Ten Tips to Avoid Pig Butchering Schemes

1. Be wary of unsolicited messages or invitations, especially from strangers or in group chats.

2. Verify the legitimacy of brokerages before investing. Check for recently created domains using Whois lookup tools to verify legitimacy (whois.domaintools.com or whois.net).

3. Be extremely skeptical of high-return, low-risk investment promises. If it sounds too good to be true, it probably is.

4. Never share personal or financial information with unverified contacts or websites.

5. Research and understand common scam tactics to recognize warning signs early.

6. Avoid making quick investment decisions under pressure. Take time to think and verify.

7. Use only official, well-established investment platforms and financial institutions.

8. Monitor your personal information for potential identity theft or data breaches regularly. Here are three trusted and free sources:

    i. **AnnualCreditReport.com:** Access your free credit reports from Equifax, Experian, and TransUnion annually.

    ii. **IdentityTheft.gov:** Use this FTC resource for guidance and alerts if your identity is compromised.

iii. **Your bank or credit card apps:** Many offer free fraud monitoring and alerts for suspicious activity.

9. Trust your instincts. If something feels off about an investment opportunity, step back.

10. Report suspicious activities to law enforcement promptly, especially if you've transferred funds.

Top Ten Tips to Avoid Online Sextortion Scams and What to Do if Victimized

1. Never share explicit content online. Assume that every photograph you send could be used by a criminal. *Never* send a nude or explicit photograph to *anyone*, regardless of how much you trust them.

2. Protect your online presence by setting your social media profiles to private and only accept connections from people you know personally.

3. Be cautious of video chats and platform changes. Be suspicious of anyone who asks you to switch to video chat or another platform, as this is often a tactic used by scammers to make their activities harder to trace.

4. Don't trust everything you see online. Online identities can be deceptive. The image or persona someone presents could be entirely fabricated to lure you into a trap.

5. Avoid interacting with strangers online. Block or ignore people you do not know who try to connect with you on social media or other platforms.

6. Be aware of common tactics used by scammers. Scammers often manipulate emotions to gain trust and use that trust to pressure you into sharing personal information or content. Stay vigilant and skeptical of anyone asking for personal details or photos.

7. Report all extortion attempts immediately. You are not alone in what is a widespread crime. Report any extortion attempts to law enforcement and seek help from trusted adults or professionals. Learn how to report your incident at https://report.cybertip.org/.

8. Preserve evidence for law enforcement. Don't delete any information or messages from your device. This evidence could be crucial for law enforcement to track down and arrest the person extorting you.

9. If your images have been shared, request their removal from major search engines and any other platforms where they might have been posted at http://takeitdown.ncmec.org.

10. Seek help! Being a victim of sextortion can be emotionally devastating. Reach out to a trusted friend, family member, or counselor for support, and remember that help is available.

For more resources, visit the wealth of information at Take It Down at https://takeitdown.ncmec.org/resources-and-support/.

Top Ten Tips on How to Help Prevent Ransomware Attacks

1. Keep software and operating systems updated with the latest patches.

2. Implement robust backup and recovery procedures, storing backups offline or in the cloud.

3. Use strong, unique passwords and multifactor authentication for all accounts.

4. Train employees on cybersecurity best practices and how to identify phishing attempts.

5. Implement network segmentation to limit the spread of potential infections.

6. Install and maintain comprehensive, up-to-date antivirus and antimalware software.

7. Restrict administrative privileges and access rights on a need-to-know basis.

8. Use secure networks and avoid public wi-fi for sensitive operations.

9. Develop and regularly test an incident response plan.

10. For businesses, invest in cyber insurance for additional protection and support in the event of a ransomware attack.

Remember to report any ransomware attacks to the Cybersecurity and Infrastructure Security Agency (CISA), the FBI IC3, your local FBI field office, or a Secret Service field office. To report ransomware to my friends at the FBI Internet Crime Complaint Center (IC3), point your browser to the following website and click "File a Ransomware Complaint": https://www.ic3.gov/Home/Ransomware.

If you are the victim of a ransomware attack, discover whether you can seek a decryption key from the No More Ransom initiative.

Law enforcement and IT security companies have collaborated to combat ransomware through the No More Ransom initiative, led by the National High Tech Crime Unit of the Netherlands' police, Europol's European Cybercrime Centre, and cybersecurity companies Kaspersky and McAfee. This project helps ransomware victims recover their encrypted data without paying criminals, while also educating users on how ransomware works and how to prevent infections. Visit https://www.nomoreransom.org/en/about-the-project.html.

Top Ten Tips to Prevent Your Social Media Applications from Disclosing Private Information

1. Review default settings. Locate the "Settings," "Preferences," or "Privacy" section on your social media platform. Most platforms have preset privacy settings. Check and adjust them according to your preferences. The more private, the better.

2. Limit post visibility. Decide who can see your posts (e.g., Public, Friends, Only Me). Use privacy settings to control who can tag you in photos or posts.

3. Manage friend requests. Choose whether to approve friend requests or automatically accept them. Determine who can see your friend list.

4. Control profile information. Decide what information is publicly visible (e.g., name, profile picture, location). Consider limiting contact information (email, phone number).

5. Manage location services. Decide whether to allow apps to access your location. Disable location sharing for posts and check-ins if desired.

6. Use privacy tools.

7. Mute: Temporarily stop seeing content from specific people or groups.

8. Block: Prevent someone from contacting you.

9. Report: Flag inappropriate or harmful content.

10. Be cautious of third-party apps. Only use trusted apps that connect to your social media accounts. Avoid sharing sensitive information.

11. Review privacy policies. Understand how platforms collect, use, and share your data. Avoid platforms that sell your data to advertisers.

12. Use strong passwords. Create unique, complex passwords for all your accounts. Turn on multifactor authentication for all social media accounts. Better yet, get and use a trusted password manager like 1Password or Bitwarden.

13. Stay updated. Keep your software and apps up to date to address potential security vulnerabilities.

Platform-Specific Tips:

- Facebook: Explore settings for "Public Posts," "Friends of Friends," and "Only Me."

- Instagram: Adjust "Post Visibility" and "Story Highlights."

- X (formerly Twitter): Use "Privacy Settings" to control who can see your tweets and follow you. Take note! X's "block" function is more like a "mute" feature. Users you block on X can see your public posts, but cannot like, reply to, or repost your posts.

- LinkedIn: Manage "Visibility Settings" for your profile and posts.

Remember to check the specific privacy settings available on each social media platform you use. Regular reviews and adjustments can help protect your privacy online.

Stay informed, Spy Hunter! Subscribe to my weekly newsletter at https://www.ericoneill.net/newsletter.

ACKNOWLEDGMENTS

I began writing this book when the world shut down. The pandemic struck, and suddenly IT and cybersecurity professionals like me found ourselves overwhelmed, underprepared, and working from kitchen tables while defending business as usual. The tele-everything world had arrived—and we weren't ready. To paraphrase the Rolling Stones, we don't always get what we want.

The pandemic also split my family in two. Juliana took Lukas and Emma—our youngest—to her parents' home in Germany to avoid school closures. Hannah, in seventh grade, stayed with me in Maryland, where her school remained open. For six months, I was a single dad, juggling a teenager, multiple businesses, and the chaos of a global crisis. Naturally, I thought it was the perfect time to start writing a book. Many great friends and colleagues helped me along the way.

To my friend and agent Ken Sterling at BigSpeak—thank you for reading my rough first draft, seeing the vision, and offering both encouragement and the occasional necessary shove. Every author needs a kind word and a kick in the pants. You gave me both. Thanks also to Barret Cordero, Cara Tracy, Eleanor Linton, and the entire BigSpeak team for always being in my corner and helping to strategize the book release. Special thanks to Laura Yellen for her ideas, support, and frequent texts with fascinating cybercrime stories.

To Carolyn Monaco and Barbara Carabello at Monaco Associates: Thank you for giving this spy a squad. Your rebranding, marketing road map, and social media strategy turned chaos into clarity. Special thanks to Sarah Mattern for my amazing new website.

To Michael Palgon—publishing special agent extraordinaire. You believed in this project from the start and helped shape it into the spy hunter's manual it became. You were right: No one wanted a pandemic book. Thank you for telling me so.

To Matthew Daddona—your editorial insight sharpened the proposal that sold this book and polished the manuscript before it landed on my editor's desk. You were the compass keeping my writing accessible, grounded, and clear.

At William Morrow/HarperCollins, thank you to Mauro DiPreta—editor, leader, and the mind behind DI^{2}CED. You believed in this book from the outset. Thank you for trusting my instincts on the release. Andrew Yakira—your quiet precision, smart suggestions, and timely return from paternity leave made all the difference. Allie Johnston—you stepped in and carried the book over the goal line. And Jane Cavolina—your copyediting was so meticulous I'm convinced you moonlight as a CIA analyst. Thanks to Melissa Esner, Martin Wilson, Taylor Turkington, and the rest of the HP team. Special thanks to the team at Smith Publicity.

To Safi Bahcall—thank you for your wisdom, friendship, and our exchange of ideas while exploring lunch spots in Bethesda. To my closest friends, Michael Diokno and Christian Spain—you appear often in my writing because you've always shown up in my life. Your constant presence has shaped more than just stories; it's shaped me. To Josh Thurmond and Richard Mead—I never forgot John Brown's cave. To Rick McElroy and Dave Balcar—your experience and insight as former CISOs were invaluable. Thanks to your guidance, the PAID section speaks to real-world defenders with clarity and purpose. To Janek Claus—*vielen Dank* for your friendship and insights into quantum physics in front of the fire at Butternut. To my Uncle John Gemelli and Cousin Gabby, your stories helped shape this book. And to Tom Alioto—diving into the dark web with you felt like swallowing the red pill and waking up inside the Matrix. Here's to more digital deep dives and cybercrime takedowns ahead.

This book is dedicated to my father, who taught my brothers and me to forge our own path—and somehow always managed to be there to catch us when we stumbled. Your calm during chaos taught me how to be the kind of father I want to be. Yes, Dad, I fixed the part about fire insurance.

To Juliana, Hannah, Lukas, and Emma—you appear in these pages and on my stages (whether you know it or not). Hannah, thank you for your patience with a pandemic-era dad who should've spent less time writing and more time trying to beat your Beat Saber score. Juliana, thank you for being my guiding star and the force that drove this book across the finish line. Writing requires solitude—not always ideal for marriage—but your daily reminders to "go write" turned good intentions into a finished book. You and our children are my foundation and the source of all my joy.

Finally, to you, dear reader. I wrote this book for the same reason I take the stage or publish my newsletter: to entertain, inform, and inspire. If you close this book with a spy hunter's mindset and a sharper eye for cyberthreats, then we've already won. Every time you channel your inner digital detective and suit up as an email archaeologist, you're helping to take down the dark web—one cybercriminal at a time.

Eric O'Neill
Washington, D.C.

NOTES

Prologue: The Deepest, Darkest Cave

1. "Data Never Sleeps 11," Domo.com, https://www.domo.com/learn/infographic/data-never-sleeps-11.

Introduction: It's Now or . . . *It's Now!*

1. Europol Innovation Lab, "Facing Reality: Law Enforcement and the Challenge of Deepfakes," https://www.europol.europa.eu/cms/sites/default/files/documents/Europol_Innovation_Lab_Facing_Reality_Law_Enforcement_And_The_Challenge_Of_Deepfakes.pdf.

Chapter One: The House Is Burning Down

1. U.S. Department of State, "Reward for Information: LockBit Ransomware-as-a-Service," https://www.state.gov/reward-for-information-lockbit-ransomware-as-a-service.

Chapter Four: Impersonation: How to Skip School

1. FBI Alert Number: I-091124-PSA, September 11, 2024, https://www.ic3.gov/PSA/2024/PSA240911.
2. Gina Kolata, "A.I. Chatbots Defeated Doctors at Diagnosing Illness," *New York Times*, November 17, 2024, https://www.nytimes.com/2024/11/17/health/chatgpt-ai-doctors-diagnosis.html.
3. "How Many AI Tools Are There," Workmind.ai, August 22, 2024, https://workmind.ai/blog/how-many-ai-tools-are-there/.
4. Kristin Houser, "Watch the First AI Vs. Human Dogfight Using Military Jets," Freethink.com, April 22, 2024, https://www.freethink.com/robots-ai/ai-fighter-pilot.

5. Caitlin McFall, "US Scrambles as Drones Shape the Landscape of War: 'The Future Is Here,'" Fox News, November 23, 2024, https://www.foxnews.com/world/us-scrambles-drones-shape-landscape-war-future-here.

Chapter Five: Impersonation: Deepfakes

1. Jennifer DeStefano, Testimony before the U.S. Senate Judiciary Committee, June 13, 2023, accessed August 8, 2024, https://www.judiciary.senate.gov/imo/media/doc/2023-06-1320PM20-20Testimony20-20DeStefano.pdf.
2. New Hampshire Department of Justice, "Voter Suppression AI Robocall Investigation Update," February 6, 2024, https://www.doj.nh.gov/news-and-media/voter-suppression-ai-robocall-investigation-update.
3. Federal Communications Commission, "Report and Order and Further Notice of Proposed Rulemaking: In the Matter of Advanced Methods to Target and Eliminate Unlawful Robocalls, adopted February 2, 2024," https://docs.fcc.gov/public/attachments/FCC-24-17A1.pdf.

Chapter Six: Infiltration: The Trojan Horse

1. "A Worst Nightmare Cyberattack: The Untold Story of the SolarWinds Hack," *All Things Considered*, NPR, April 16, 2021, https://www.npr.org/2021/04/16/985439655/a-worst-nightmare-cyberattack-the-untold-story-of-the-solarwinds-hack.
2. "A Worst Nightmare Cyberattack."
3. Chainalysis, "Ransomware Trends in 2024: The Latest Insights on Payments and Attacks," https://www.chainalysis.com/blog/ransomware-2024/.
4. Sergiu Gatlan, "Lincoln College to Close After 157 Years Due to Ransomware Attack," BleepingComputer, May 9, 2022, https://www.bleepingcomputer.com/news/security/lincoln-college-to-close-after-157-years-due-ransomware-attack/.

Chapter Seven: Infiltration: Indomitable Weeds

1. U.S. Department of Justice, "Multiple Foreign Nationals Charged in Connection with Trickbot Malware and Conti Ransomware," September 27, 2023, https://www.justice.gov/opa/pr/multiple-foreign-nationals-charged-connection-trickbot-malware-and-conti-ransomware.
2. "Russia Arrests Alleged REvil Ransomware Hackers at the Request of U.S.," uploaded by Bloomberg Quicktake, January 14, 2022, YouTube, https://www.youtube.com/watch?v=OqEWuFmzhzs.

3. Statista, "Average Number of Days to Patch a Vulnerability Worldwide as of 2023, by Severity," Statista.com, https://www.statista.com/statistics/1363099/average-days-to-patch-vulnerability-by-severity/.
4. Christopher Snowbeck, "UnitedHealth Group Falls on Report of High Medical Costs, Dampened Outlook," *Star Tribune,* October 14, 2024, https://www.startribune.com/unitedhealth-group-beats-analysts-estimates-despite-higher-medical-expenses-in-q3/601162413.
5. Change Healthcare, HIPAA Substitute Notice, https://www.changehealthcare.com/hipaa-substitute-notice.

Chapter Eight: Confidence: "I Want to Believe"

1. FBI, "$1 Billion in Losses Reported by Victims of Romance Scams," https://www.fbi.gov/contact-us/field-offices/houston/news/press-releases/1-billion-in-losses-reported-by-victims-of-romance-scams.
2. Federal Trade Commission, "Reports of Romance Scams Hit Record Highs in 2021," https://www.ftc.gov/news-events/data-visualizations/data-spotlight/2022/02/reports-romance-scams-hit-record-highs-2021.
3. Federal Trade Commission. "Love Stinks (When a Scammer Is Involved)." FTC Business Blog, February 12, 2024, https://www.ftc.gov/business-guidance/blog/2024/02/love-stinks-when-scammer-involved.

Chapter Ten: Exploitation: Spelunking into a Nightmare

1. Javelin Strategy & Research, "Child Identity Fraud: A Web of Deception and Loss," November 2021, https://javelinstrategy.com/research/child-identity-fraud-web-deception-and-loss.
2. Javelin Strategy & Research, "Child Identity Fraud: The Perils of Too Many Screens and Social Media," October 2022, https://javelinstrategy.com/whitepapers/child-identity-fraud-perils-too-many-screens-and-social-media.
3. Javelin Strategy & Research, "Child ID Theft: Social Cyber Risks and the Persistent Threat to Families," November 2023, http://javelinstrategy.com/whitepapers/child-id-theft-social-cyber-risks-and-persistent-threat-families.
4. Lawrence Abrams, "LockBit Ransomware Admin Identified, Sanctioned in US, UK, Australia," BleepingComputer, May 7, https://www.bleepingcomputer.com/news/security/lockbit-ransomware-admin-identified-sanctioned-in-us-uk-australia.

5. Safe4Us, "INTERPOL's Child Exploitation Database," January 1, 2024, https://www.safe4us.org/blog/interpols-child-exploitation-database.
6. Nurmi, J., Paju, A., Brumley, B.B. et al. "Investigating child sexual abuse material availability, searches, and users on the anonymous Tor network for a public health intervention strategy." Scientific Reports 14, 7849 (2024). https://doi.org/10.1038/s41598-024-58346-7.
7. U.S. Department of Justice, Dark Web Child Pornography Facilitator Sentenced to 27 Years in Prison for Conspiracy to Advertise Child Pornography, accessed August 8, 2024, https://www.justice.gov/opa/pr/dark-web-child-pornography-facilitator-sentenced-27-years-prison-conspiracy-advertise-child.
8. Gareth Owen and Nick Savage, "The Tor Dark Net," Centre for International Governance Innovation, September 2015, CIGI Paper No. 20, https://www.cigionline.org/publications/tor-dark-net/.
9. U.S. Immigration and Customs Enforcement, "HSI, Brazil Law Enforcement Partners Take Down International Child Exploitation Ring," May 19, 2022, https://www.ice.gov/news/releases/hsi-brazil-law-enforcement-partners-take-down-international-child-exploitation-ring.

Chapter Eleven: Exploitation: No Blank Pages

1. U.S. Department of Justice, "Nigerian Brothers Sentenced for Sextortion Scheme That Resulted in the Death of a Teen," 2024. https://www.justice.gov/opa/pr/nigerian-brothers-sentenced-sextortion-scheme-resulted-death-teen.
2. Federal Bureau of Investigation, "Sextortion: A Growing Threat Targeting Minors," FBI, Nashville Field Office, March 27, 2024, https://www.fbi.gov/contact-us/field-offices/nashville/news/sextortion-a-growing-threat-targeting-minors.
3. Gassó, AM, Klettke, B, Agustina, JR, Montiel, I. "Sexting, Mental Health, and Victimization Among Adolescents: A Literature Review." *International Journal of Environmental Research and Public Health* 16, no. 13 (July 3, 2019): 2364, doi: 10.3390/ijerph16132364. PMID: 31277335; PMCID: PMC 6650829.
4. CyberTipline, National Center for Missing & Exploited Children, https://www.missingkids.org/gethelpnow/cybertipline.
5. Take It Down, https://takeitdown.ncmec.org/about-us/.
6. Javelin Strategy & Research, "Child ID Theft: Social Cyber Risks and the Persistent Threat to Families."

7. Santiago Lakatos, "A Revealing Picture: A Look into Coordinated Influence Operation," December 8, 2023, Graphika.com, https://graphika.com/reports/a-revealing-picture.

Chapter Twelve: Destruction: Inside the Fishbowl

1. Kelly Jackson Higgins, "What the CEO Saw: Colonial Pipeline & Accellion Execs Share Cyberattack War Stories," Dark Reading, October 6, 2021, https://www.darkreading.com/threat-intelligence/what-the-ceo-saw-colonial-pipeline-accellion-execs-share-cyberattack-war-stories.
2. U.S. House Committee on Homeland Security, "Cyber Threats in the Pipeline: Using Lessons from the Colonial Ransomware Attack to Defend Critical Infrastructure," June 9, 2021, https://www.govinfo.gov/content/pkg/CHRG-117hhrg45085/html/CHRG-117hhrg45085.htm.
3. Snir Ben Shimol, "DarkSide Ransomware," Varonis, updated December 21, 2022, https://www.varonis.com/blog/darkside-ransomware.
4. "FBI Deputy Director Paul M. Abbate's Remarks at Press Conference Regarding the Ransomware Attack on Colonial Pipeline," FBI News, June 7, 2021, https://www.fbi.gov/news/press-releases/press-releases/fbi-deputy-director-paul-m-abbates-remarks-at-press-conference-regarding-the-ransomware-attack-on-colonial-pipeline.
5. Robert McMillan and Dustin Volz, "Web Site of DarkSide Hacking Group Linked to Colonial Pipeline Attack Is Down," *Wall Street Journal*, updated May 14, 2021, https://www.wsj.com/articles/web-site-of-darkside-hacking-group-linked-to-colonial-pipeline-attack-is-down-11621001688.
6. U.S. Department of Health and Human Services, Breach Portal: Notice to the Secretary of HHS Breach of Unsecured Protected Health Information, "Cases Currently Under Investigation," https://ocrportal.hhs.gov/ocr/breach/breach_report.jsf.
7. Center for Strategic and International Studies (CSIS), "Significant Cyber Incidents," https://www.csis.org/programs/strategic-technologies-program/significant-cyber-incidents.
8. "The City of Dallas Ransomware Incident: May 2023: Incident Remediation Efforts and Resolution," The City of Dallas Department of Information & Technology Services, September 20, 2023, https://dallascityhall.com

/DCH%20Documents/dallas-ransomware-incident-may-2023-incident-remediation-efforts-and-resolution.pdf.

9. Cybersecurity and Infrastructure Security Agency, "Threat Actors Exploit Progress Telerik Vulnerability in Unpatched Systems," March 2, 2023, https://www.cisa.gov/news-events/cybersecurity-advisories/aa23–061a.

10. Cybersecurity and Infrastructure Security Agency, #StopRansomware: "Blacksuit (Royal) Ransomware," August 26, 2024, https://www.cisa.gov/news-events/cybersecurity-advisories/aa23-061a.

Chapter Thirteen: Destruction: Up at Night

1. Sahil Raina, "Geopolitical Instability Raises Threat of Catastrophic Cyberattack in Next Two Years," World Economic Forum, January 18, 2023, https://www.weforum.org/press/2023/01/geopolitical-instability-raises-threat-of-catastrophic-cyberattack-in-next-two-years/.

2. Internet Crime Report 2021, FBI Internet Crime Complaint Center (IC3). https://www.ic3.gov/Media/PDF/AnnualReport/2021_IC3Report.pdf.

3. Internet Crime Report 2023, FBI Internet Crime Complaint Center (IC3), https://www.ic3.gov/Media/PDF/AnnualReport/2023_IC3Report.pdf.

4. Business Standard. "NotPetya: How a Russian Malware Created the World's Worst Cyberattack Ever." https://www.business-standard.com/article/technology/notpetya-how-a-russian-malware-created-the-world-s-worst-cyberattack-ever-118082700261_1.html.

5. O'Neill, Eric M. *Gray Day: My Undercover Mission to Expose America's First Cyber Spy*. Crown, 2019.

6. National Security Agency, "CSA: Sandworm Actors Exploiting Vulnerability in Exim Transfer Agent." Available at: https://media.defense.gov/2020/May/28/2002306626/-1/-1CSA20Sandworm20Actors20Exploiting20Vulnerability20in20Exim20Transfer20Agent2020200528.pdf.

7. Andy Greenberg, "Russia's Fancy Bear Hackers Are Hitting US Targets Again," *Wired*, July 24, 2020, https://www.wired.com/story/russia-fancy-bear-us-hacking-campaign-government-energy/.

8. Cybersecurity and Infrastructure Security Agency (CISA), "Ongoing Cyber Threats to U.S. Water and Wastewater Systems," https://www.cisa.gov/news-events/cybersecurity-advisories/aa21–287a.

9. Chrissy Suttles, "Federal, State Investigators Probing Aliquippa Water Authority Hack, *USA Today*, updated November 28, 2023, https://www.usatoday.com/story/news/local/2023/11/27/federal-state-investigators-probing-aliquippa-water-authority-hack/71720634007/.
10. Rewards for Justice, U.S. Department of State, https://www.state.gov/rewards-for-justice/.
11. 2023 Cyber Strategy Summary, U.S. Department of Defense, September 2023, https://cdn01.dailycaller.com/wp-content/uploads/2023/09/2023-DoD-Cyber-Strategy-Summary-1.pdf.
12. "Director Wray's Opening Statement to the House Select Committee on the Strategic Competition Between the United States and the Chinese Communist Party," FBI News, January 312, 2024, https://www.fbi.gov/news/speeches/director-wrays-opening-statement-to-the-house-select-committee-on-the-chinese-communist-party.
13. Kevin Williams, "Cyber-Physical Attacks Fueled by AI Are a Growing Threat, Experts Say," CNBC, March 3, 2024, https://www.cnbc.com/2024/03/03/cyber-physical-attacks-fueled-by-ai-are-a-growing-threat-experts-say.html.
14. Peter Landers, "IBM, Google Give $150 Million for U.S.-Japan Quantum Computing Push as China Looms," *The Wall Street Journal*, May 17, 2023, https://www.wsj.com/articles/ibm-google-give-150-million-for-u-s-japan-quantum-computing-push-as-china-looms-26e614d4.
15. "Quantinuum Launches Industry-First Trapped-Ion 56-Qubit Quantum Computer That Challenges the World's Best Supercomputers," Quantinuum, June 5, 2024, https://www.quantinuum.com/news/quantinuum-launches-industry-first-trapped-ion-56-qubit-quantum-computer-that-challenges-the-worlds-best-supercomputers.
16. Michael Bogobowicz, Kamalika Dutta, Martina Gschwendtner et al., "Steady Progress in Approaching the Quantum Advantage," McKinsey Digital, McKinsey & Company, April 24, 2024, https://www.mckinsey.com/capabilities/mckinsey-digital/our-insights/steady-progress-in-approaching-the-quantum-advantage.
17. Victoria Bela, "China and Russia Test Hack-Proof Quantum Communication Link for BRICS Countries," *South China Morning Post*, December 30, 2023, https://www.scmp.com/news/china/science/article/3246752/china-and-russia

-test-hack-proof-quantum-communication-link-brics-countries?module=inline
&pgtype=article.

Chapter Fifteen: Prepare

1. CISA Secure Our World Blog, *Protect Our World With MFA*, https://www.cisa.gov/MFA
2. Cybersecurity Framework, National Institute of Standards and Technology, https://www.nist.gov/cyberframework.

Chapter Sixteen: Assess

1. "What We Learned: Change Healthcare Cyber Attack," U.S. House of Representatives, Committee on Energy and Commerce News, May 12, 2024, https://energycommerce.house.gov/posts/what-we-learned-change-healthcare-cyber-attack.
2. Dwight D. Eisenhower, "Remarks at the National Defense Executive Reserve Conference," American Presidency Project, November 14, 1957, https://www.presidency.ucsb.edu/documents/remarks-the-national-defense-executive-reserve-conference.
3. Brian Fung, "We Finally Know What Caused the Global Tech Outage—And How Much It Cost," CNN, July 24, 2024, https://www.cnn.com/2024/07/24/tech/crowdstrike-outage-cost-cause/index.html.

Chapter Seventeen: Investigate

1. FBI Internet Crime Complaint Center (IC3), "PSA: FBI Public Service Announcement—Alert Number: I-091124-PSA," FBI Internet Crime Complaint Center (IC3), September 11, 2024, https://www.ic3.gov/PSA/2024/PSA240911.

Chapter Eighteen: Decide

1. Mary Louise Kelly, "Colonial Pipeline CEO Explains the Decision to Pay Hackers a $4.4 Million Ransom," *All Things Considered*, NPR, June 3, 2021, https://www.npr.org/2021/06/03/1003020300/colonial-pipeline-ceo-explains-the-decision-to-pay-hackers-4-4-million-ransom.
2. Ryan McCarthy, "Oversight Committee Releases More Details on JBS Cyberattack," Meat+Poultry, November 24, 2021, https://www.meatpoultry.com/articles/25834-oversight-committee-releases-more-details-on-jbs-cyberattack.

About the Author

Eric O'Neill's career began in the FBI's counterintelligence trenches as an undercover operative. Since then, he has spent decades working in the field as a cybersecurity analyst, corporate investigator, and national security attorney. He is the founder of The Georgetown Group, a competitive intelligence firm, and serves as national security strategist for NeXasure AI. O'Neill speaks to thousands across the globe on cybercrime, cybersecurity, hacking and fraud, corporate diligence, espionage, and national security. He has appeared as a national security expert on CNN and Fox, and his writing has been featured in NPR, *USA Today*, *The Boston Globe*, *The Hill*, TechCrunch, and Mashable. A graduate of Auburn University and the George Washington University School of Law, O'Neill is also a highly sought-after keynote speaker. Learn more at EricONeill.net.